Twayne's English Authors Series

Sylvia E. Bowman, *Editor*

INDIANA UNIVERSITY

Oliver Goldsmith

 47

Oliver Goldsmith

By CLARA M. KIRK

TWAYNE PUBLISHERS
A DIVISION OF G. K. HALL & CO., BOSTON

To
RUDOLF KIRK
"Nullum quod tetigit non ornavit."

Contents

About the Author

Clara M. Kirk brings to bear upon the study of Goldsmith an extensive background in English literature. After taking a doctor's degree at the University of Chicago, she taught at Vassar, Bryn Mawr, and Rutgers. She had studied at the University of Brussels and spent a year in Belgium as a Fulbright Research Scholar. Among her publications are *Mr. Pepys and Mr. Evelyn, Types of English Poetry* (an anthology), *W. D. Howells, Traveler From Altruria,* and *Howells and the Art of His Time.*

Preface

"Were angels to write books, they never would write folios,"
observed Oliver Goldsmith. We shall in this brief study of Goldsmith attempt to stay on the side of the angels and focus our
discussion on the comparatively few masterpieces by which he
is known and loved today: *The Deserted Village, The Vicar of
Wakefield,* and *She Stoops to Conquer.* Without writing a folio,
however, we shall add to these three most famous titles others,
which, though less frequently read, are also important: *The Citizen of the World, The Traveler, The Memoirs of M. de Voltaire,*
and *The Life of Richard Nash.* Goldsmith experimented in every
form of writing popular in his day; beginning his career as an
essayist, he turned, not consecutively but concurrently, poet,
novelist, dramatist, and finally biographer. Under these five head-
ings we will consider the complex genius of Oliver Goldsmith, and
hope not to offend the angels by our frequent excursions into
other areas of Goldsmith's extensive writing.

Goldsmith declared that he admired above all "the art of
writing which is but another name for good sense," and in so
saying he voiced one of the most accepted criteria for "the art
of writing" current in his time. His style was admired then and
now for its lucidity, its simplicity, its reasonableness. However,
Goldsmith did not believe that "good sense" completely described
the "art of writing," for he always knew that imagination was
superior to reason. "Innocently to amuse the imagination in this
dream of Life is wisdom," he wrote. A range of humor, from
subtle irony to broad farce; a sense of poetry, sometimes nobly
rhetorical, sometimes witty, and sometimes as simple as a ballad;
and the impulse to tell a story, real or imagined, old or new, carried his imagination far beyond the scope of "good sense."

The balance of reason and imagination in the writing of Goldsmith was as delightful and as confusing to his contemporaries

as to the modern reader. James Boswell called Goldsmith "a curious, odd, pedantic fellow with some genius"; Dr. Johnson considered him "one of the first men we now have as author"; and Sir John Hawkins, another member of the Library Club, spoke of him as "a mere literary drudge." To many a London beggar Goldsmith was a generous benefactor, but to Horace Walpole he was only an "inspired ideot" who was always in debt. It is probable that Goldsmith understood himself no better than he was understood by others, for, as he claimed, "the opinion we form of ourselves is generally measured by what we hear from others."

Goldsmith's baffled effort at self-realization might be said to underlie all that he wrote. His quest of "the ghost of departed happiness" goes far to explain why he turned from one literary form to another, frequently assumed a fresh literary disguise, and then cast it aside as casually as he discarded a new coat just purchased from his tailor. Though he was always homesick for Ireland, which he left in his early twenties, he never returned to his country. Instead, he transformed his feelings into the brooding melancholy of one of his characters or into the simple cheerfulness of another, for both were projections of his own personality. In the Preface to *The Citizen of the the World*, Goldsmith wrote of his darker side: "I resemble one of those solitary animals that has been forced from its forest to gratify human curiosity. My earliest wish was to escape unheeded through life; but I have been set up, for halfpence, to fret and scamper at the end of my chain" (III, 11–12).[1]

With equal validity Goldsmith wrote of his gayer self when he described George Primrose's approach to London: "The first misfortune of my life [the loss of the family fortune], which you all know, was great; but though it distressed, it could not sink me. No person ever had a better knack at hoping than I. . . . I proceeded, therefore, towards London, in a fine morning, no way uneasy about to-morrow; but cheerful as the birds that carolled by the road" (I, 155–56).

Which was Goldsmith? Was he the "solitary animal" forced from its native haunts to amuse the world, like a monkey at the end of a chain? Or was he the gay and casual George, cheerful as the birds, sauntering down the road to London to make his

fortune? He was both, of course, for this Irish poet and advent
was marked not only by a moodiness that prompted him to draw
within himself from time to time, but also by a sociable nature
familiar to the friends among whom he loved "to play the fool a
little." The dark and the light, the sad and the gay, were inter-
twined in Goldsmith's writing because they were two sides of
his unique personality.

[The question as to the way in which Goldsmith's life was
related to his writing is complicated by the fact that no one has
ever been able to determine when Goldsmith was truthfully recounting his own experiences—whether, indeed, he was capable
of telling the truth in any but a poetic sense—or whether he was
frankly imagining when apparently speaking of his actual life.]
So intermingled were reason and imagination in the mind and
temperament of Goldsmith that he would himself have been unable to untangle the story of his own experiences—had he been
willing to make such an attempt. Though he began in April, 1773,
a year before his death, to dictate a Memorandum[2] of his life to
his friend, Thomas Percy; and, though Bishop Percy attempted
soon after Goldsmith's death, to verify this account by inquiries
among his relatives and friends, scholars today are in doubt as
to how to interpret the information thus assembled.

(That Goldsmith survives today as one of the most readable
writers of that age of heroic couplets and sententious moralizing
is due, in part, to the fact that he was born in an Irish country
parsonage, full of children, and presided over by a kind, good-
humored father and a more practical mother,) later to be im-
mortalized as Dr. and Mrs. Primrose of Wakefield. Oliver, the
fifth child and second son of the Reverend Charles Goldsmith,
was born in 1728 or 1730, at Pallas, County Longford. A plain,
stocky little boy, he was, at the age of seven, cruelly marked for
life by smallpox. Oliver was considered dull by several of his
teachers, but promising enough by others to encourage his father
to send him to the University of Dublin as a sizar in 1745. His
brother Henry by that time had completed his studies and had
returned to his father's rectory at Lissoy. However, the money
intended for Oliver's education had already been used as the
dowry of an older sister who had married "above herself."

At Trinity College, Dublin, Oliver was not only humiliated by his menial position as a "poor student," destined to sweep the courtyard and wait at table, but he was also bored by his academic studies and painfully conscious of his awkward body and pale, ugly countenance. Frolicsome by nature, Oliver soon became known as the kind of student who neglected his lectures. When a bailiff of the town was dipped in the pump on the square by a group of riotous students, no one was surprised to find Oliver among them. Oliver further damaged his reputation by celebrating an award he won in a poetry contest with a party involving both wine and women in his college room. Attracted by the noise of song and merriment, an angry tutor burst through the door and knocked down the helpless host. This incident so enraged Oliver that he packed up his small supply of books the next day, sold them, and left the university with vague plans of migrating to America. Fortunately, he was persuaded by his brother Henry to return to Trinity, where he was awarded his Bachelor of Arts in 1749. Perhaps Goldsmith's pleasantest memories of his experiences at Trinity College were of the nights when he slipped through the portals of the courtyard and wandered around the streets of Dublin hoping to hear the boys and girls of the town sing the ballads that he had sold to the printshop for five shillings apiece.

When Oliver returned to his home with his degree, his mother was a widow living in a cottage in Ballymahon; Henry was a curate in a near-by village; and his sister's husband, Daniel Hodson, was the Rector of Lissoy. Oliver and his family assumed that he too would follow the family tradition and in due time take orders. However, since he could not be ordained until he was twenty-three, he was willing enough to idle away his time in fishing, fluting, and playing cards in the village inn.[3]

Oliver's preparation for the ministry naturally proved inadequate, but the singing and the story-telling that he enjoyed in the public-house of the village with his friends might have been the best possible preparation for the future writer. When he presented himself as a candidate for ordination in the diocese of Elphin, he was rejected by the Bishop for unspecified reasons—perhaps because of his college record, perhaps because he had wasted his time, perhaps because he chose to wear a pair of crimson breeches to the interview.

Preface

Goldsmith's uncle, the Reverend Thomas Contarine, was determined that Oliver, in spite of his wayward nature, should be properly started in life. He endeavored to launch him twice, first into the career of law in Dublin, and then into that of medicine in Edinburgh. Oliver managed to lose his money, as well as his impulse to study, on both occasions. Without further help from his uncle, he now continued his useful education in roadside scamps and scoundrels on the Continent.

After two years of wandering in Europe, Goldsmith landed in Dover and made his way to London, perhaps joining on the way a group of strolling players.[4] Since the good Uncle Contarine was now dead and since Oliver's family had not replied to his requests from Italy for money, Goldsmith was forced to earn his daily bread as best he could. Writing reviews, compiling books for children, and editing other men's poems and plays seemed preferable to mixing powders in an apothecary's shop or to teaching in a boys' school. Goldsmith hinted that on more than one occasion he begged for money on the streets of London; certain it is that necessity, as well as talent, turned this wandering Irishman into a writer for the London booksellers.

A hackwriter of a most industrious and useful kind Goldsmith might have remained had he not felt impelled to re-live, again and again, in essays, poems, stories, and plays his memories of Ireland. The transforming veil which he cast over the simple scenes of his youth may be found in all that Goldsmith wrote, from his essays for *The Bee* to *The Life of Richard Nash*. Equally apparent to the reader is the vein of melancholy in the writing of this travel from "the unambitious retirement" of an Irish parsonage to the streets of London. Though Goldsmith discovered that "age and knowledge only contribute to sour our dispositions," he never returned to Ireland; instead, he transformed himself, between 1757 and 1774, from an assistant in an apothecary shop to the "very great man" lauded by David Garrick, Sir Joshua Reynolds, Edmund Burke, Dr. Samuel Johnson, and many others.

Not many of Goldsmith's friends and admirers were aware of the melancholy beneath the surface of his apparently gay, and playful personality. When Goldsmith disappeared for a few days —or a few months—members of the Literary Club no doubt merely observed that Goldsmith had gone to the country, and thought no more about their odd and gifted friend until he re-appeared in their midst. One member of the Club, however, Sir John Hawkins, remarked of him: "Goldsmith is well known by his writings to have been a man of genius and of very fine parts; but of his character and general deportment, it is the hardest task anyone can undertake to give a description."[5]

Difficult as the task is to relate Goldsmith's writing to his life we shall, in the following chapters, at least recognize that such is the critical problem involved in any consideration of Gold-smith as an essayist, poet, novelist, dramatist, or biographer. Both the triumph and the failure of Goldsmith's writing grew from the triumph and the failure of his life. We shall not, in the small compass of this study, do more than suggest the scope of Goldsmith's writing for the journals and magazines of his day; we will confine ourselves to the few books by which he will always be remembered.

I wish to express my appreciation of the many courtesies ex-tended to me by the library staffs of the University of Texas, the University of Wisconsin, and Southwest Texas State College. I wish also to thank Miss Katharine C. Balderston and the Cam-bridge University Press for permission to quote from *The Collected Letters of Oliver Goldsmith*.

CLARA M. KIRK
San Marcos, Texas

May 10, 1966

Chronology

1728   Oliver Goldsmith, born November 10, Pallas, County Long-
or   ford, Ireland. Father, The Reverend Charles Goldsmith,
1730   Rector of Kilkenny West, Ireland. Goldsmith's childhood
       home was in Lissoy, Westmeath, Ireland.

1737   Attended schools in Elphin, Athlone, and Edgeworths-
to   town. Contracted smallpox at seven.
1744

1745   Entered Trinity College, Dublin, as a sizar.

1747   Death of his father. Oliver involved in a college riot. Left
       college temporarily.

1749   February 27, B.A. degree.

1750–   Idled at home. Prepared to take holy orders. Rejected by
1752   the Bishop of Elphin. Left Ireland permanently.

1753   Studied medicine in Edinburgh. Did not take a degree.

1754   Imprisoned briefly. Took ship for Leyden to study medi-
       cine.

1755   Left Leyden for unknown reasons. Probably studied medi-
       cine at Padua for about six months. Traveled on foot
       through Northern Italy, Switzerland, France, and perhaps
       Germany.

1756   Landed at Dover, England, on February 1. Apothecary
       assistant in London; then an usher at the Peckham School.

1757   Editorial work on the *Monthly Review*, under Ralph Grif-
       fiths and his wife, with whom he lived. Moved to Salisbury
       Court. Proofreader for Samuel Richardson, printer.

1758   Published, in February, a translation of *The Memoirs of
       a Protestant, Condemned to the Galleys of France for His
       Religion,* by Jean Marteilhe. 2 vols. Moved Green Arbour
       Court, off Ludgate Hill. Failed to qualify as a hospital
       mate.

9   April 2, publication of *An Enquiry into the Present State of Polite Learning in Europe.* October 6 to November 24, *The Bee* (nos. I–VIII) appeared. Tobias Smollett enlisted Goldsmith for the *British Magazine;* John Newbery employed him for the *Public Ledger.*

1760–   January 24 to August, 1761, publication of the "Chinese
1761   Letters" in the *Public Ledger.* Moved to 6 Wine Office Court, Fleet Street. Editor of *Lady's Magazine* for which he wrote *Memoirs of M. de Voltaire.* Thomas Percy brought Samuel Johnson to visit Goldsmith.

1762   May 1, publication of *The Citizen of the World.* October 14, *The Life of Richard Nash, Esq.* October 28, sold a third share of *The Vicar of Wakefield.*

1763   *Plutarch's Lives,* 5 vols. Moved to Garden Court, the Temple; joined the Literary Club.

1764   June 26, published *An History of England in a Series of Letters of a Nobleman to His Son,* 2 vols. December 19, *The Traveller.*

1765   June 4, *Essays by Mr. Goldsmith.* Private edition of *Edwin and Angelina* for the Countess of Northumberland.

1766   March 12, *The Vicar of Wakefield.* Translation of *History of Philosophy and Philosophers,* by M. Formey. *Poems for Young Ladies.* Wrote *The Good-Natured-Man.*

1768   January 29, first night at Covent Garden of *The Good-Natured Man.* Moved to 2 Brick Court, Middle Temple. Cottage on the Edgeware Road with Edward Bott.

1769   May 18, *The Roman History,* 2 vols.

1770   January 9, made Professor of Ancient History to the Royal Academy. May 26, published *The Deserted Village. Life of Bolingbroke* and *Life of Parnell.*

1771   Wrote *The Haunch of Venison* (1776), and *She Stoops to Conquer.* Lived with Farmer Selby, "near the six-mile stone, on Edgeware Road."

1772   Began *An History of Earth, and Animated Nature.* February 20, published *Threnodia Augustalis;* in December, *The Roman History,* an abridgment for schools.

1773   March 15, first night at Covent Garden of *She Stoops to Conquer.*

1774   Wrote *Retaliation* (April 19, 1774). Taken seriously ill on March 25; died on April 4 at 2 Brick Court. Buried on April 9 in the Temple Churchyard. *The Grecian History,* 2 vols., and *An History of the Earth and Animated Nature,* 8 vols., published in June.

Oliver Goldsmith

CHAPTER 1

"*A Whimsically Dismal Figure*"

I Grub Street, London

GOLDSMITH landed at Dover, England, early in 1756, without any intention of earning his living by writing. Four years later, on January 24, 1760, the first of his "Chinese Letters"[1] was published in the *Public Ledger*. To understand how this penniless Irishman turned himself into a popular writer of essays so soon after his arrival in London, one might begin by considering a letter he wrote home to his brother Henry sometime in January, 1759,[2] a few months before the appearance of his first book, *An Enquiry Into the Present State of Polite Learning in Europe*.[3] This letter fully displays the "whimsically dismal figure" of the essayist.

"You scarce can conceive how much eight years of disappointment anguish and study have worn me down," wrote Oliver to his brother. Goldsmith was at that time living miserably in a room on the ground floor of a filthy courtyard, ironically called Green Arbour Court, which was crowded with children and strewn with drying laundry. One reached the court by Breakneck Steps, off Ludgate Hill, after making one's way across Fleet Street Ditch.[4] No doubt the chill of Goldsmith's chamber and the dim light of his solitary candle contributed to his mood as he wrote to his brother whom he thought of as "grown fat sleek and healthy" in Ireland and as passing happy days among his children and his friends. As for himself, Oliver wrote, the intervening years had turned him into a misanthrope: "Immagine to yourself a pale melancholly visage with two great wrinkles between the eye brows, with an eye disgustingly severe and a big wig, and you may have a perfect picture of my present appearance." He was neither "that strong active man" Henry once knew, nor the simple, laughing fellow who used to enjoy a round of songs, a game of cards, or a day's fishing. "I can now neither partake of the pleasure of a revel

nor contribute to raise its jollity," he wrote dolefully. "I can neither laugh nor drink, have contracted an hesitating disagreeable
manner of speaking, and a visage that looks illnature itself."

Though Goldsmith was a favorite among the children of Green
Arbour Court, for whom he played the flute as they danced on the
cobblestones in the evening, and though he had completed for
publication his *Enquiry Into the Present State of Polite Learning
in Europe,* he was overcome with self-pity and a sense of the hard
realities of his struggles as he contrasted his life in London with
the pleasant ease he imagined to be characteristic of the existence
of his brother in Ireland. Declaring that he detested the society he
found himself forced "to partake of" in London, he also felt himself to be "unfit" for the society of his old associates at home. "In
short," wrote Goldsmith, "I have thought myself into settled melancholly and an utter disgust of all that life brings with it."

Goldsmith himself realized that this moodiness which he for the
moment indulged was only one side of his mercurial temperament; but he could hardly have known, at this early stage of his
career, that without it he could never have become the witty,
charming, ironic, melancholy, and sometimes sentimental writer
of a varied collection of the world's most treasured essays. Like
the "whimsically dismal" essayist he was, however, he preferred
his rapidly shifting moods to any "settled" views. "I perceive my
dear Sir," he wrote, following a sudden reversal of feeling, "that I
am at intervals for indulging this splenetic manner and following
my own taste regardless of yours." But "whence this romantic turn
that all our family are possessed with," he pondered in his letter to
his brother; "whence this love for every place and every country
but that in which we reside? For every occupation but our own,
this desire of fortune and yet this eagerness to dissipate!"

The immediate reason for Goldsmith's "falling into [his]
gloomy habits of thinking" was that Henry had written him that
he intended to turn his son, then three years old, into a scholar.
Why? asked Goldsmith. Books failed to introduce one to life; the
boy should be taught the rudiments at home and then prepared
for a hard world by a little sound advice:

Preach, then my dear Sir, to your son, not the excellence of human nature, nor the disrespect of riches, but endeavour to teach him thrift and

"A Whimsically Dismal Figure"

œconomy. Let his poor wandering uncles example be placed in his eyes. I had learn'd from books to love virtue, before I was taught from experience the necessity of being selfish. I had contracted the habits and notions of a Philosopher, while I was exposing myself to the insidious approaches of cunning; and often, by being even from my narrow finances charitable to excess, I forgot the rules of justice, and placd myself in the very situation of the wretch who thank'd my bounty.

Goldsmith himself does not appear to have been cast down by his melancholy musings about his fellow man's avarice and cunning. Having composed a fine paragraph on the subject, he wrote; "Your last letter was much too short. . . . Just sit down as I do, and write forward 'till you have filld all your paper, it requires no thought, at least if I may judge from the ease with which my own sentiments rise when they are addressd to you. For believe me my head has no share in all I write my heart dictates the whole." One imagines that in just such a manner Goldsmith learned to fill the sheets of paper which he later sold to various periodicals.[5] By an harmonious interplay of "head" and "heart," he seemed to have been able to banish an awareness of his grim surroundings and to earn enough money to keep himself out of the debtors' prison.

Before Goldsmith brought to a close his long, discursive letter to his brother, he referred to several "triffles" of his, which he saw no reason to conceal. One was the life of "a very extraordinary man. No less than the great Mr. Voltaire." Goldsmith called the work, on which he had spent four weeks, "a catchpenny," written, it is supposed, in order to pay off a debt to his former employer, Ralph Griffiths, then threatening to sue him for some books he had borrowed and failed to return. The other was a portion of an "heroicomical poem," the design for which he had sent his brother in an earlier letter. Oliver reminded Henry that he had intended to "introduce the hero of the Poem as lying in a paltry alehouse," which "may be described somewhat this way":

> [A] Window patch'd with paper lent a ray,
> That feebly shew'd the state in which he lay.
> The sanded floor, that grits beneath the tread
> The humid wall with paltry pictures spread.
> . . . .

The morn was cold he views with keen desire,
A rusty grate unconscious of a fire.
An unpaid reck'ning on the freeze was scor'd,
And five crack'd teacups dress'd the chimney [board.] [6]

"All this is taken you see from Nature," wrote Goldsmith gayly. "It is a Good remark of Montaign's that the wisest men often have friends with whom they do not care how much they play the fool. Take my present follies as instances of regard. Poetry is much an easier and more agreeable species of composition than prose, and could a man live by it, it were no unpleasant employment to be a Poet."

Realizing that the life of a poet would mean permanent poverty, Goldsmith determined to attract the attention of the learned world by *An Enquiry Into the Present State of Polite Learning*. Thomas Percy, later Bishop of Dromore, who called on Goldsmith[7] at 12 Green Arbour Court, on March 31, 1759, found him hard at work on the proof-sheets of this book. Percy wrote in his notebook that he had discovered Goldsmith

in lodgings so poor and uncomfortable that I should not think it proper to mention the circumstance, if I did not consider it the highest proof of the splendor of Dr. Goldsmith's genius and talents, that by the bare exertion of their powers, under every disadvantage of person and fortune, he could gradually emerge from such obscurity, to the enjoyment of all the comforts and even luxuries of life, and admission into the best societies of London. The Doctor was writing his *Enquiry, etc.*, in a wretched dirty room in which there was but one chair, and when he from civility offered it to his visitant, himself was obliged to sit in the window.[8]

The interview was interrupted by the appearance at the door of a ragged but respectable little girl who, after delivering the compliments of her "mamma," begged her neighbor for a "chamberpot of coals." Though a witness to Goldsmith's charity in spite of his own distress, Percy could not have known that Goldsmith, at that time, had just escaped the threat of debtors' prison by hastily writing his "catchpenny" life of Voltaire, that he had appealed in vain to his family and friends in Ireland to take up a subscription to *An Enquiry* to tide him over until the book should appear, and that, in fact, he was precisely the cold and hungry drudge he seemed to be.[9] No doubt the very gaiety of his tone, both to Percy and to his family, kept them from imagining his actual need. In any case, wasn't a garret the very setting for a writer? With "little reputation as an author," he wrote his brother-in-law, Daniel Hodson, in Ireland, in 1757.

I make a shift to live. Nothing more apt to introduce us to the gates of the muses than Poverty; but it were well if she only left us at the door; the mischief is, she sometimes chooses to give her company during the entertainment, and Want, instead of being gentleman-usher, often turns master of the Ceremonies. Thus upon hearing, I write, no doubt, you immagine, I starve, and the name of an Author naturally reminds you of a garret, in this particular I do not think proper to undeceive my Friends; but whether I eat or starve, live in a first floor or four pair of stairs [   ] high, I still remember them with ardour, nay my ve[ry coun]try comes in for a share of my affection.[10]

The chagrin of this hungry young Irishman at finding himself merely the slave of booksellers who, he thought, exploited his talents and left him penniless, was the inspiration of *An Enquiry Into Polite Learning.* The fact that the "dunces of society" combined to make the position of an author "ridiculous and unhappy" was the real subject of this bitter but also amusing analysis of the literary scene in England, Germany, Holland, France, and Italy. But one wonders whether *The State of Polite Learning in Europe* or *The State of Oliver Goldsmith in Green Arbour Court* inspired the following paragraph: "The poet's poverty is a standing topic of contempt. His writing for bread is an unpardonable offence. . . . His taking refuge in garrets and cellars, has of late been violently objected to him. . . . Is poverty the writer's fault? No doubt he knows how to prefer a bottle of champaign to the nectar of the neighbourghing alehouse, or a venison pasty to a plate of potatoes. Want of delicacy is not in him, but in us, who deny him the opportunity of making an elegant choice" (III, 507).

"Wit," continued Goldsmith, is sometimes the only property the poet has for sale. "We must not underrate him who uses it for subsistence, and flies from the ingratitude of the age even to a bookseller for redress." If "stupids" are allowed to laugh at the profession of an author, isn't it better to be "contemptibly rich, than contemptibly poor?" Indeed, Goldsmith's letter to Henry on the subject of the proper education for his son in economy and thrift—not to mention avarice and cunning—suggests that his own struggle to survive occasioned the grim remark in *An Enquiry* that "a long habit of writing for bread thus turns the ambition of every author at last into avarice. . . . He finds that money procures all those advantages, that respect, and that ease, which he vainly expected from fame. Thus the man who, under the protection of the great, might have done honour to humanity, when only patronized by the bookseller, becomes a thing little superior to the fellow who works at the press" (III, 509). The fact that Goldsmith addressed the reader in the third person does not make one any the less aware that he is speaking in his own person. As he observed elsewhere in *An Enquiry*, "the most diminutive son of fame, or of famine, has his *we* and his *us*, his *firstlies* and his *secondlies*, as methodical as if bound in cow-hide, and closed with clasps of brass" (III, 514).

Goldsmith found himself, when he was writing *An Enquiry*, not only friendless and unknown, but also attempting to find his footing in the new conditions of eighteenth-century Grub Street. Authors were now reliant on the booksellers of St. Paul's Churchyard rather than on the favor of the great noblemen to whom the poet of an earlier age had addressed his dedication in the hopes, usually justified, of generous support. Harsh experience taught Goldsmith that this dependence was one of the basic reasons for the enfeebled taste of his day. "The author, when unpatronized by the great, has naturally recourse to the bookseller," wrote Goldsmith who had wielded his pen for Ralph Griffiths and for Samuel Richardson, and who was about to enter into new agreements with John Newbery and Tobias Smollett.[11]

Helpless though Goldsmith was to do otherwise, he was not unaware of the dilemma of the seeker after literary fame when forced to remain in the pay of the bookdealers. "There cannot be a combination more prejudicial to taste than this," he wrote; for "it is to the interest of the one to allow us little for writing, and of the other to write as much, as possible." Describing the writer's fate that he had struggled to elude, Goldsmith stated that "tedious compilations and periodical magazines" are the inevitable result of the collaboration of writer and bookdealer. The author must

A Whimsically Dismal Figure

forego fame and write for bread alone, and this kind of writing requires no imagination: "He sits down to address the venal muse with the most phlegmatic apathy. . . . His reputation never spreads in a wider circle than that of the trade, who generally value him, not for the fineness of his compositions, but for the quantity he works off in a given time" (III, 509).

When Goldsmith wrote these words, he had just escaped from Ralph Griffiths and his wife, who not only had employed him to write without pause from nine in the morning until two in the afternoon, but had also kept him on starvation wages. Perhaps Goldsmith's bitterest complaint was that the Griffiths had ruthlessly and stupidly "edited" in the afternoon what he had written in the morning. Such treatment gives writers "an hatred of their kind," he well knew, and forces them to fly "from thought to drunkenness, yielding to the united pressure of labour, penury, and sorrow" until at last they sink "unheeded, without one friend to drop a tear on their unattended obsequies, and indebted to charity for a grave."

Certainly, Goldsmith described his own character, as well as foresaw the trials and suffering that lay before him, when he wrote that an author should be accorded "proper consideration, as a child of the public, not a rent-charge on the community." A *child* of the public he most certainly is, wrote Goldsmith, "for while so well able to direct others, how incapable he is frequently found of guiding himself!"

His simplicity exposes him to all the insidious approaches of cunning; his sensibility, to the slightest invasion of contempt. Though possessed of fortitude to stand unmoved the unexpected bursts of earthquake, yet of feelings so exquisitely poignant as to agonize under the slightest disappointment. Broken rest, tasteless meals, and causeless anxiety, shorten his life, or render it unfit for active employment; prolonged vigils and intense application still farther contract his span, and make his time glide insensibly away (III, 508).

Though Goldsmith was avowedly incapable of directing himself, he did not for a moment doubt that he was of great value to society as a guide and legislator. Just as Addison and Steele had considered themselves in the *Spectator Papers* as the proper castigators of the follies of the day, so Goldsmith declared, in *An En-*

quiry, that "new fashions, follies, and vices, make new monitors necessary in every age. An author may be considered as a merciful substitute to the legislature. He acts, not by punishing crimes, but preventing them. However virtuous the present age, there may be still growing employment for ridicule or reproof, for persuasion, or satire" (III, 507–8).

II The Bee

Thus Goldsmith defined his own aim as an essayist six months before the first issue of *The Bee* appeared. John Wilkes, a bookseller in St. Paul's Churchyard who was quick to recognize the promise of the little known author of *An Enquiry*, proposed that Goldsmith edit a weekly journal to be printed at Wilkes' shop and sold at the "Sign of the Bible." Many of the ideas on the stage, on universities, on travel, and on critics already presented in *An Enquiry* found fresh expression in *The Bee*. But now the style was light and airy, for, as the reader was told at the opening, "Like bees at large about the flowery fields,/So in our turn we sip of everything." [12]

Again like the bee, Goldsmith warned his readers, the editor "would rove from flower to flower, with seeming inattention, but concealed choice, expatiate over all the beauties of the season," and make his industry his amusement (II, 305–6). A glance at the table of contents—or "the bill of entertainment," to use Goldsmith's phrase—of this little journal that lasted only eight weeks, shows that the bee, in its flight across the "flowery fields" of wit and learning, certainly made an attempt to "sip of everything"— frequently of the works of others which Goldsmith incorporated into his own essays without mentioning his sources. [13]

Urged forward by the sheer necessity of paying off his debts and of escaping from the various discomforts of Green Arbour Court, Goldsmith quickly learned how deftly and effortlessly he could transform the thoughts of others into essays which the next day would please the coffee-house readers. In order to allow himself free scope for any turn chance might throw in his way, he assured his publisher "that as I intended to pursue no fixed method, so it was impossible to form any regular plan; determined never to be tedious, in order to be logical, wherever pleasure presented, I was resolved to follow."

"A Whimsically Dismal Figure"

Goldsmith fell into step with the tradition of the essay, from the time of Montaigne to the twentieth century, which depends for its effect as much on the free and natural expression of the writer as on the ideas advanced. The very opening sentence of these "Essays on the Most Interesting Subjects" puts the reader in touch with the author, who was soon recognized by Londoners as Oliver Goldsmith. Perhaps, wrote the anonymous editor, referring to himself, there is not "a more whimsically dismal figure in nature than a man of real modesty, who assumes an air of impudence— who, while his heart beats with anxiety, studies ease, and affects good-humour."

This humorous-dismal fellow assured his readers when he made his first bow to the public in *The Bee* of Saturday, October 6, 1759, that he was at a loss to know "whether to be merry or sad on this solemn occasion." Should he resolve to be merry, he might soon be "censured as *vastly low*"; should he be prevailingly sorrowful, he might soon be allowed to "mourn in solitude and silence." In short, wrote this laborer in the "Magazine trade," who was determined to write himself out of his poverty, whichever way he looked he saw only "prospects of terror, despair, chandlers' ships, and waste paper." How, then, could a writer hope to achieve any "degree of reputation," he asked, especially when "A *bon mot*, for instance, that might be relished at White's, may lose all its flavour when delivered at the Cat and Bag-pipes in St. Giles's. A jest calculated to spread at a gaming table, may be received with a perfect neutrality of face, should it happen to drop in a mackerel boat. We have all seen dunces triumph in some companies, where men of real humour were disregarded by a general combination in favour of stupidity" (II, 306). "Whatever the merit of his intention may be," Goldsmith concluded, "every writer is now convinced that he must be chiefly indebted to good fortune for finding readers willing to allow him any degree of reputation." A writer who meets with success knows that he owes it, at least in part, "to a happy concurrence of circumstances in its favour."

Several weeks later, in the fourth issue of *The Bee* (II, 362–79), Goldsmith was forced to admit that, were he to attempt to estimate the merit of his recent venture into journalism by the rapidity of the sale of his journal, his "pride as an author" would certainly suffer. The fame of many other writers for newspapers and magazines, he noticed, covered a wide circle of London, "some as far as Islington"; but his "has hardly travelled beyond the sound of Bow-bell." Though the writing of others "fly like unpinioned swans, I find my own move as heavily as a new-plucked goose." Should the editor show his "indignation against the public" by discontinuing his "endeavours to please"? Further reflection suggested to him that the absence of *The Bee* might hardly be noticed by those who daily hurried through St. Paul's Churchyard in pursuit of their private business or pleasure: "The sun, after so sad an accident, might shine next day as bright as usual . . . and not a single creature feel any regret but myself." Instead of causing Apollo to go into mourning, and giving the Muses "a fit of the spleen," the untimely demise of *The Bee* might only cause Grub Street to laugh at the fall of its ambitious editor.

"In short," Goldsmith concluded, "I am resolved to write on, if it were only to spite them." If all who criticised him should be "clapped in the pillory, kept fifteen days upon bread and water, and obliged to run the gauntlet through Pater-noster Row," Goldsmith would be "perfectly content." However, since posterity alone seems to be able to administer literary justice, Goldsmith decided to adopt a more practical plan and to render *The Bee* more generally popular by addressing himself to the "vulgar" rather than to the "learned" and the "witty": "Considering things in a prudential light, perhaps I was mistaken in designing my paper as an agreeable relaxation to the studious, or a help to conversation among the gay; instead of addressing it to such, I should have written down to the taste and apprehension of the many, and sought for reputation on the broad road. Literary fame, I now find, like religious, generally begins among the vulgar" (II, 364).

The importance of *The Bee* for the reader today is that one sees in the eight issues the young Goldsmith struggling to discover his own vein as a writer: whether to be merry or sad; whether to address himself to the vulgar or to the learned; whether to "lay by a proper stock of popular subjects"; or to write instead a critical comment on the preachers and orators to be heard in London. Goldsmith never settled these questions; instead, he mingled the serious and the humorous, for both were deep in his nature. Whether or not his readers cared for the results, write he must.

"A Whimsically Dismal Figure"

When one of his subscribers declared that he intended to throw away no more threepences on purchasing *The Bee* and, further, would not recommend the sheet to his neighbors, Goldsmith, forgetting both bread and fame, laughed off this threat to retort: "Were my soul set upon threepences, what anxiety might not a denunciation produce! But such does not happen to be the present motive of publication: I write partly to show my good nature, and partly to show my vanity; nor will I lay down my pen till I am satisfied one way or another" (II, 365–66).

Unsuccessful though *The Bee* was, it at least brought Goldsmith into contact with the important writers, editors, and publishers of London. One of the essays included in the fifth issue of *The Bee* brought him the attention of Samuel Johnson and Tobias Smollett by the simple device of praising their writing. The essay "A Reverie" (II, 388–94) was written, declared the author, "in order to eke out the present page." It grew, he said, from the reflection that "though our present writers had not equal merit with their predecessors, it would be politic to use them with ceremony." It was easy to pay compliments to Dryden and Pope, whose immortality was assured; but should not the critic assume that in the republic of letters, which "hangs at present so feebly together," some at least were "laying in stores for immortality?"

"Indulging these reflections," Goldsmith conceived of a "Fame Machine," a great stage-coach, which, having delivered Addison, Swift, Pope, Steele, Congreve, and Colley Cibber at the Temple of Fame, had now returned to the innyard for the next batch of passengers bound for Immortality. No one was allowed to climb aboard unless he could prove to the coachman that the luggage he carried was of sufficient value to serve as security for the price of his ticket. Goldsmith, with only a few copies of *The Bee* under his arm, was invited by the coachman to stand aside while his more notable contemporaries took their places.

Among the would-be passengers was "a very grave personage" who seemed at a distance to be "a very reserved, even disagreeable figure." In spite of his severity, however, he proved on closer inspection to have "one of the most good-natured contenances that could be imagined." He attempted to place "a parcel of folios" on the seat of the coach, but "our inquisitorial coachman" promptly shoved them onto the ground:

"What! not take in my Dictionary?" exclaimed the other in a rage. "Be patient, Sir," replied the coachman, "I have drove a coach, man and boy, these two thousand years; but I do not remember to have carried above one dictionary during the whole time. That little book which I perceive peeping from one of your pockets, may I presume to ask what it contains?"—"A mere trifle," replied the author; "it is called the *Rambler*." "*The Rambler!*" says the coachman, "I beg, Sir, you'll take your place" (II, 392).

After Dr. Johnson was safely seated, Goldsmith's attention was drawn to a crowd which was urging forward a man who seemed to prefer "the Stage-coach of Riches" to "the Stage-coach of Fame." Impelled by his admirers against his will towards the "Fame Machine," this writer waved before the eyes of the coachman the pages of a voluminous history, and asked whether that would give him the right to enter: " 'Sir, I have formerly heard your name mentioned,' says the coachman, 'but never as an historian. Is there no other work upon which you may claim a place?' —'None,' replied the other, 'except a romance; but that is a work of too trifling a nature to claim further attention.'—'You mistake,' says the inquisitor, 'a well-written romance is no such easy task as is generally imagined' " (II. 393–94). This passenger was none other than Tobias Smollett, historian, novelist, and editor of the *British Magazine* to which Goldsmith was soon a contributor.

Goldsmith attempted, for his part, to "dazzle" the coachman with "the splendour" of a page of *The Bee*; he, never having heard of the author before, read in silence the title and the table of contents "without any emotion," and refused him a place on the "Fame Machine." "I expect better passengers," he assured the supplicant; "but as you seem a harmless creature, perhaps, if there be room left, I may let you ride a while for charity." "So he drove away," Goldsmith wrote in conclusion, "and for myself, as I could not get in, I mounted behind, in order to hear the conversation on the way" (II, 394).

III   The Citizen of the World

Though Goldsmith's name was unknown in 1759 to the driver of the "Fame Machine," it was soon familiar to the passengers in the coach as well as to the crowd which stood about the innyard. When Tobias Smollett and John Newbery invited Goldsmith tc contribute to their new venture, the *British Magazine,* he cheerfully responded by writing at least twenty essays, among them "A Reverie of the Boars Head Tavern in Eastcheap," and "Adventures of a Strolling Player." Always ready to assume a burden of work beyond his strength, he also agreed to contribute to the *Public Ledger,* a journal only recently begun by Newbery, publisher of children's books.[14]

The essays that Goodsmith wrote anonymously for the *Public Ledger* were known as the "Chinese Letters," for they purported to be the naïve reflections of a gentleman from China on his first visit to London. Beginning on January 24, 1760, and continuing to August 14, 1761, these ninety-eight essays were immediately collected into one volume, *The Citizen of the World,* which appeared on May 1, 1762.

Goldsmith's position, after the publication of *The Citizen of the World,* was sufficiently assured to enable him to move to a two-room apartment at No. 6 Wine Court Office, Fleet Street, and also to maintain a room in Canonbury House, Islington, to which he retreated to escape—or elude—the various pressures of London. Both of these chambers were controlled by John Newbery, well-known to the coachman of the "Fame Machine" as one of the more liberal publishers in St. Paul's Churchyard.

Though John Newbery was more generous and fair in his treatment of writers than Ralph Griffiths, he was equally firm with Goldsmith in money matters. Since Goldsmith was incapable of living within any budget, Newbery subtracted the amount Goldsmith needed for room and board, gave him advances on forthcoming books, kept careful records of all his transactions with his wayward and gifted writer, and passed the accounts on to his nephew Francis Newbery at his death some ten years later. Thus Goldsmith remained, in a sense, permanently enslaved to the Newberys and to other less generous publishers for the remainder of his comparatively short career. Unable to deny the solicitations of any beggar, especially if he proved to be an Irishman; unable, too, to resist the promise of merriment, either at a gambling table, a nearby tavern, or a gentleman's mansion; careless in the payment of debts; and subject to seizures of personal vanity which found expression in velvet coats and in costly dinner parties in his Temple chambers, Goldsmith was hounded by problems of

[33]

money all of his life; and, though moderately well paid by his publishers, he was seldom out of debt.

The two sides of Goldsmith's nature—the one, reasonable, ironically critical, and gay; the other, gloomy, suspicious, and secretive—are clearly defined in his first book to achieve permanent success, *The Citizen of the World*. The Chinese Philosopher and the Man in Black, both projections of their author, reflect the dichotomy of Goldsmith's mind, which was discernible in his earlier essays in *The Bee*. The character of the philosophising Chinaman was proposed and discussed by Goldsmith in a letter to his boyhood friend, Robert Bryanton,[15] several years before his "Chinese Letters" appeared, just as Oliver had sketched the outlines of the Man in Black in his letter to his brother Henry at this same time. Similarly the character of Lien Chi Altangi had already been treated in *The Bee* by a little story Goldsmith retold in order to illustrate the point he reiterated in his "Chinese Letters": that by travel alone one learns to overcome one's parochialism (II, 416). So also Goldsmith had suggested the Chinaman's foil, the Man in Black, in the somber night-wanderer presented in *The Bee* in an essay entitled "A City Night Piece."[16] The two finally met in Letter XIII of *The Citizen of the World* (III, 47-52), as they strolled about Westminster Abbey, examining the monuments erected to the honor of poets, statesmen, warriors, and kings. Goldsmith was again considering the meaning of fame.

"Alas!" Lien had sighed as he studied the monuments, "how does pride attend the puny child of dust even to the grave!" All of these great men must have "toiled for an hour to gain a transient immortality, and are at length retired to the grave, where they have no attendant but the worm, none to flatter but the epitaph." As Altangi was "indulging such reflections, a gentleman dressed in black, perceiving that he was a stranger, politely offered to be his instructor and guide through the great Abbey. "If any monument," said he, "should particularly excite your curiosity, I shall endeavour to satisfy your demands."

The Chinese Philosopher, who eagerly accepted the gentleman's offer, stated, without a touch of cynicism, that he had come to the Abbey "to observe the policy, the wisdom, and the justice of the English, in conferring rewards upon deceased merit." In the lofty style of the Oriental, the Chinese visitor enlarged upon the duty of every good government to provide such a "glorious incentive" as a monument in Westminster. The Man in Black, however, appeared impatient of the stranger's observations, so he lapsed into silence, as they "walked on together to take a view of every particular monument in order as it lay." The monuments, tombs, statues, and busts—all were examined by the two philosophers; the Chinaman was eager to admire the memory of great men, and the cynic by his side patiently explained to his astonished companion that, if one but had enough money, one might purchase a monument from "the guardian of the temple."

One overhears the voice of Goldsmith himself in the remarks of the Man in Black as the two approach the Poet's Corner. Here, he explained, true genius is seldom rewarded, for reputations are determined by reviewers for the journals. "There are a set of men called answerers of books," he explained, "who take upon them to watch the republic of letters, and distribute reputations by the sheet." Such wretches, kept in the pay of booksellers, are especially employed to "praise the dead, and revile the living."

But the true character of the Man in Black, like Goldsmith's, is neither cynical nor harsh; he is actually so moved by compassion for others that he with difficulty conceals his feelings beneath his apparent bluntness. As Lien describes him to his friend, Fum Hoam, in Letter XXVI (III, 95–98), the manners of the Man in Black are "tinctured with some strange inconsistencies, and he may justly be termed a humourist in a nation of humourists." [17] Though his conversation was filled with "the most sordid and selfish maxims," his heart was "dilated with the most unbounded love. I have known him profess himself a man-hater, while his cheek was glowing with compassion; and, while his looks were softened into pity, I have heard him use the language of the most unbounded ill-nature." Pretending to indifference to the pleas of a beggar with a dying wife and five hungry children, he had pressed a piece of silver into his hand, just as Goldsmith had done in a similar situation with a poor student in Dublin. The Man in Black, wrote the Chinese Philosopher, "takes as much pains to hide his feelings, as any hypocrite would to conceal his indifference."

The "History of the Man in Black," which fills Letter XXVII (III, 99–105), purports to be an account of the early life of Lien's new friend, but is in fact the story only slightly veiled of Goldsmith's own youth.[18] After "repeated solicitations" on the part of the Chinese visitor, Mr. Drybone, as the Man in Black was called, thus began: "If you are fond," said he, "of hearing hairbreadth 'scapes, my history must certainly please; for I have been for twenty years upon the very verge of starving, without ever being starved."

My father, the younger son of a good family, was possessed of a small living in the church. His education was above his fortune, and his generosity greater than his education. Poor as he was, he had his flatterers still poorer than himself; for every dinner he gave them, they returned an equivalent in praise; and this was all he wanted. The same ambition that actuates a monarch at the head of an army, influenced my father at the head of his table. He told the story of the ivy-tree, and that was laughed at; he repeated the jest of the two scholars and one pair of breeches, and the company laughed at that; but the story of Taffy in the sedan-chair, was sure to set the table in a roar. Thus his pleasure increased in proportion to the pleasure he gave; he loved all the world, and he fancied all the world loved him.

An earnest believer in "universal benevolence," the Rector taught his children to prefer learning to money, for "that was dross," and took as much pains to form the morals of his brood as to improve their understanding. "We were taught to consider all the wants of mankind as our own," so that the minister's children could never afterwards withstand any appeal of distress. In short, "we were perfectly instructed in the art of giving away thousands, before we were taught the more necessary qualifications of getting a farthing." Indeed, the father succeeded in winding his children up to be "mere machines of pity," rendering them "incapable of withstanding the slightest impulse made either by real or fictitious distress." Armed with "a stock of wisdom" which enabled him to talk like his father "upon subjects that once were useful," but were so no longer, the Man in Black "made his first entrance into the busy and insidious world." There he found himself at a loss as to how to deal with the cunning, the distress, the avarice, and the cruelty he encountered on every side.

How long the Man in Black might have remained in "this torpid state of simplicity," in regard to money, he hardly knew. He was roused at last by seeing a former acquaintance, "whom I knew to be a prudent blockhead," given a fine position by the government. This discovery made him realize that he "had pursued a wrong track, and that the true way of being able to relieve others, was first to aim at independence" himself. "For a free, open, undesigning deportment," the Man in Black "put on that of closeness, prudence, and economy," and made it his "immediate care" to leave his humble habitation and to reform his too liberal character. Mr. Drybone, once the generous friend of those in need, now told his Chinese friend that "one of the most heroic actions I ever performed, and for which I shall praise myself as long as I live, was the refusing half-a-crown to an old acquaintaince, at the time when he wanted it and I had it to spare." Pursuing a course of "uninterrupted frugality," he "seldom wanted a dinner, and was consequently invited to twenty." The Man in Black soon began to be known as a man who had money, and thus grew into general esteem:

Neighbors have asked my advice in the disposal of their daughters; and I have always taken care not to give any. I have contracted a friendship with an alderman, only by observing, that if we take a farthing from a thousand pounds, it will be a thousand pounds no longer. . . . If ever I am asked a question, whether I know it or not, instead of answering, I only smile and look wise. If a charity is proposed, I go about with my hat, but put nothing in myself. If a wretch solicits my pity, I observe that the world is filled with imposters, and take a certain method of not being deceived, by never relieving. In short, I now find the truest way of finding esteem, even from the indigent, is—to give away nothing, and thus have much in our power to give.

After this initial conversation in Westminster Abbey, the Chinese Philosopher, armed with the book on Confucius and a bank account, and the Man in Black, equipped with a cloak of cynicism and a knowledge of London, pursued their investigation of the world in the best of humor. Each in his own way having achieved a fundamental understanding of the human heart, the two were able to discuss profitably such questions as "the great number of old maids and bachelors in London," the concept of justice held by the English, or the art of gardening in China and in England. All conversation led to delightful observations, cheerful satire, and wise conclusions; for these commentators on the ways of the world were gay of heart, in spite of their awareness of human cruelty and impending disasters. As the reader accompanies the pair through the parks of London, into the coffee houses and clubs, to the theaters, to the churches, and to Bedlam, he comes to recognize them as two sides of Goldsmith's nature, already made familiar to him by Goldsmith's earlier venture, *The Bee.*

Lien Chi Altangi is as characteristic of Goldsmith's sociable nature as Mr. Drybone is of his withdrawing, solitary impulses. Expecting little of "human nature," calmly aware of the approach of old age and death, accepting his precarious position on "the wheel of fortune" without complaint, the Chinese Philosopher said of himself: "Though naturally pensive, yet I am fond of gay company, and take every opportunity of thus dismissing the mind from duty. From this motive, I am found in the centre of a crowd; and wherever pleasure is to be sold I am a purchaser." Without attracting the notice of the passersby, Altangi freely joins in "whatever goes forward," consciously works his "passions into a similitude of frivolous earnestness," and shouts as the crowd shouts or condemns "as they happen to disapprove." With his customary dignity, he justifies his actions by the thought that "a mind thus sunk for a while below its natural standard, is qualified for stronger flights, as those first retire who would spring forward with greater vigour." (III, 203).

IV *Goldsmith as a Character-Writer*

A novelist at heart, Goldsmith in the course of the "Chinese Letters" made the contrast between the character of Lien Chi Altangi and Mr. Drybone still more evident by introducing a number of minor characters. One of the most charming of these is Beau Tibbs, "an important trifler," who, curiously enough, also bears a certain resemblance to Goldsmith. On a serene summer evening, Lien Chi and his friend in black "went to gaze upon the company in one of the public walks near the city," as they frequently did. One sees them, in Letter LIV (III, 203–6), sauntering along the paths beneath the trees, "either praising the beauty of such as were handsome, or the dresses of such as had nothing else to recommend them." They were thus deliberately making their way through the throng of evening strollers, when, wrote Altangi, "my friend caught me by the elbow, and led me out of the public walk" in a vain endeavor to avoid the little gentleman approaching them. They were soon overtaken, however, and the Man in Black was addressed "with all the familiarity of an old acquaintance" by the intrusive and persistent Beau. "My dear Drybone," cried he, shaking his friend's hand, "Where have you been hiding this half a century? Positively, I had fancied you were gone down to cultivate matrimony and your estate in the country."

While Beau Tibbs was thus addressing Mr. Drybone, the Chinese Philosopher was carefully studying the appearance of their new companion, whom he later described to his distant correspondent. "His hat was pinched up with peculiar smartness," he wrote; "his looks were pale, thin, and sharp; round his neck he wore a broad black riband, and in his bosom a buckle studded with glass; his coat was trimmed with tarnished twist; he wore by his side a sword with a black hilt; and his stockings of silk, though newly washed, were grown yellow by long service."

Beau Tibbs, after a merry exchange of gossip, withdrew with a flourish of his hat and the usual afterthought—"But, dear Drybone, you are an honest creature; lend me half-a-crown for a minute to two, or so, just till—but harkee, ask me for it the next time we meet, or it may be twenty to one but I forget to pay you." The sober Man in Black reached in his pocket for the half-crown, in spite of his resolution not to indulge his weakness. After the withdrawal of the Beau, he turned to the Chinese Philosopher, and cried, "His very dress is not less extraordinary than his conduct. If you meet him this day, you find him in rags; if the next, in embroidery. With those persons of distinction of whom he talks so familiarly, he has scarce a coffeehouse acquaintance." This "harmless, amusing little thing," who appeared and reappeared in the course of the subsequent Letters, offered Goldsmith a chance to enlarge upon the ramifications of the relationship of man and money, especially interesting when viewed against the rigid pattern of eighteenth-century class distinctions. Beau Tibbs was not merely a borrower of shillings; he was also a flatterer, a name-dropper, a braggart, a snob—and, at the same time, a charming and pathetic little creature.

The Beau gave Goldsmith just the opportunity he needed to put into practice what he had observed from a study of Samuel Butler's skill as a "character-writer" that had been learned, noted Goldsmith, from La Bruyère, who "has the happy art of varying his manner; when the bare description of nature begins to disgust, he has recourse to a story, and when this has ceased to surprise, he finds refuge in a bon mot" (IV, 379). Following this practical formula, Goldsmith presented Beau Tibbs first in abstract terms. Had Goldsmith been a seventeenth-century character writer, he might have entitled this paragraph on the Beau "An Important Trifler":

Both for the interests of society, and perhaps his own, Heaven has made him poor, and while all the world perceives his wants, he fancies them concealed from every eye. An agreeable companion, because he understands flattery; and all must be pleased with the first part of his conversation, though all are sure of its ending with a demand on their purse. While his youth countenances the levity of his conduct, he may thus earn a precarious subsistence; but when age comes on, the gravity of which is incompatible with buffoonery, then will he find himself forsaken by all; condemned in the decline of life to hang upon some rich family whom he once despised, there to undergo all the ingenuity of studied contempt, to be employed only as a spy upon the servants, or a bugbear to fright the children into obedience.

Although Goldsmith thus presented Beau Tibbs in terms of a seventeenth-century character writer at the end of Letter LIV, in the next Letter he showed that he had mastered "the happy art of varying his manner" by having "recourse to a story." Overtaking the Chinese Philosopher in the park the day after their first meeting, Beau Tibbs slapped him on the shoulder and saluted him "with an air of the most perfect familiarity." He was dressed as usual, "except that he had more powder in his hair, wore a dirtier shirt, a pair of temple spectacles, and his hat under his arm." After a stroll about the park—which, though thronged, Tibbs declared "devoid of company"—the Beau led Lien Chi to his flat at the very top of a shabby little house near the park. There the visitor was introduced to Mrs. Tibbs, "at once a slattern and a coquette," and waited in vain for dinner which never appeared. As his appetite increased, his curiosity began to abate; the only comfort to the Chinese Philosopher was the aphorism he composed for Fum Hoam: "The company of fools may at first make us smile, but at last never fails of rendering us melancholy."

"A Whimsically Dismal Figure"

Letter LXXI (III, 266–70) described a trip to Vauxhall for an evening of fun. Squeezed together in one hackney coach were Beau Tibbs, with his wife on his lap; the Chinese Philosopher; the Man in Black; and the pawnkeeper's widow, "dressed out in green damask, with three gold rings on every finger." In spite of the foreboding of Tibbs that he would see no personages there worth his attention, and of Mrs. Tibbs' insistence that all should be conducted in the most "genteel" manner possible, and of the widow's ardent wish to see the fireworks, their two more serious companions, Altangi and Mr. Drybone, manage to enjoy the evening. Ample opportunity was afforded them to observe the absurd snobbery of Beau Tibbs, the ridiculous pretensions of Mrs. Tibbs, and the hearty vulgarity of the widow.

V Two Philosophers

Though a study of "human nature" was for these two philosophers a large part of the entertainment, they at the same time enjoyed the gay scene before them. "Head of Confucius!" cried Altangi to his friend, "this is fine! this unites rural beauty with courtly magnificence! If we except the virgins of immortality, that hang on every tree, and may be plucked at every desire, I do not see how this falls short of Mahomet's Paradise!" Like Goldsmith, whose capacity for enjoyment was as marked as his ability to moralize, Lien was lifted into "an ecstasy of admiration" when the orchestra began to play and he suddenly heard "the full-bodied concert bursting on the stillness of the night." Here, at last, nature and art were harmoniously joined: "The natural concert of the birds, in the more retired part of the grove, vieing with that which was formed by art; the company gaily dressed, looking satisfaction, and the table spread with various delicacies, all conspired to fill [Altangi's] imagination with the visionary happiness of the Arabian lawgiver." Lien Chi Altangi, master of the sublime style, trained in the seventeen books of Chinese courtesy, expounder of the wisdom of Confucius, was also capable of rapture when he beheld the illuminated lamps among the trees of the park, especially when they were reflected in the canal and caught in a hundred fountains. Strolling crowds, soft music, and delicious food served in leafy arbors invited visions of Paradise. Lien Chi Altangi reflected not only Goldsmith's more "rational" side, as opposed to the more "feeling" nature of the Man in Black, but also Gold-smith's gayer, vainer, and more worldly self. For he, too, liked to spend evenings at Vauxhall, sauntering through the groves, and mingling with the crowds.

It was the Chinese Philosopher, rather than Mr. Drybone, who strayed one day into the shop of a London mercer, and was flat-tered into buying a morning-coat—"rich, tasty, and quite the thing"—which he by no means wanted. Returning to his lodging, he reflected in Letter LXXVII, as no doubt Goldsmith often had, "I knew he was only answering his own purposes, even while he attempted to appear solicitous about mine: yet, by a voluntary infatuation, a sort of passion compounded of vanity and good-nature, I walked into the snare with my eyes open." Just as Gold-smith's pleasure in a new coat outweighed his discretion, so also the wisdom of the Chinese Philosopher was no match for the per-suasion of the London tailor. "The wisdom of the ignorant," ob-served Lien to his correspondent, "somewhat resembles the in-stinct of animals; it is diffused in but a very narrow sphere, but within that circle it acts with vigour, uniformity, and success."

In Letter XC the two sides of Goldsmith's nature—the merry and the sad—met and conversed with that harmony which oppo-sites sometimes experience. Expounding on this state of mind, Lien Chi described an encounter with his English companion for the benefit of Fum Hoam. "Some days ago," he wrote, "I went to visit the man in black, and entered his house with that cheerful-ness which the certainty of a favourable reception always in-spires." Opening the door of his friend's chamber, however, he "found him with the most rueful face imaginable, in a morning gown and flannel nightcap, earnestly employed in learning to blow the German flute." Lien ventured to ask him what could have persuaded him to attempt so difficult an instrument, so late in life, especially "without the consolation of being musical." When he found he was met only with groans and angry looks, he sought to cheer his friend by the means he had previously discov-ered to be effective. "I began to discant," he wrote, "on those gloomy topics by which philosophers often get rid of their own spleen, by communicating it: the wretchedness of a man in this life; the happiness of some wrought out of the miseries of others; the necessity that wretches should expire under punishment, that rogues might enjoy affluence in tranquillity." Thus the Chinese Philosopher led the Man in Black, who by now had laid aside his flute, "from the inhumanity of the rich to the ingratitude of the beggar; from the insincerity of refinement to the fierceness of rusticity; and at last had the good fortune to restore him to his usual serenity of temper, by permitting him to expatiate upon the modes of human misery."

Beguiled by the doleful philosophizing of his Chinese visitor, the Man in Black attempted to explain that he had taken up a study of the flute, for which he had no gift, in order to combat his tendency to melancholy. Some nights ago, he said, sitting alone by his expiring fire, he read until too late an hour an account of "the hideous cruelties" of certain "haters of mankind." He threw down the book in an agony of rage" and "began to think with malice of all the human kind." The ticking of his watch, the wind at the window, the cry of the nightwatchman—all seemed "noisy and troublesome" to the solitary man. "I strove to find a resource in philosophy and reason," but all to no avail.

In words which recall Goldsmith's projection of himself in "A City Night Piece," he now wrote: "Morning came, I sought for tranquillity in dissipation, sauntered from one place of public resort to another, and found myself disagreeable to some of my acquaintance, and ridiculous to others." In his earlier essay for *The Bee,* Goldsmith had described the same character, ending with similar painful reflections, which he removed after the first edition, as being perhaps too autobiographical: "He has passed the whole day in company he hates, and now goes to prolong the night among company that as heartily hate him. May his vices be detected; may the morning rise upon his shame! Yet I wish to no purpose: villany, when detected, never gives up, but boldly adds impudence to imposture."

Which predominated in the "whimsically dismal" character of Goldsmith, the Man in Black or the Chinese Philosopher? Probably, at this point in his career, the more cheerful, the more rational "Citizen of the World" controlled the darker moods of his companion when the two were together. Mr. Drybone alone could hardly cope with his "black" moods. Both characters have behind them long traditions in literature; in the former, we recognize the familiar Renaissance picture of "the malancholy man," suffering from the "humour" of black bile, and easily identify Goldsmith's Man in Black as a younger brother of Shakespeare's Hamlet. In the case of the latter, we encounter the well-known figure of the philosophic traveler from the Orient, made famous in the eighteenth century by Montesquieu's *Lettres Persanes* and by Voltaire's *Asiatic*—to mention only two of many such publications.[19]

Goldsmith, however, breathed into these traditions so much of his own genius that he transformed the material from which he borrowed. When the Chinese described his first sight of London to Fum Hoam, for example, the reader is conscious of how Goldsmith must have felt when he, alone and friendless, first strolled through the great city. The letter Lien Chi wrote home to China might have been written by Goldsmith to his brother Henry soon after his arrival in London. "Judge, then, how great is my disappointment on entering London," wrote Altangi, after two days in that great city, "wherever I turn, I am presented with a gloomy solemnity in the houses, the streets, and the inhabitants: none of that beautiful gilding which makes a principal ornament in Chinese architecture." Though Goldsmith was a traveler from Ireland rather than from China, he, too, had been amazed by the "gloomy solemnity" of the metropolis, its muddy streets crowded with heavy carts and lumbering coaches.

Goldsmith, no doubt, recalled the streets of his Irish village through a golden haze, as did the Chinese traveler when he wrote, "The streets of Nankin are sometimes strewed with gold leaf; very different are those of London: in the midst of their pavements a great lazy puddle moves muddily along; heavy-laden machines, with wheels of unwieldly thickness, crowd up every passage; so that a stranger, instead of finding time for observation, is often happy if he has time to escape from being crushed to pieces" (III, 15). Goldsmith here described Fleet Street Ditch, meandering down Ludgate Hill, at the foot of Breakneck Step which led to his chamber in Green Arbour Court.

In the character of the Man in Black, Goldsmith himself might have retired to his lonely room, there to "pour over the page of antiquity, or the sallies of contemporary genius" until the town clock had struck two. Then he roused himself and exclaimed, "Let me no longer waste the night . . . but pursue the solitary walk, where vanity, ever changing, but a few hours past, walked before me. . . . What a gloom hangs all around! The dying lamp feebly emits a yellow gleam; no sound is heard but of the chiming clock, or the distant watch-dog. All the bustle of human pride is forgotten and this hour may well display the emptiness of human vanity." But now how empty are the streets which only a few hours ago were crowded; those who hasten by him "no longer now wear their daily mask, nor attempt to hide their lewdness or their misery." Who are these creatures "who make the street their couch" and sleep in the dark doorways of "the opulent?" They are "strangers, wanderers, and orphans," some of them "without the covering even of rags," and others "emaciated with disease," people "too humble to expect redress," with "distresses too great even for pity." Goldsmith shared the hunger and cold of these "poor, houseless creatures." One cannot question the sincerity of his despair when he cried out in his own voice rather than that of his assumed role, "Why, why was I born a man, and yet see the sufferings of wretches I cannot relieve!" (II, 376–78). Goldsmith had been a stranger and a wanderer in London, and had not learned to suppress his personal emotions when he wrote "A Night Piece."

The initial shock felt by the Chinese Philosopher at the sight of London's filthy streets and dismal buildings inspired him with no such melancholy thoughts, for he was a Citizen of the World armed with objectivity and common sense, and reflected the other side of Goldsmith's nature. In Letter III, addressed to Fum Hoam, "First President of the Ceremonial Academy at Pekin, in China," Lien Chi established the philosophic outlook of a traveler which was sustained throughout all of his Letters. "I consider myself here as a newly created being, introduced into a new world," he wrote. "Every object strikes with wonder and surprise. The imagination, still unsated, seems the only active principle of the mind. The most trifling occurrences give pleasure, till the gloss of novelty is worn away." For over a year, Lien Chi Altangi reported on the costumes, the journals, the parks, the theaters, the coffee-houses of London, with the same wonder and surprise that he felt on his arrival. "When I have ceased to wonder, I may possibly grow wise," he added. "I may then call the reasoning principle to my aid, and compare those objects with each other, which were before examined without reflection" (III, 17).

Thus the reader is introduced to the character of the Chinese Philosopher who remains precisely the same reasoning creature when one leaves him at the end of the "Chinese Letters" as he was when one first made his acquaintance. Though one views all the people and places of London through his eyes alone, he himself is no more than the rational factor in a philosophic equation. Though his character is incapable of further development, the reader continues to enjoy him for the wit and wisdom which the exercise of reason always reveals. The opportunities for irony, satire, humor, and wit presented to Goldsmith by such an imagined personality are limitless. "Behold me, then, in London, gazing at the strangers and they at me," wrote this seeming-simple Chinaman in the same Letter III to his friend: "It seems they find somewhat absurd in my figure; and had I been never from home, it is possible I might find an infinite fund of ridicule in theirs: but by long travelling, I am taught to laugh at folly alone, and to find nothing truly ridiculous but villany and vice." Before quitting his native land and passing over the Chinese Wall, Lien had naturally supposed that "every deviation from the customs and manners of China was a departure from nature." Now he has learned to disregard the prejudices of all countries and to realize that people everywhere are intent upon improving on "nature's simple plan" but according to their own limited views. By travel alone one learns to combat one's parochialism and become a true "citizen of the world," who, because of his wide, objective view of many civilizations, does not identify himself with the vanity, the misery, or the illusions of any.

Altangi's wisdom was soon put to the test by the news he learned of his family. Before many days had passed, Lien Chi Altangi received a communication from his friend, which, after the usual flowery opening, informed him "with a heart full of sorrow" that "what the world calls happiness" could no longer be his. The Emperor, displeased with his sudden departure, had seized Lien's wife, daughter, and the rest of his household, and appropriated them to his use. Only his fifteen-year-old son had Fum managed to secrete from the Emperor. "You see, my dearest friend," wrote Fum, not able to resist his opportunity to moralize, "what imprudence has brought thee to. . . . Want of prudence is too frequantly the want of virtue. . . . How long, my friend, shall an enthusiasm for knowledge continue to obstruct your happiness, and tear you from all the connections that makes life pleasant?" (III, 29–30). Lien replied in Letter VII that, though as a human being he had shed tears over the fate of his family, as a philosopher he could but "submit to the stroke of Heaven." He was prepared to outface disaster, for "I hold the volume of Confucius in my hand, and, as I read, grow humble, and patient, and wise" (III, 31–33).

The wit and wisdom of the Chinese Philosopher prevail over the sad experiences of life, and thus he becomes the perfect companion for the Man in Black, who was "tinctured with some strange inconsistences." In the end, Altangi resolved to spend the remainder of his life in travel, "examining the manner of different countries"; and he "prevailed upon the man in black to be [his] companion." Like so many of Goldsmith's characters, the two resolved their difficulties by becoming travelers. "They must often change," says Confucius, "who would be constant in happiness or wisdom" (III, 446).

The year after the publication of the "Letters" as *The Citizen of the World* (1762), Goldsmith was asked to join Percy, Johnson, and others as one of the original members of a club, later known as the Literary Club. By accepting this invitation, Goldsmith moved forever from the lonely isolation in which he had lived in London while writing *An Enquiry, The Bee,* and many other essays and reviews. Though Goldsmith showed that he was able to maintain a delicate balance in the essays which make up his first important book between the rational and the emotional, and that, indeed, the rational, in the figure of the Chinese Philosopher, was plainly in the ascendancy throughout, one is reminded by the Preface to *The Citizen of the World* that the bland good humor and intrepid optimism of the supposed writer of the "Letters" does not reflect the range of the author's feeling. Here Goldsmith reminded his readers of the other side of his character: "Though none are injured by my rage, I am naturally too savage to court any friends by fawning—too obstinate to be taught new tricks; and too improvident to mind what may happen. I am appeased, though not contented: too indolent for intrigue, and too timid to push for favour, I am—but what signifies what I am?" (III, 12).

The private rage that here broke through the surface of Goldsmith's assumed role as a Chinese Philosopher is also felt in the poetry and prose he was about to attempt, for Goldsmith was always, in certain moods, the Man in Black. Though much of Goldsmith's power was squandered in hackwork, all that he wrote that has survived the test of time proves to be an attempt to complete his unfinished sentence, "I am—what signifies what I am?"

In one of his earliest known letters to a friend of his youth, Robert Bryanton,[20] Goldsmith, in playfully unfolding his future hopes, and lightly revealing his present distresses, wrote: "Where the d—l *is I?* Oh, Gods! Gods! here in a garret writing for bread, and expecting to be dunned for a milk score!" Goldsmith at that time was a penniless drudge of Grub Street, whose days were spent in servitude to Ralph Griffiths and his wife. But, as he wrote Bob Bryanton, he had just completed *An Enquiry,* and was looking forward to fame from a series of "Chinese Letters" taking shape in his mind. "I shall soon make our Chinese talk like an Englishman," he wrote. Professors of literature in China generations hence might begin a lecture on "Oliver Goldsmith" thus: "Oliver Goldsmith flourished in the eighteenth and nineteenth centuries. He lived to be an hundred and three years old, [and in that] age may justly be styled the sun of [literature] and the Confucius of Europe."

After a lengthy paragraph in this vein, Goldsmith suddenly broke off, not wishing "to tire my Chinese Philosopher, nor you, nor myself," and remembering perhaps that at the moment his "ill-natured contemporaries" were suffering his "genius to lie neglected." With mocking rage he exclaimed, "God's curse, Sir! who am I? Eh! what am I?" The answer to these impatient questions Goldsmith never found; the search, however, continued during the fifteen years of his harried writing career. His friend Bob, still living in pleasant ease in the Ireland of Goldsmith's imagination, seemed to dwell "at the very center of fortune's wheel," quite unaware of the motion of the whirling wheel. "I seem to have been tied to the circumference," he wrote, "and [turned] disagreeably round like an wh—in a whirligig."

Though Goldsmith, in his personal life, remained "in a whirligig," he was able at times to approach, "the center of fortunes's wheel" through his writing. The wisdom of his own Lien Chi Altangi, for example, taught him how to face the "distress" that the

Man in Black found incomprehensible. "We should feel sorrow," he wrote in Letter VII "but not sink under its oppression," for "The wheel of fortune turns incessantly round; and who can say within himself I shall to-day be uppermost? We shall hold the immutable mean that lies between insensibility and anguish; our attempts should not be to extinguish nature, but to repress it; not to stand unmoved at distress, but endeavour to turn every disaster to our own advantage."

But Goldsmith was more than the sum total of the Man in Black and the Chinese Philosopher, for he often preferred the whirligig of the circumference to the center of the wheel. He was also, for example, the poet Scroggen, whom we meet after a night of revelry, lying on the floor of his desolate room in the Red Lion Tavern: "There, in a lonely room, from bailiffs snug,/The Muse found Scroggen stretch'd beneath a rug." Goldsmith added these lines to the verse he had sent in his letter to his brother in 1759 and included the whole in Letter XXX of *The Citizen of the World*, at the same time humorously admitting to the reader that the hero of the poem was himself.

CHAPTER 2

"The Lengthening Chain"

IN Letter LXXXIV of *The Citizen of the World* Goldsmith
painted a perfect portrait of himself as a poet, though he called
it the character of *a* poet. "I fancy," he wrote, "the character of a
poet is in every country the same: fond of enjoying the present,
careless of the future; his conversation that of a man of sense, his
actions those of a fool; of fortitude able to stand unmoved at the
bursting of an earthquake, yet of sensibility to be affected by the
breaking of a tea-cup" (III, 313).

In Goldsmith's two long, rhetorical poems, *The Traveller*
(1764) and *The Deserted Village* (1770), one is aware both of
the man of "sense," who is the interested observer of the manners
of men in different countries, and of the man of "sensibility," the
somber traveler, who "drags at each remove the lengthening
chain." The former may be compared to the Chinese Philosopher;
the latter, to the Man in Black. In these poems, on which his position as a poet depends, Goldsmith succeeded in harmonizing the
conflicting sides of his temperament and in finding for his divided
self a unified expression. *The Traveller,* moreover, brought the
poet in the garret both fame and money; why, then, did he at the
end of *The Deserted Village*, published only four years later, bid a
sad farewell to "the charming nymph" of poetry with these lines?

> And thou, sweet Poetry, thou loveliest maid,
> Still first to fly where sensual joys invade;
> Unfit, in these degenerate times of shame,
> To catch the heart, or strike for honest fame;
> Dear, charming nymph, neglected and decried,
> My shame in crowds, my solitary pride;
> Thou source of all my bliss, and all my woe,
> That found'st me poor at first, and keep'st me so;

> Thou guide by which the nobler arts excel,
> Thou nurse of every virtue, fare thee well!   (II, 44)

To discover why Goldsmith thus turned from the writing of serious poetry, the source of all his "bliss" and all his "woe," one must consider in some detail *The Traveller* and *The Deserted Village.*

I   The Traveller

The Traveller, or a Prospect of Society, which he wrote while in retirement at Islington, was published and sold by John Newbery, St. Paul's Churchyard, in December, 1764. The poet was paid twenty guineas for the piece, which was the first work to carry on its title-page the name of the author, "Dr. Goldsmith." [1] More important still, it was the first book by the author to command definitely the respect of the literary élite of London, especially after Dr. Johnson considered it the best poem in the English language since Pope's death.[2] Befriended thus by the great Doctor himself, "little Goldy" could never again be patronized by Sir John Hawkins, James Boswell, and other members of the Literary Club as "a mere literary drudge." [3] Though usually (like Scroggen) hiding from bailiffs, landlords, and tailors, for the remainder of his short life, his poverty, after the appearance of *The Traveller,* was caused more by his generous, profligate, improvident character than by the fact that he occasionally snatched time from the burden of hackwork for various booksellers and followed the Muse of Poetry.

Goldsmith's thoughts usually returned to Ireland when he removed himself from the dissipation, the confusion, and the triviality of his actual life in London, and, in his loneliness, sought refuge in poetry, his "solitary pride." *The Traveller* was dedicated to the Reverend Henry Goldsmith, whom Oliver had not seen since he left Ireland forever in 1753. The general reader, wrote Goldsmith, will better understand the import of the poem if he knows that it is "addressed to a man who, despising fame and fortune, has retired early to happiness and obscurity, with an income of forty pounds a year." Contemplating in his imagination the picture of his brother's contented life, Goldsmith remarked, "I now perceive, my dear brother, the wisdom of your humble choice." He himself, less wise, was moved by the ambition of being a poet though he knew that such an aim was hopelessly impractical: "Of all kinds of ambition—what from the refinement of the times, from different systems of criticism, and from the division of party—that which pursues poetical fame is the wildest." [4]

By "refinements of the times" Goldsmith meant that poetry belonged to an age more simple and primitive than the eighteenth century. By referring to "the different systems of criticism," he was casting aspersions on "the mistaken efforts of the learned" who amused themselves and harmed poetry by their endless discussions of "blank verse, and Pindaric odes"; and, by "division of party," he was deploring the fact that the "tawdry lampoons" of the politicians, mistakenly called "satires," filled the daily journals and brought discredit to "sweet Poetry." How true poetry can succeed in this sophisticated age of dilletantes, scholars, and rhyming politicians, Goldsmith could not imagine: "What reception a poem may find, which has neither abuse, party, nor blank verse to support it, I cannot tell, nor am I solicitous to know. My aims are right" (II, 4–5).

What his aims were in writing *The Traveller* Goldsmith stated clearly to his brother: "Without espousing the cause of any party, I have attempted to moderate the rage of all." He thus warned the reader that the long poem in heroic couplets that he was preparing to read was philosophical in aim. According to Goldsmith, he had in *The Traveller* "endeavoured to show, that there may be equal happiness in states that are differently governed from our own; that every state has a particular principle of happiness, and that this principle in each state, and in our own in particular may be carried to a mischievous excess. There are few can judge better than yourself how far these positions are illustrated in this Poem" (II, 3–5).

One might ask why such philosophic abstractions should be cast in the form of poetry at all; why should they not be expressed instead by the Man in Black in the course of his midnight broodings or by the Chinese Philosopher in a more rational mood? To understand the impact in its day of this now outmoded rhetorical expression, we might return to the "club of authors" described by Goldsmith in *The Citizen of the World,* and observe the poet as he prepared to declaim his heroic couplets. Placing his shilling on the table as a fine for the offense, "then putting himself into the attitude of an orator, with all the emphasis of voice and action, he proceeded." With the other members of the club, one may imagine listening in "profound silence" as the poet Goldsmith recites the opening lines of *The Traveller:*

> Remote, unfriended, melancholy, slow,
> Or by the lazy Scheldt, or wandering Po;
> Or onward, where the rude Carinthian boor
> Against the houseless stranger shuts the door;
> Or where Campania's plain forsaken lies,
> A weary waste expanding to the skies;
> Where'er I roam, whatever realms to see,
> My heart untravell'd fondly turns to thee;
> Still to my brother turns, with ceaseless pain,
> And drags at each remove a lengthening chain. (II, 6)

Like most poets, Goldsmith only partially understood what he called his "aims" in writing these lines which are not merely didactic but also rhetorical. Every reader unconsciously sounds them aloud, throwing himself "into the attitude of an orator, with all the emphasis of voice and action." Though we discover in the seventh line the identity of the traveler, the reader feels, from the melancholy fall of the opening line, that he himself is the traveler who "drags at each remove a lengthening chain," as his "heart untravell'd fondly turns" to some lost dream of childhood. "I only beg you'll endeavour to make your souls unison with mine, and hear with the same enthusiasm with which I have written," Goldsmith urged the members of the "club of authors." When "this tempest of poetry and praise was blown over," one member sought to change the subject from the poem itself "by wondering how any man could be so dull as to write poetry at present, since prose itself would hardly pay" (III, 113–14).

Goldsmith frequently debated the same question; he found before he had been long in London that he could cast his thoughts as readily into balanced prose as into heroic couplets, and that he could in this way earn more money. One should consider, for example, Lien Chi Altangi's letter to Fum Hoam, which so closely resembles the lines Goldsmith addressed to his brother at the opening of *The Traveller*. "Think not, O thou guide of my youth!" began Altangi, "that absence can impair my respect, or interposing tractless deserts blot your reverend figure from my memory. The farther I travel, I feel the pain of separation with stronger force; those ties that bind me to my native country and you, are still unbroken. By every remove, I only drag a greater length of chain" (III, 17).

Similarly, when Goldsmith was writing *The Traveller* in heroic couplets, he was also beginning to cast the story of Dr. Primrose and his family, *The Vicar of Wakefield*, into the delicately ironic but nonetheless poetic prose of his only novel. Here he also contrasted the pleasures of home with those of the larger world. "As we lived near the road," explained the Doctor, "we often had the traveller or stranger visit us to taste our gooseberry wine" (I, 72). In the more solemn tones of verse, Goldsmith in *The Traveller* (II, 6–19) wrote of the same family circle; but on this occasion his "earliest friend" was probably his father, the Reverend Charles Goldsmith, rather than his brother:

> Eternal blessings crown my earliest friend,
> And round his dwelling guardian saints attend:
> Blest be that spot, where cheerful guests retire
> To pause from toil, and trim their ev'ning fire:
> Blest that abode, where want and pain repair,
> And every stranger finds a ready chair.

Goldsmith never returned to Ireland to join that family group, but he wrote with moving simplicity and feeling,

> Blest be those feasts with simple plenty crown'd,
> Where all the ruddy family around
> Laugh at the jests or pranks that never fail,
> Or sigh with pity at some mournful tale,
> Or press the bashful stranger to his food,
> And learn the luxury of doing good!   (II, 6)

Just as Goldsmith had written to his brother in 1759, "I perceive, my dear Sir, that I am at intervals for indulging this splenetic manner and following my own tastes regardless of yours," so now he turned abruptly from these parochial joys and indulged his own "splenetic manner," which he shared with the Man in Black:

> But me, not destin'd such delights to share,
> My prime of life in wandering spent and care,
> Impell'd, with steps unceasing, to pursue
> Some fleeting good, that mocks me with the view;
> That, like the circle bounding earth and skies,
> Allures from far, yet, as I follow, flies;
> My fortune leads to traverse realms alone,
> And find no spot of all the world my own.   (II, 7)

Lord Byron is said to have admired extravagantly everything Goldsmith wrote; though cast in the perfectly balanced couplets of Neoclassic eighteenth-century verse, one can easily see in this restless and melancholy philosophic journey of Goldsmith's traveler the early signs of the romantic wanderings of Byron's *Don Juan*. It is not impossible, indeed, that the Man in Black and his somber explorations of sin, suffering, and injustice through the byways of the world might have suggested to Byron the long black cape and the turned-down collar as the appropriate garb for his own Continental journeys. The poetic pilgrimages of Goldsmith and Byron were, in any case, philosophical in intent; both took their seats on mountaintops in order to survey the towns, the rivers, the forests, and the busy ways of men below. Goldsmith's couplet foreshadows the Byronic attitude of another generation: "E'en now, where Alpine solitudes ascend,/I sit me down a pensive hour to spend" (II, 7).

Though "humbler bosoms vain" (like that of the parish priest, for example) might be pleased with "little things," the "philosophic mind" asks for more, and is willing to pay for the knowledge thus gained by the loneliness and pain of the homeless wanderer. From his Alpine perch, at least for the moment, he can exclaim:

> Ye glitt'ring towns, with wealth and splendour crown'd;
> Ye fields, where summer spreads profusion round,
> Ye lakes, whose vessels catch the busy gale,
> Ye bending swains, that dress the flow'ry vale,
> For me your tributary stores combine;
> Creation's heir, the world, the world is mine!   (II, 7)

But like "some lone miser," who counts and recounts his treasure, the poet is still a prey to "alternate passions" of rapture and despair "to see the hoard of human bliss so small." Where, in all the panorama below him, could the poet find his proper place?

> And oft I wish, amidst the scene to find
> Some spot to real happiness consign'd,
> Where my worn soul, each wand'ring hope at rest,
> May gather bliss to see my fellows blest.   (II, 8)

Here begins, one might suppose, the fulfillment of Goldsmith's aim in writing *The Traveller:* "to show that there may be equal happiness in states that are differently governed from our own." With the detachment of the Chinese Philosopher, who journeyed beyond the Chinese Wall for exactly the same purpose, Goldsmith surveyed the "frigid zone" of the northern people and the golden sands of the "naked negro." "But where to find that happiest spot below/Who can direct, when all pretend to know?" (II, 8), he asked, as Lien Chi Altangi had demanded before him. Both were aware that "the patriot's boast" in every land is that "his first best country, ever is at home." However, wrote the poet, if we compare all countries, and estimate their blessings and their woes,

> Though patriots flatter, still shall wisdom find
> An equal portion dealt to all mankind;
> As different good, by art or nature given,
> To different nations makes their blessing even.   (II, 8)

Such were the general suppositions of this philosopher-poet, still upon his mountaintop. The poet, however, soon descended to the valley, "these truths with closer eyes" to try; and he continued his quest through Italy, Holland, France, and Switzerland—the countries, indeed, through which Goldsmith had wandered with his flute several years earlier. One is tempted to linger with Goldsmith in France, "gay, sprightly land of mirth and social ease," where he had loitered along the Loire and paused to play his flute on village greens: "How often have I led thy sportive choir,/With tuneless pipe beside the murmuring Loire!" Though his "harsh touch" on the flute "mock'd all tune," "Yet would the village praise my wondrous power,/And dance, forgetful of the noon-tide hour" (II, 13). Intent on discovering "the particular principle of happiness" of every country, which "may be carried to a mischievous excess," Goldsmith marked with a stern philosophic eye the evidences of degeneration and corruption which he saw on every side. Indeed, of Italy he wrote that "all evils here contaminate the mind."

It is a pleasure to learn that, before Goldsmith had completed his survey of Italy, a knock came on his door and a friend, possibly Reynolds, entered unceremoniously. The anecdote[5] goes that he discovered Goldsmith engaged in an effort to teach a small dog to sit on his haunches. The friend glanced at the lines lying on Goldsmith's desk and read from his description of Italy, "By sports like these are all their cares beguil'd,/The sports of children satisfy the child" (II, 11). He laughingly suggested that the lines were related to Goldsmith's game with the dog, and Goldsmith with his usual good humor admitted that playing with the dog had suggested to him the idea for the couplet. High spirits were constantly breaking through Goldsmith's most serious thought. In spite of his sternest strictures, with what pleasure he must have written of France and Italy, "So blest a life these thoughtless realms display;/Thus idly busy rolls their world away" (II, 14).

But away with all enfeebling thought of the vain and frivolous south, and let our glance fly "where Britain courts the western spring." Here, in England,

> Stern o'er each bosom Reason holds her state,
> With daring aims irregularly great,
> Pride in their port, defiance in their eye,
> I see the lords of human kind pass by.   (II, 16)

"Fierce in their native hardiness of soul," the simple peasant "boasts these rights to scan,/And learns to venerate himself as man." But even on the blessed island of Britain, certain "ills" were beginning to appear. Perhaps, indeed, "That independence Britons prize too high,/Keeps man from man, and breaks the social tie." Thus "self-dependent lordlings" often stand alone, "all claims that bind and sweeten life unknown." What is the sad consequence?

> Here, by the bonds of nature feebly held,
> Minds combat minds, repelling and repell'd;
> Ferments arise, imprison'd factions roar,

> Represt ambition struggles round her shore;
> Till, overwrought, the general system feels
> Its motion stop, or frenzy fire the wheels.   (II, 16)

"Nor this the worst," wrote Goldsmith, who thus presaged the age of revolution so soon to overtake the eighteenth-century world. "As Nature's ties decay,"—by which he meant the age-old bonds of "duty, love, and honour,"—then "fictitious bonds," those of "wealth and law," wax in strength to the ultimate harm of all that men know as civilization. One might imagine oneself strolling again with the Chinese Philosopher and the Man in Black through the aisles of Westminster Abbey as one reads that, when wealth and law assume the ascendency, then

> Hence all obedience bows to these alone,
> And talent sinks, and merit weeps unknown:
> Till time may come, when, stript of all her charms,
> The land of scholars, and the nurse of arms,
> Where noble stems transmit the patriot flame,
> Where kings have toil'd, and poets wrote for fame,
> One sink of level avarice shall lie,
> And scholars, soldiers, kings, unhonour'd die.   (II,16–17)

Though Goldsmith was not to complete *The Deserted Village* until 1769, he was already beginning to brood upon the effects of trade and of the new industrial era on the English peasantry. Have we not seen, he asked, in *The Traveller,* "Opulence" lead "stern Depopulation in her train?"

> Have we not seen, at pleasure's lordly call,
> The smiling, long frequented village fall?
> Beheld the duteous son, the sire decay'd,
> The modest matron, and the blushing maid,
> Forced from their homes, a melancholy train,
> To traverse climes beyond the western main.   (II, 18)

Goldsmith's survey of many lands ended where all such meditations must close:

> Vain, very vain, my weary search to find
> That bliss which only centres in the mind:

> Why have I stray'd from pleasure and repose,
> To seek a good each government bestows?   (II, 19)

The concluding lines of *The Traveller*,[6] Boswell reported in his *Journal*, were written by Dr. Johnson. Whether or not Boswell's statement is true can never be determined; what is perhaps more important to notice is that they are so in the spirit of Johnson's own poem, "The Vanity of Human Wishes," that the poetic style of the two men is interchangeable:

> How small, of all that human hearts endure,
> That part which laws or kings can cause or cure!
> Still to ourselves in every place consign'd,
> Our own felicity we make or find:
> With secret course, which no loud storms annoy,
> Glides the smooth current of domestic joy. . . .
> To men remote from power but rarely known,
> Leave reason, faith, and conscience, all our own.   (II, 19)

The publication of *The Traveller* not only made Goldsmith the most sought after poet in London literary circles, but also brought him enough financial independence to enable him, early in 1764, to take a room "on the library stairs" in Garden Court of the Temple.

Johnson, then living in Inner Temple Lane, was already a friend of the author of *The Traveller*, whom he loved, teased, cajoled, and advised for the rest of his life. Their first recorded meeting had taken place on May 31, 1761, when Johnson was invited to a dinner party given by Goldsmith to which he was escorted by Percy. Remarking on the fact that the Doctor was wearing that evening a clean and freshly powdered wig and a neat, new suit, Percy ventured to ask him why he was thus honoring the occasion. "Why, Sir," replied Johnson, "I hear that Goldsmith, who is a very great sloven, justifies his disregard of cleanliness and decency by quoting my practice, and I am desirous this night to show him a better example." [7] Though Doctor Minor was said by the members of the Literary Club to imitate Doctor Major in his manner of speaking and in his bearing, there is no record that he thereafter followed Johnson's example.

II *Ballads and Songs*

Laughter as well as serious discussion must have marked Goldsmith's dinner party, though Percy had no more to say on what transpired behind those closed doors. The conversation might well have turned to the subject of Percy's *Reliques of Ancient Poetry* on which he was at that time working. It was, indeed, their common interest in ballads—an interest not shared by Johnson—which first brought Goldsmith and Percy together. Goldsmith wrote the ballad of "Edwin and Angelina" in imitation of one of the "reliques" Percy had shown him several years earlier, for both Percy and Goldsmith amused themselves by attempting to write in the spirit of the medieval poems.[8]

Though Goldsmith called his ballad "Edwin and Angelina" when he published it in his collection *Poems for Young Ladies* (1767), he used the title "The Hermit" when referring to it among his friends. Goldsmith loved songs and ballads as much as he did the heroic couplets of his more ambitious poems. "The Hermit," which he worked over for many years, was one of his favorites. "As to my Hermit, that poem, . . . cannot be amended," he said to Joseph Cradock not long before his death when he was considering the publication of his works.[9]

Goldsmith's final version of "The Hermit" is to be found in Chapter VIII of *The Vicar of Wakefield* (I, 99–102), which appeared two years after *The Traveller* and four years before *The Deserted Village*. The recitation of the ballad to the Primrose family by their mysterious visitor, Mr. Burchell, not only forms an integral part of the action of the story, but also, because of the enjoyment of the ballad, leads to a discussion of the nature of poetry which reflects Goldsmith's own views on the subject in a half-serious, half-satiric manner wholly characteristic of this poet-novelist-critic. Though Goldsmith had come to the conclusion that one could not earn a living by poetry, he remained the poet in his various experiments in prose and was always, as a critic, fascinated by the question of the nature and source of true poetry.

One of Goldsmith's fundamental beliefs concerning poetry was that it should be simple, direct, and unstrained. He believed that poetry originated among primitive people and survived in such country places, as those he had known in Ireland. We must picture the Primrose family sitting—or rather, "reclining"—around the haystack in the fields where a luncheon cloth had been spread. Mr. Burchell, a frequent guest at the Primrose home, whose "wit" seemed to improve daily as his "simplicity assumed the superior air of wisdom," had joined the family in haying. "To lend cheerfulness to the feast," Mr. Burchell proposed now to introduce to the company a ballad, which he drew forth from his pocket after the cloth had been folded. While two black birds sang on a neighboring tree, Mr. Burchell stepped forth and thus began:

> 'Turn, gentle hermit of the dale,
>   And guide my lonely way,
> To where yon taper cheers the vale,
>   With hospitable ray.
>
> 'For here, forlorn and lost I tread,
>   With fainting steps and slow;
> Where wilds immeasurably spread,
>   Seem length'ning as I go.'

Burchell, too, was a melancholy traveler, conscious of "the lengthening chain" that wanderers drag behind them. All the kindness of the simple hospitality of Dr. Primrose to his guest—whose true identity he at that time did not know—flows through the next six stanzas that end, as Goldsmith's meditation in *The Traveller* ended, with a final statement on man and his wants "here below." The lonely, restless journey of the far-wanderer, and the beauty of simple compassion can find expression in the old, familiar ballad form, loved by all country folk, as well as in the heroic couplet which the eighteenth century adopted as its favorite poetic form. In a ballad, as in his more formal poems, Goldsmith is essentially rhetorical. Who can doubt that Mr. Burchell gestured appropriately as he spoke the words of the hermit's reply to the pilgrim?

> 'Forbear, my son,' the hermit cries,
>   'To tempt the dangerous gloom;
> For yonder faithless phantom flies
>   To lure thee to thy doom.

'Here, to the houseless child of want,
    My door is open still;
And though my portion is but scant,
    I give it with good will.

'Then turn to-night, and freely share
    Whate'er my cell bestows;
My rushy couch, and frugal fare,
    My blessing, and repose.

'No flocks, that range the valley free,
    To slaughter I condemn;
Taught by that Power that pities me,
    I learn to pity them.'

How strangely akin in feeling are these lines to those of a poet of the next generation, William Blake, who also turned to ballads to express his deeper intuitions. The hermit continued:

'But from the mountain's grassy side,
    A guiltless feast I bring;
A scrip with herbs and fruits supply'd,
    And water from the spring.

'Then, pilgrim, turn, thy cares forego,
    For earth-born cares are wrong,
Man wants but little here below,
    Nor wants that little long.'

Thirty years later, two young poets tramped through Europe and discussed the "new poetry," at the same time attempting to illustrate in their own poems a simpler poetic expression. They called the little volume which resulted from these discussions, *Lyrical Ballads*, for they, too, found fresh meaning in the almost forgotten music of ballads. The stanzas quoted above bring overtones of Wordsworth's "Lucy poems," "Michael," and "Resolution and Independence," while the following verses remind one that Coleridge's Ancient Mariner conversed with a hermit in his cell and learned from him the need for compassion. Strange as the analogy is, the stanzas recited by Burchell are not unlike those of "The Rime of the Ancient Mariner."

Soft, as the dew from heav'n descends,
    His gentle accents fell:
The modest stranger lowly bends,
    And follows to the cell.

Far in a wilderness obscure
    The lonely mansion lay;
A refuge to the neighb'ring poor,
    And strangers led astray.

No stores beneath its humble thatch
    Requir'd a master's care;
The wicket, opening with a latch,
    Receiv'd the harmless pair.

And now, when busy crowds retire
    To take their evening rest,
The hermit trimm'd his little fire,
    And cheer'd his pensive guest.   (I, 99–100)

The "pensive guest" is discovered to be Angelina in disguise, and the hermit none other than Edwin himself, turned hermit because so cruelly spurned by Angelina. She, the only daughter of a "wealthy lord," had treated her many suitors with "fickle art," and was then too selfish and disdainful to recognize in time the true qualities of Edwin. Now repentant, she was determined to waste away her life as a pilgrim. Perhaps the tale is no more absurd than a ballad should be, but Goldsmith's own satiric sense of humor broke through when he incorporated it into *The Vicar of Wakefield*. Just as the lovers stand clasped in each other's arms, swearing never to part, Goldsmith takes up the thread of the story of the Primrose family. In the words of Dr. Primrose,

While this ballad was reading, Sophia seemed to mix an air of tenderness with her approbation. But our tranquillity was soon disturbed by the report of a gun just by us, and, immediately after, a man was seen bursting through the hedge, to take up the game he had killed. The sportsman was the Squire's chaplain, who had shot one of the blackbirds that so agreeably entertained us. So loud a report, and so near, startled my daughters; and I could perceive that Sophia, in the fright, had thrown herself into Mr. Burchell's arms for protection. (I-102)

Thus does poetry, even that found in old ballads, lead the young astray by causing them to forget their customary "prudence."

But poetry also provides the balm with which to comfort, Goldsmith seems to say, when "Fresh Calamities" (I, 182–86) overtake the Primroses. Though their habitation has been burned to the ground, and Olivia betrayed by Squire Thornhill, nevertheless, with the aid of song and poetry, "cheerfulness" again condescended to hover around the saddened family. One finds the family at breakfast "on the honey-suckle bank"—the very spot where "poor Olivia first met her seducer." The Doctor, however, mused aloud, soothing his family with the thought that "that melancholy which is excited by objects of pleasure, or inspired by sounds of harmony, soothes the heart instead of corroding it." Mrs. Primrose, too, "felt a pleasing distress, and wept, and loved her daughter as before." Wiping her tears, the mother turned to her erring daughter with a cheering suggestion, "Do, my pretty Olivia, let us have that little melancholy air your papa was so fond of; your sister Sophy has already obliged us. Do, child; it will please your old father." Olivia "complied in a manner so exquisitely pathetic" as to move not only her old father but thousands of readers since she joined her voice with the birds and sang,

> When lovely woman stoops to folly,
> And finds, too late, that men betray,
> What charm can soothe her melancholy,
> What art can wash her guilt away?

> The only art her guilt to cover,
> To hide her shame from every eye,
> To give repentance to her lover,
> And wring his bosom,—is to die.   (I, 183)

Life, as usual, breaks in upon poetry. Just as the shot of a pistol recalled the reader to reality after the reading of the ballad, so now, the Doctor reported, "the appearance of Mr. Thornhill's equippage at a distance, alarmed us all, but particularly increased the uneasiness of my eldest daughter, who, desirous of shunning her betrayer, returned to the house with her sister."

The Primrose family was not only trained in the art of poetry, and well aware of its uses both to rouse and to soothe the passions, but also versed in the art of criticism. Before Mr. Burchell, for example, refreshed the family by his reading of "Edwin and Angelina," a discussion took place in the hayfield between Mr. Burchell, Sophia, and Moses, as to what makes "fine poetry." The reading of the ballad, indeed, was the outcome of the argument for simplicity in poetry advanced by Mr. Burchell. Sophia lent support to his remark by glancing about "the tranquil scene," and remarking, "I never sit thus, but I think of the two lovers, so sweetly described by Mr. Gay, who were struck dead in each others arms. There is something so pathetic in the description, that I have read it a hundred times with new rapture."

Moses, oblivious to the coquetry which lay behind his sister's remarks, pronounced on the question as follows: "In my opinion, the finest strokes in that description are much below those in the Acis and Galatea of Ovid. The Roman poet understands the use of *contrast* better, and upon that figure, artfully managed, all strength in the pathetic depends." Mr. Burchell then expressed his views (those of Goldsmith) and thus set straight both Sophia and Moses. "It is remarkable," cried he, "that both the poets you mention have equally contributed to introduce a false taste into their respective countries, by loading all their lines with epithet. Men of little genius found them most easily imitated in their defects; and English poetry, like that in the latter empire of Rome, is nothing at present but a combination of luxuriant images, without plot or connection; a string of epithets, that improve the sound without carrying on the sense" (I, 98).

By "false taste," Goldsmith meant "deviation from common sense," which he had already discussed in *An Enquiry* as "a mark of literary decay." Poets and critics alike are guilty of "false taste," he had declared; and "from this proceeds the affected security of our odes, the tuneless flow of our blank verse, the pompous epithet, laboured diction, and every other deviation from common sense, which procures the applause of the month; he [the poet] is praised by all, read by a few, and soon forgotten" (III, 512).

In simpler terms, the Chinese Philosopher, exponent of common sense as he was, had complained (III, 358) that the poetry which he had examined at the London booksellers seldom held his attention, for in the poems he found "very good words, truly, and much exactness of rhyme, but no information. A parcel of gaudy images pass on before his imagination like the figures in a dream; but curiosity, induction, reason, and the whole train of affections, are fast asleep." In order to be pleased by a book of contemporary English poetry, he wrote his friend, a reader must be willing to "leave his good sense behind him." Worse still, "those sallies which mend the heart, while they amuse the fancy" are also neglected. The poets of England appeal neither to the reason nor to the feelings of their readers to whom they offer merely "laboured vanity." Goldsmith's reviews of the English poets, to be found in *The Critical Review, The Monthly Review,* and in many other periodicals of the day, show how deeply read in the poetic tradition of England, France, and the Classics, he was, as well as how wide were his sympathies with poetry of any period or country, which displayed common sense, genuine feeling, and disciplined form.

III *"Agreeable Trifling"*

A follower of tradition at heart, Goldsmith complained of "erroneous innovation" in poetry in *An Enquiry* (III, 510–16). Above all, he objected to "a disgusting solemnity of manner," which, he thought, afflicted both the prose writers and the poets of his day. To Goldsmith, "agreeable trifling" often "deceives us into instruction," which he considered one of the great objects of writers. Who could fail to perceive that "the finest sentiment and the most weighty truth may put on a pleasant face [or that] it is even virtuous to jest when serious advice must be disgusting. But, instead of this, the most trifling performance among us now assumes all the didactic stiffness of wisdom" (III, 514).

Even "dull and dronish" reviews and essays in the journal might be pardoned if they would consent to be "frothy, pert, or absurd." Goldsmith's sense of the proper uses of the light and the fanciful, as opposed to the solemn and the heavy, explains, perhaps, the well-known anecdote, reported by Boswell, of a conversation between Johnson and Goldsmith as to the difficulties of writing old fables. Goldsmith gave as an illustration the story of "the little fishes who saw birds fly over their heads, and envying them, petitioned Jupiter to be changed into birds." While he was earnestly enlarging on the difficulty of making them talk like little fishes, Johnson broke in with a laugh. Goldsmith turned to him sharply and said, "Why, Dr. Johnson, that is not so easy as you think, for if *you* were to make little fishes talk, they would talk like *whales.*" [10]

Goldsmith himself, when attending the meetings of the Literary Club at the Turk's Head Tavern in Gerrard Street, was never dull and seldom wise. Boswell, Sir John Hawkins, Sir Joshua Reynolds, and many others testify that he was frequently "frothy, pert, and absurd." William Cooke noted that the "literati" of London "took a pleasure in the Doctor's conversation, and by turns laughed at his blunders, and admired the simplicity of the man, and the elegance of his poetical talents." [11] Goldsmith's ill-timed fooling, said Reynolds, impelled him at times to strut before mirrors in admiration of his new coat, to dance about the floor, and even to stand on his head. His taste in real life, one is forced to conclude, was as "false" as it was "true" in his writings.

"To paint the absurdities of the vulgar," in verse as well as in prose, had been one of Goldsmith's amusements since he first came to live on Grub Street. Goldsmith's Wednesday evenings in Fleet Street at the Globe Tavern, where the rafters rang with song, were very different in tone from his Monday evenings at the Turk's Head, but equally important to him. Indeed, Goldsmith's association with "men of eminence" was not altogether a gain, for now he felt he had to cease visiting "many of those public places" that were both cheap and amusing. "In truth," said he, "one sacrifices something for the sake of good company, for here I'm shut out of several places where I used to play the fool very agreeably." [12] For here he came into contact with the "vulgar," whom, he said, the critics were too stupid to realize were the very best source of humor and fun.

Poetry which introduces characters from the London streets is dubbed by the critics "low"; and, "by the power of one single monosyllable," they have almost gained complete "victory over humour amongst us," wrote Goldsmith in Chapter XI of *An Enquiry.* And if the poet is carried away by the foolish behavior of the common people, as Goldsmith often was, and dares to "exaggerate the features of folly to render it more thoroughly ridiculous, he is then *very low.*" Beyond a doubt, Goldsmith admitted, high life, as well as low life, abounds in fools. However, good breeding teaches people to cover up their absurdity as far as they are able. "Among well-bred fools we may despise much, but have little to laugh at; nature seems to present us with a universal blank of silk, ribbons, smiles, and whispers." Goldsmith, the homely, eccentric poet who never lost his Irish brogue, had begun to move among the damask drawing rooms of London, and to match his manners—never successfully—with those of Horace Walpole and Lord Chesterfield.

"Absurdity is the poet's game," he concluded, "and good-breeding is the nice concealment of absurdities" (III, 515). Never a good story-teller at the Club, and frequently the butt of other members, Goldsmith was able to "shine" only at his desk—or with his companions at the tavern. Borrowing the mock-heroic tone of Gay and Swift, Goldsmith composed "An Elegy on That Glory of Her Sex, Mrs. Mary Blaize"; or a song, reminiscent of Lovelace and Suckling, to "Cruel Iris, pretty rake, dear mercenary beauty"; or a tale in the manner of Pope, of Jack bookworm and Flavia, his wife, "by turns a slattern and a belle." These he published anonymously in *The Bee*, or he inserted them in the play he was writing, or he casually included a verse or two in a letter to his brother. The poet's "absurdity" was seldom appreciated in the drawing rooms of men of "good breeding."

Goldsmith had already pointed out the distinction between *wit* and *humor* in *An Enquiry* in terms which throw light on his own character: "Wit raises human nature above its level; humour acts a contrary part, and equally depresses it." When a person is "*humourously* described, our burst of laughter proceeds from a very different cause; we compare the absurdity of the character represented with our own, and triumph in our conscious superiority." "Thus, then, the pleasure we receive from wit turns on the admiration of another; that which we feel from humour, centres in the admiration of ourselves" (III, 515–16).

The poet, therefore, must necessarily place the character of humorous verse in a position of inferiority for "the subject of humour must be *low*." The poet should occasionally forget the "inflated style," "lofty expressions," and the "loaded epithet"; he should lay aside his velvet coat and enjoy the life around him in the parks and in the streets of London, "low" though it undoubtedly was. "On my conscience," he wrote, "I believe we have all forgot to

[68]

laugh in these days," which is a pity; for laughter encourages the "natural style" of writing (III, 516). Goldsmith needed companions from "low life" as well as from "high life" with whom he could feel at ease, and was determined, he confided to Cooke, to "hunt after *nature* and *humour* in whatever walks of life they were most conspicuous." [13]

Restlessly moving from city to country, changing his lodgings frequently according to the whim of the moment, Goldsmith never discovered a mode of living satisfactory to him for more than a brief interval. In 1768, having suddenly come into possession of what was to him a large sum of money for the production of his play, *A Good-Natured Man,* he moved to a three-room apartment at No. 2 Brick Court, Middle Temple. After spending most of his windfall for the lease of the chambers, he spent the rest on Wilton carpets, card tables, mahogany sofas and chairs, draperies and long mirrors, all of which required the services of a charwoman and a valet. Goldsmith's money was soon exhausted, but he borrowed from Edmund Bott, a young Irish barrister, who lived on the opposite landing and, like Goldsmith, enjoyed good dinners and cheerful company. The faithful Bott, indeed, was found on Goldsmith's death, to be his largest creditor.

Happily for posterity, overtones of the talk at one of Goldsmith's dinner parties have come down to us in the reminiscences of a certain "Mr. Roach" of Ireland,[14] who reported that the dinner he attended was "lavish," and that in the course of the evening Goldsmith "waxed eloquent with great animation" on the relative merits of Shakespeare, Milton, Otway, Congreve, and Farquhar. He amused his guests by reading aloud, with elaborate solemnity, a Prologue written by Boswell in honor of the opening of the Edinburgh Theatre Royal, and thus kept the table in roars of laughter. Goldsmith remarked, as he laid aside the newspaper clipping, "Why, how simple a man must be to write such lines, and call them poetry! And then to advertise them in the newspaper as his own by a formal letter to the printer! What were his friends about to let him expose himself?" Dr. Johnson, Goldsmith thought, when he learned of Boswell's verses, would either be "very angry or very witty" on the subject. Goldsmith, who was so often to appear a fool in Boswell's *Journal,* could laugh away at his own dinner table the pretensions of Boswell as a poet. Humor, in real life as well as in poetry, restored one to one's rightful position of superiority.

IV   The Deserted Village

In 1768 and again in 1769, Goldsmith and Edmund Bott rented on the Edgeware Road a small cottage called by Goldsmith the "Shoemaker's Paradise" in honor of the trade of his landlord.[15] Here Goldsmith worked—when he could seize the time from his *Roman History*—on his greatest poem, *The Deserted Village*. The poem appeared in 1770, six years after the publication of *The Traveller*, and was an immediate success. It was dedicated to Sir Joshua Reynolds, his kindly older friend, in whose home he had spent many sociable evenings. Just as Goldsmith told his brother the purpose of his poem in his Dedication of *The Traveller*, so now, in his Dedication of *The Deserted Village* (II, 31–32), Goldsmith clearly stated his aim to Sir Joshua Reynolds. He intended, he wrote, to present in his poem a picture of the sad effects of the depopulation of rural areas. Wealthy landlords, grown rich by industry and trade, were indolent in their opulence; and, oblivious to the needs of the poor, they wished to maintain their parks and hunting preserves. Lest Reynolds think that these "disorders are only found in the poet's imagination," Goldsmith assured him, "I have taken all possible pains in my country excursions, for these four or five years past, to be certain of what I allege."

As has been seen, the theme of *The Deserted Village* was foreshadowed in *The Traveller*. Though the later poem was, in a sense, the fulfillment of the earlier, *The Deserted Village* (II, 33–45) stressed the social and the economic aspects of the problem, but the political implications were uppermost in Goldsmith's mind when he wrote *The Traveller*. Both are philosophical in intent, and both are written from the point of view of Goldsmith the lonely wanderer. Just as the "Traveller" placed himself upon a mountaintop to pass "a pensive hour" reflecting on the happiness of men under various governments, so now the same figure returns to his native village to survey the effects of time and man's depredations on sweet Auburn: "Here, as with doubtful, pensive steps I range,/Trace every scene, and wonder at the change."

The first four lines of the poem, we are told, were written and

"The Lengthening Chain"

then laid aside, perhaps because of the demands of the booksellers.

> Sweet Auburn! loveliest village of the plain,
> Where health and plenty cheer'd the labouring swain,
> Where smiling spring its earliest visit paid,
> And parting summer's lingering blooms delay'd.

Re-reading this evocation one morning in the cottage on the Edgeware Road, Goldsmith added ten delightful lines which call up once more the vision of his Irish village:

> Dear lovely bowers of innocence and ease,
> Seats of my youth, when every sport could please,
> How often have I loiter'd o'er thy green,
> Where humble happiness endear'd each scene!
> How often have I paused on every charm,
> The shelter'd cot, the cultivated farm,
> The never-failing brook, the busy mill,
> The decent church that topt the neighbouring hill,
> The hawthorn bush, with seats beneath the shade,
> For talking age and whispering lovers made.   (II, 33)

Goldsmith had just completed this last line, William Cooke says,[16] when his friend walked into the room. As usual, Goldsmith greeted Cooke with cheerful gaiety; then he held up his paper and exclaimed, "Come, let me tell you this is no bad morning's work; and now, my dear boy, if you are not better engaged, I should be glad to enjoy a Shoe-maker's holiday with you." Cooke explains that "a Shoe-maker's holiday," "a day of great festivity to poor Goldsmith," was spent with four or five companions who enjoyed strolling across fields with him and dining in country taverns. For all that he was a poet and a philosopher, Goldsmith to his dying day loved to "convivialize" with practically anyone who would talk, walk, play cards, or dance a jig with him. He did not feel above a merry game of blind-man's-buff, nor a round of old songs in a country inn, nor an evening of card-tricks in a London drawing room.

In spite of this gaiety of heart, one must not think that poetry flowed with ease from his pen. "Goldsmith, though quick enough at prose," wrote Cooke, who no doubt had often sat in his chambers while his friend completed his couplet, "was rather slow in his poetry—not from tardiness of fancy, but the time he took in pointing the sentiment, and polishing the versification. . . . His manner of writing poetry was this: he first sketched a part of his design in prose, in which he threw out his ideas as they occurred to him; he then sat carefully down to versify them, correct them, and add such other ideas as he thought better fitted to the subject." Cooke observed that Goldsmith would sometimes "exceed his prose design by writing several verses impromptu, but these he would take uncommon pains afterwards to revise, lest they should be found unconnected with his main design."

Goldsmith's habit, as described by Cooke, of writing out in prose the "main design" of his long poems, to which he added "other ideas" as they occurred to him, explains in part the striking similarity between the thought expressed in *The Deserted Village* and in many letters of the Chinese Philosopher. Altangi never tired of pointing out to his friend in China that the decay of English manners was the inevitable accompaniment of the gain in trade. Trade, said he, leads to opulence, opulence to luxury, luxury to pride, and pride to ruthless treatment of the poor. Only a good monarch, said Lien, and Goldsmith agreed with him, could uphold the rights of the peasantry against the grasping landlords. These ideas appear throughout Goldsmith's prose and poetry. Perhaps the most often quoted lines of *The Deserted Village* are the ones that can fairly be said to express the "main design" of the whole poem:

> Ill fares the land, to hastening ills a prey,
> Where wealth accumulates, and men decay:
> Princes and lords may flourish, or may fade;
> A breath can make them, as a breath has made;
> But a bold peasantry, their country's pride,
> When once destroy'd, can never be supplied. (II, 34)

A natural democrat, Goldsmith was in spontaneous sympathy with people in all walks of life; and he always refused to assume the grand airs of a superior. In his political philosophy, however, he was as thorough a Tory as Dr. Johnson himself, and believed with him that lords and peasants alike gain freedom by continuing in their accustomed places under a strong monarchy. Instead of looking ahead to the revolution of the people soon to manifest itself in France, and, later, in England, Goldsmith glanced wistfully backward to a supposed "golden age" before the industrial era that was, indeed, no more real than the "Sweet Auburn" of his imagination. "A time there was," lamented Goldsmith,

> A time there was, ere England's grief began,
> When every rood of ground maintain'd its man:
> For him light labour spread her wholesome store,
> Just gave what life required, but gave no more:
> His best companions, innocence and health,
> And his best riches, ignorance of wealth.   (II, 34–35)

What the poor peasant actually enjoyed was, one might think, not so much "ignorance of wealth" as merely ignorance. However, the eighteenth century achieved a certain economic, political, religious, and artistic unity which, to men like Johnson and Goldsmith—and, indeed, to most men of the times—must have seemed both right and permanent. To Goldsmith, signs of change in the picture brought only wistful regret, and perhaps this melancholy endears the poem to all who feel the sadness of change. Who does not join Goldsmith in his lament?

> But times are alter'd: trade's unfeeling train
> Usurp the land, and dispossess the swain;
> Along the lawn, where scatter'd hamlets rose,
> Unwieldy wealth and cumbrous pomp repose,
> And every want to opulence allied,
> And every pang that folly pays to pride.
> These gentle hours that plenty bade to bloom,
> Those calm desires that ask'd but little room,
> Those healthful sports that graced the peaceful scene,
> Lived in each look, and brighten'd all the green,—
> These, far departing, seek a kinder shore,
> And rural mirth and manners are no more.   (II, 35)

Though Goldsmith chose to live in London all of his life, he frequently sought the solitude of the open country still to be found within walking distance of Temple Bar. One cannot doubt the feeling—perhaps he would have called it "passion"—that swept across him as he brooded over the desolate villages near London, and thought of the hamlets he had known in Ireland. Since he seems to have enjoyed the glitter and the pomp, and perhaps the misery of London, even more than the quiet of the village, one smiles somewhat ruefully at his painting of the great city in *The Deserted Village*. The poor boy is forced to earn his living

> Here, while the courtier glitters in brocade,
> There the pale artist plies his sickly trade;
> Here, while the proud their long drawn pomps display,
> There the black gibbet glooms beside the way.
> The dome where Pleasure holds her midnight reign,
> Here, richly deck'd, admits the gorgeous train;
> Tumultuous grandeur crowds the blazing square,
> The rattling chariots clash, the torches glare.
> Sure scenes like these no troubles e'er annoy,
> Sure these denote one universal joy!   (II, 42)

Could these be "thy serious thoughts?" asked Goldsmith, assuming the guise of the Man in Black. "Ah, turn thine eyes/Where the poor houseless shivering female lies." She was once a modest maiden in just such a village as Auburn, but "Now lost to all—her friends, her virtue fled,/Near her betrayer's door she lays her head."

In *The Deserted Village*, Goldsmith so blended the feelings of the Man in Black for the village preacher, the lonely wanderers, and the forlorn "female" of the city streets with the thoughts of the Chinese Philosopher on the subject of opulence and poverty, luxury and corruption, simplicity and dissipation, that the two characters can no longer be distinguished. For behind these two familiar phantoms, one is aware of the sensitive, sad spirit of Goldsmith the poet, looking back with brooding affection on the dream of his youth. Not only did Goldsmith weep to see "the rural virtues leave the land," but he also lamented the departure of the Muse of Poetry, to whom he now bade farewell.

Though Goldsmith amused himself with epigrams, rhymed letters, occasional poems of various kinds for the remainder of his short life, *The Deserted Village* was, in fact, his last great poem. Poetry, he claimed, could hardly keep a writer from starving in a garret on Grub Street. Perhaps had he continued to devote his time to the writing of verse, he could not have paid for the apartment in the Temple, for the elegant coats from Filby's, for the man servant to care for the coats and to supervise the dinners, for the gambling debts he incurred when he disappeared to enjoy "the pleasures of the town," and for the shillings and the guineas he freely bestowed on friends, relatives, and mere spongers.

Robert Day,[17] a young Irish barrister who came to live at the Temple in 1769, has left a picture of Goldsmith at that time which helps us to understand why the "dear, charming nymph" of poetry was forced to quit his quarters. As a retired judge of eighty, Day wrote down his memory of Goldsmith as follows:

The Poet frequented much the Grecian Coffee-house, then the favourite resort of the Irish and Lancashire Templars; and delighted in collecting around him his friends, whom he entertained with a cordial and unostentatious hospitality. Occasionally he amused them with his flute or with whist, neither of which he played well, particularly the latter, but in losing his money, he never lost his temper. In a run of bad luck and worse play, he would fling his cards on the floor and exclaim, "*Bye-fore* George! I ought for ever to renounce thee, fickle, faithless Fortune."

In person he was short, about five feet five or six inches; strong, but not heavy in make; rather fair in complexion, with brown hair, such at least as could be distinguished from his wig. His features were plain, but not repulsive,—certainly not so when lighted up by conversation. His manners were simple, natural, and perhaps on the whole we may say not polished. . . . He was always cheerful and animated, often indeed boisterous in his mirth; entered with spirit into convivial society; contributed largely to its enjoyment by solidity of information and the naïveté and originality of his character; talked often without premeditation and laughed loudly without restraint.

Day remembered that Goldsmith wrote much for the booksellers, and that he usually spent his money as soon as he received it: "His purse replenished by labours of this kind, the season of relaxation and pleasure took its turn in attending the Theatres, Ranelagh, Vauxhall, and other scenes of gaiety and amusement, which he continued to frequent as long as his supply held out. He was fond of exhibiting his muscular little person in the gayest apparel of the day, to which was added a bag wig and sword."

Day recalled a morning when, as he walked down the Strand with the poet thus arrayed, two passing "coxcombs" called out, "Look at that fly with a long pin stuck through it!" Without a moment's hesitation, Goldsmith shouted a warning to the passers-by against "that brace of disguised pickpockets," and backed into a nearby driveway. Flourishing his sword, he challenged the scoffers to approach. The two amazed young men, needless to say, disappeared amid the laughter of the crowd. Goldsmith was as quick and tempestuous in actual life as he was serene and noble as the pensive poet of the changing times.

On May 26, 1770, the *Public Ledger* carried the following notice: "This day, at twelve, will be published, price two shillings, 'The Deserted Village,' a Poem. By Dr. Goldsmith. Printed for W. Griffin, at Garrick's Head, Catherine Street, Strand." Robert Day ended his reminiscences with the remark, "I was in London when the Deserted Village came out. Much had been expected from the Author of the Traveller, and public expectation and impatience were not disappointed. In fact it was received with universal admiration, as one of the most fascinating and beautiful effusions of British genius."

Goldsmith's poem met with immediate and unprecedented popularity. "This man is a poet," exclaimed Thomas Gray, to whom *The Deserted Village* was read aloud at his retreat in Oxford; and Gray's approval was echoed through the land. Indeed, a general outcry was raised immediately in the magazines and journals at the very idea that Goldsmith should be allowed to say farewell to poetry. "Apollo and the Muses forbid," cried the *St. James's Chronicle*. What! should the author of *The Traveller* and *The Deserted Village* be permitted to lay aside his pen? In more sober terms the *Monthly Review* (June, 1770) wrote: "We hope for the honour of the art and the pleasure of the public, Dr. Goldsmith will retract his farewell to poetry and give us other opportunities of doing justice to his merit." An unnamed critic in one of the journals wrote in the poet's own language:

> Pathetic warbler of the pensive plain,
> Cast forth this demon with thy magic strain;

> O sooth our troubled minds, renew thy song,
> And as alone thou charms't us, charm us long.
> From royal George the royal means shall spring,
> To give thee strength to fly and power to sing;
> So shall his reign this long wish'd truth declare,
> That Kings can feel and genius smile at care.[18]

George III, who had other affairs on his mind, showed no interest then or later in Goldsmith or in poetry. Though Goldsmith would certainly have welcomed a pension from the king who had bestowed one on Dr. Johnson, he was both proud and tactless, and refused to bend his knee to king, lord, or minister.

Thus Goldsmith remained a poor man, tied "to the wooden desk of drudgery," permanently in debt to the booksellers. While stealing time for his poetry, Goldsmith wrote a *History of Philosophy* (1766), his *Roman History* (1769) for school boys, and the beginning of his *History of Animated Nature* in eight volumes, the last of which did not appear until after his death. The "draggle-tail muses" would let him starve, he said to a friend;[19] "but by pursuing plain prose, I can make a shift to eat, and drink, and wear good clothes." Had the muses been even more generous to Goldsmith than they were, they might not have supplied him with the funds he thought he needed. Both before and after the success of *The Deserted Village*, Goldsmith actually was living in comfort in the Temple, where he entertained freely and, no doubt, noisily. Sir William Blackstone, who had recently completed his *Commentaries* in the apartment directly under that of Goldsmith, wearily complained of the loud laughter, the singing, and the stamping of feet, which kept him awake until the dawn. Finally, in despair, he was forced to abandon his chambers and hunt for quieter quarters. No one could moderate the gaiety of this small Irishman when he found himself "in spirits."

IV *Occasional Verse*

It is equally true that no one could buy the pen of one of the most prolific, effective of hackwriters of the day. After Goldsmith had become known in London as a poet as well as a journalist, he was approached by a certain "Parson Scott," chaplain to the Earl of Sandwich, and invited to write political propaganda for the North ministry. Goldsmith turned down the suggestion without a moment's hesitation, and he had the fun of satirizing Scott as that "d—d Scottish rogue" in *The Haunch of Venison* (II, 46–50), a *jeu d'esprit* which was not published until 1776, two years after the poet's death.

Goldsmith never laid aside his playfully poetic pen, even though he had decided that he could earn more money by "plain prose." "The Haunch of Venison," "A Poetical Epistle to Lord Clare" was sent to Robert Nugent, Lord Clare, in thanks for a "haunch of venison" that he had sent as a gift to Goldsmith's chambers. In 1771 Goldsmith had stayed at Gosfield Hall, Essex, the country house of this jovial lord, who was himself something of a poet and, like many of Goldsmith's friends, an Irishman. Here Goldsmith had met men and women of rank, including the Earl of Northumberland, from whom he asked no favors. Lord Clare, when he received the following witty lines from his guest, had become in a sense the poet's patron. The *Epistle* begins:

> Thanks, my lord, for your venison, for finer or fatter
> Never rang'd in a forest, or smok'd in a platter.
> The haunch was a picture for painters to study,
> The fat was so white, and the lean was so ruddy.   (II, 46)

But how should a poor bachelor in the Temple deal with so large a "haunch"? Though "to poets, who seldom can eat,/Your very good mutton's a very good treat," the question remained as to how to prepare it and how to consume it as well: "Such dainties to them their health it might hurt,/It's like sending them ruffles, when wanting a shirt" (II, 47). And so on—through several pages of pleasant fooling written for the private pleasure of a noble patron who dispatched mutton rather than money to his not-impecunious poet.

Goldsmith was, in fact, at the height of his popularity and fame after the appearance of *The Deserted Village*. He was welcomed at the Literary Club by such men as Edmund Burke, Sir Joshua Reynolds, Topman Beauclerk, and the good Dr. Johnson himself. In appreciation of the fact that *The Deserted Village* was dedicated to him, Reynolds, the first president of the newly founded Royal Academy, had appointed Dr. Goldsmith Professor of Ancient History, a purely honorary position, which added to Goldsmith's prestige. At this time, too, Reynolds painted the famous picture of his friend—without his wig—engravings from which were seen immediately in all the shop windows of London.

It was at the home of Reynolds, recently knighted by the king, that Goldsmith first met Mrs. Horneck, and her two beautiful daughters, Catherine, age nineteen, and Mary, seventeen. Catherine, named by Goldsmith "Little Comedy," and Mary, called by the poet "The Jessamy Bride," made Goldsmith feel at home in a drawing room presided over by three intelligent, witty, and respectable women. The verses exchanged between these sisters and their much older friend show once more the pleasure Goldsmith found in the wayward muse of poetry. An invitation, written in verse by the Horneck sisters, was answered in kind; an evening of whist and blind-man's bluff with the family was described in a bit of doggerel sent in thanks. Reynolds's painting of "The Jessamy Bride" in Turkish costume suggests the charades which Goldsmith also enjoyed. The caricature of their guest, made by the husband of "Little Comedy," gives a realistic and amusing sense of Goldsmith's appearance which one would never catch from Reynolds' dignified painting.[20]

Both Johnson and Goldsmith—Ursa Major and Ursa Minor, as Gray called them—were considered great poets in their day. Of the two, Goldsmith is now the more readable, perhaps because, though both made use of the traditional poetic forms in their verse and shared most of the current philosophic views on man and his position in the world, Goldsmith expressed himself with more simplicity and naturalness. Instead of adopting the solemnity of his learned friend, Goldsmith caught the very tone of the eighteenth-century conversation that he listened to in the taverns and parks of London, as well as around the table at the Literary Club and in the Reynolds' drawing room. Moreover, the attitude of the two men toward themselves as poets differed profoundly, as the following anecdote suggests. Strolling one day together in Westminster Abbey, Johnson and Goldsmith paused and surveyed the Poet's Corner. Johnson said, under his breath, "Forsitan ut nostrum nomen miscebitur istis" ("Perhaps one day both of our names will be here"), to which Goldsmith made no reply. Continuing their walk down the Strand, after they had left the Abbey, they passed under Temple Bar, on which, affixed to tall spikes,

were the severed heads of state criminals. Goldsmith pointed to
the heads above them and said with a smile, "Forsitan ut nostrum
. . . miscebitur ISTIS." [21]

Goldsmith was less sure than Dr. Johnson of a place in Westminster Abbey after his death, and perhaps more aware of his
kinship with the erring. The two sides of his nature, the melancholy misanthrope and the wise and cheerful sage—the Man in
Black and the Chinese Philosopher—were harmonized in Goldsmith's greatest poetry. No one knew better than he that poetry
was his "solitary pride"; perhaps it seemed to him his "shame in
crowds" because in crowds he constantly betrayed his better self.
As a result, Goldsmith remained a bookseller's hack and could not
manage to achieve the position of those men "whom fortune has
blessed with affluence, to whom the muse pays her morning visit,
not like a creditor but a friend" (III, 512 footnote).

Goldsmith's lines on the death of a fellow bookseller's hack, Edward Purdon,[22] whom he had attempted to help when both were
employed by Griffiths, have a special quality because Goldsmith
knew so well the struggle this clever young Irishman had been
through before he dropped dead from hunger on the streets of
London. Goldsmith is said to have recited the lines at the
Wednesday Club:

> Here lies poor Ned Purdon, from misery freed,
>   Who long was a bookseller's hack;
> He led such a damnable life in this world,
>   I don't think he'll wish to come back.   (II, 91)

A fellow member[23] of the Club recalled that "Doctor Goldsmith
made this epitaph in his way from his chambers in the Temple to
the Wednesday evening's club at the Globe. *I think he will never
come back*, I believe he said. I was sitting by him, and he repeated it more than twice, I *think he will never come back*. Ah!
and not altogether as a jest, it may be, the second and the third
time: it is not without a certain pathos to me, indeed, that he
should so have repeated it." Goldsmith's "Epitaph on Edward Purdon" was not published until 1777, three years after the death of
Goldsmith himself.

V   Retaliation

Shortly before his last illness Goldsmith's own epitaph was written by David Garrick at a gay party of friends and acquaintances gathered in Goldsmith's absence at St. James's Coffee-house. Since Goldsmith's "absurdities" was often the theme of the conversation when his friends foregathered, it is not surprising that someone in the group proposed that each guest write an epitaph on their absent friend for the general amusement of the party. Garrick's clever couplet is the only contribution which has survived: "Here lies Nolly Goldsmith, for shortness call'd Noll,/Who wrote like an angel, but talk'd like poor Poll."

When Goldsmith arrived later in the evening and heard the epitaph, he, for once, remained silent; and he did not accept the invitation to reply on the spot.[24] Instead, he took the matter back to his chambers for further thought; the result was a long but unfinished satire published two weeks after his death entitled *Retaliation, A Poem Including Epitaphs on some of the most Distinguished Wits of this Metropolis* (II, 52–58). Goldsmith explained in the first four lines the simple device of the satire:

> Of old, when Scarron his companions invited,
> Each guest brought his dish, and the feast was united;
> If our landlord supplies us with beef, and with fish,
> Let each guest bring himself—and he brings the best dish.

Each guest who had written a couplet on Goldsmith at the recent dinner at St. James's Coffee-house was now given a line or two describing the "dish" he represented. For example, "Our Garrick's a salad, for in him we see/Oil, vinegar, sugar, and saltness agree." The dessert turned out to be "Magnanimous Goldsmith a gooseberry fool." What a splendid feast!

> Who'd not be a glutton, and stick to the last?
> Here, waiter, more wine! let me sit while I'm able,
> Till all my companions sink under the table;
> Then, with chaos and blunders encircling my head,
> Let me ponder, and tell what I think of the dead.

Small wonder that *Retaliation* went rapidly through nine editions in the three years after Goldsmith had sunk "under the table." In the dozen or so epitaphs Goldsmith composed he managed to say precisely what he thought of many of his friends who, all too frequently, concluded that his utterances were composed of nothing but "chaos and blunders." In *Retaliation* they were devastatingly clear.

Goldsmith's epitaph on David Garrick was the longest of those included in the poem, perhaps because his relationship with his actor-friend had been the most ambiguous, as the following lines suggest:

> Here lies David Garrick, describe me who can,
> An abridgment of all that was pleasant in man;
> As an actor, confess't without rival to shine,
> As a wit, if not first, in the very first line:
> Yet, with talents like these, and an excellent heart,
> The man had his failings, a dupe to his art.

Goldsmith knew Garrick well, not only as the greatest actor of his day, but also as the theater manager who more than once had refused to accept Goldsmith's plays. He knew him, too, as fellow member of the Literary Club and delightful companion; he knew him, in short, as an artist with contradictions not unlike his own:

> On the stage he was natural, simple, affecting;
> 'Twas only that when he was off he was acting.
> With no reason on earth to go out of his way,
> He turn'd and he varied full ten times a-day.

If Garrick was "salad" and Goldsmith "gooseberry fool," Sir Joshua Reynolds was "lamb," the sustaining meat of the feast. Dr. Johnson's epitaph was not included in the collection, perhaps because he was not present at the original dinner, and perhaps because Goldsmith's illness interrupted the poem before he had time to describe Johnson, his greatest friend. The last lines Goldsmith wrote cast a benign light over the whole satire, for here Goldsmith was speaking of Reynolds who shared with him a peculiarly sweet nature. When Reynolds heard of the sudden death of Goldsmith, he is said to have closed his studio for the day to mourn his loss

alone. Two weeks later he read Goldsmith's tribute in the poem
that had already circulated in London:

> Here Reynolds is laid, and, to tell you my mind,
> He has not left a wiser or better behind;
> His pencil was striking, resistless, and grand,
> His manners were gentle, complying, and bland:
> Still born to improve us in every part,
> His pencil our faces, his manners our heart.
> To coxcombs averse, yet most civilly steering,
> When they judg'd without skill, he was still hard of hearing:
> When they talk'd of their Raphaels, Correggios, and stuff,
> He shifted his trumpet, and only took snuff,
> By flattery unspoiled. . . .

Thus ended, Goldsmith's so-called "retaliation" on his numerous
friends, who, if they had laughed at his "absurdities," had also
weaned him forever from his Irish village and made him "a citizen
of the world" of London.

Like the Chinese Philosopher, Goldsmith believed that "the
finest sentiments and the most weighty truth may put on a pleasant face," and, indeed, that "agreeable trifling" might be the way
poetry "deceives us into instruction." In this spirit, Goldsmith
dashed off many a witty, ironic, or merely playful verse, expres-
sive of the essential "conviviality" of his nature, that endeared him
to the Wednesday Club, as well as to the more distinguished Literary Club.

On quite a different level, Goldsmith had composed two long,
serious, rhetorical poems, *The Traveller* and *The Deserted Village,* in which are blended Goldsmith's melancholy vision and his
philosophic rationality. Though these poems are written in the
now unfashionable heroic couplet, the reader readily enters into
their spirit and soon comes to understand why Goldsmith called
poetry "the source of all my bliss, and all my woe." When Goldsmith was willing to forego a merry evening at the Club, or when
he felt he could put off the booksellers for a few weeks, he turned
to poetry as the perfect means of shortening the "lengthening
chain" which separated him from himself. In *The Traveller* and in
The Deserted Village Goldsmith's many-sided nature found harmonious expression.

CHAPTER 3

Philosophic Travelers

I *Publication of* The Vicar of Wakefield

HAD Goldsmith lived to complete *Retaliation,* perhaps Dr. Johnson's Epitaph would have been the final and most moving stanza, for Goldsmith owed not only a literary but also a personal debt to his great, lumbering, affectionate friend. The story of how Johnson managed to sell the manuscript of *The Vicar of Wakefield* for Goldsmith while the bailiffs were standing by to take him to prison is one of the notable anecdotes of literary history. It must be repeated in Boswell's own words, which, he claimed, were as nearly as possible the words of Johnson himself:

I received one morning a message from poor Goldsmith that he was in great distress, and, as it was not in his power to come to me, begging that I would come to him as soon as possible. I sent him a guinea, and promised to come to him directly. I accordingly went as soon as I was drest, and found that his landlady had arrested him for his rent, at which he was in a violent passion. I perceived that he had already changed my guinea, and had got a bottle of Madeira and a glass before him. I put the cork into the bottle, desired he would be calm, and began to talk to him of the means by which he might be extricated. He then told me that he had a novel ready for the press, which he produced to me. I looked into it, and saw its merit; told the landlady I should soon return, and having gone to a bookseller, sold it for sixty pounds. I brought Goldsmith the money, and he discharged his rent, not without rating his landlady in a high tone for having used him so ill.[1]

Since Boswell gave no date for these events and failed to say where either Goldsmith or Johnson was living at the time, many questions are left unsolved. The entertaining tale of Johnson's visit was, of course, repeated in the coffee-houses and drawing rooms of London immediately; and it is now imbedded in a number of eighteenth-century memories.

It is probable that Goldsmith was living at the time in the Temple, and that Johnson was staying with his new friends, Mr. and Mrs. Thrale in Streatham. Since Johnson was not introduced to the Thrales until 1764,[2] he could not have come to Goldsmith's rescue until that year. The question still remains, however, as to why the publication of the novel was delayed for two years, for it did not at last appear until March 12, 1766. It was then printed, without Goldsmith's name on the title page, by B. Collins for Francis Newbery, nephew to John Newbery, at the Crown, in Pater-Noster Row.

A further question as to the date of composition of *The Vicar* arose in the latter part of the nineteenth century when Charles Welsh, in making a study of the history of Newbery's publishing business, discovered an entry in the printer's account book which read, " 'Vicar of Wakefield', 2 vols. 12 mo. ⅓ rd. B. Collins, Salisbury, bought of Dr. Goldsmith, the author, October 28, 1762. £21."[3] Whether Goldsmith explained the circumstances of the previous sale to Dr. Johnson, who told them more briefly to Boswell, or whether, in fact, Boswell himself was inaccurate and somewhat unfriendly to Goldsmith in his retelling of the story, is not known. Perhaps the most interesting fact revealed by the Newbery account book is merely that a third of *The Vicar of Wakefield* was completed by 1762. *The Vicar of Wakefield,* according to Mrs. Thrale, seemed to Goldsmith "a novel which when finished was to be his whole fortune; but he could not get it done for distraction."

As has already been seen, Goldsmith was, at this same time, composing his "Chinese Letters," and had begun to write *The Traveller,* to mention only those titles now being considered. It was characteristic of this prolific, endlessly experimental writer that he should be working on a series of essays, a long philosophical poem, and a novel at the same time; it was also typical of Goldsmith that many of the ideas, expressed through similar characters, appear again and again, not only in these three books but in essays, poems, and plays, before and after this period. Goldsmith assumed many disguises in his lifelong effort to find expression for the thoughts and visions which crossed and recrossed his mind. The multiplication of these disguises made it difficult for Goldsmith to bring his novel to a satisfactory conclusion, and accounts, in part, for the delay in publication.

The Vicar of Wakefield, "Supposed to be written by Himself," indicates the first disguise assumed by Goldsmith in his only novel. The "Advertisement" signed "Oliver Goldsmith," reads:

There are an hundred faults in this thing, and an hundred things might be said to prove them beauties. But it is needless. A book may be amusing with numerous errors, or it may be very dull without a single absurdity. The hero of this piece unites in himself the three greatest characters upon earth: he is a priest, an husbandman, and the father of a family. He is drawn as ready to teach, and ready to obey: as simple in affluence, and majestic in adversity. In this age of opulence and refinement, whom can such a character.please? Such as are fond of high life, will turn with disdain from the simplicity of his country fire-side; such as mistake ribaldry for humour, will find no wit in his harmless conversation; and such as have been taught to deride religion, will laugh at one, whose chief stores of comfort are drawn from futurity. (I, 67)

Perhaps to Goldsmith's own surprise many readers of the day concluded, after studying this "Advertisement," that the book was in fact written by Dr. Primrose himself. Many journals, such as *Lloyd's Evening Post* and the *London Chronicle,* simply carried notices stating that "The Editor, Dr. Goldsmith" had affixed his name to the introductory advertisement of a new novel called *The Vicar of Wakefield.* Readers of today are pleased to discover in "the hero of this piece" the same country parson made familiar in the "History of the Man in Black," *The Traveller,* and later in *The Deserted Village.* Dr. Primrose he recognizes as a composite protrait of Charles and Henry Goldsmith; after the first third of the book, however, the Doctor became a spokesman for Goldsmith himself.

The "hundred faults" that Goldsmith was all too conscious of "in this thing"—and which he had no inclination to attempt to prove to be "beauties"—are perhaps to be explained by what is now known of the circumstances of its publication. Goldsmith must have shown Collins about a third of the book in 1762, for which, as already noted, he was paid twenty-one pounds, with the promise of forty pounds more upon the completion of the novel. Between 1762 and 1764, the year when Johnson probably took the manuscript to the publisher, Goldsmith had hastily huddled together the final chapters, snatching hours from the numerous jobs he was doing for the booksellers at the same time. Had he been satisfied with the result, however, he would surely himself have submitted the finished manuscript either to Newbery or to Collins (who were now partners in business) before his landlady threatened him with arrest.

One may picture Goldsmith, then, rather unwillingly reaching into the drawer of his table and producing the manuscript for Johnson after they had for some time discussed the question of how to keep Goldsmith out of the debtors' prison. Glancing through the sheets of the *Vicar*, Johnson decided that, though the tale was "a mere fanciful performance," [4] it had sufficient "merit" to warrant his making an effort to dispose of it with the publishers suggested, for good reasons, by Goldsmith. That the need for money was paramount in Goldsmith's thought at the moment is suggested by the reply he made to a friend who reproved him for not having corrected some of its obvious faults. "Had I made it ever so perfect or correct," replied the author, "I should not have had a shilling more." [5] Goldsmith knew what he was talking about, for he was quite aware of the fact that he had made his bargain with Collins two years earlier.

Readers of Goldsmith's day recognized at once that *The Vicar of Wakefield* was, indeed, a "singular tale" and that it was "needless" to try to prove its "faults" to be "beauties." The unnamed critic of the *Monthly Review* of May, 1766, for instance, wrote that, "through the whole course of our travels in the wild regions of romance, we never met with anything more difficult to characterize than the *Vicar of Wakefield*." But, he added, "with all its faults, there is much rational enjoyment to be met with in this very singular tale." [6] His criticism remains true today, as a brief consideration of the novel makes clear.

That Squire Thornhill, the wealthy landlord of the deserving Dr. Primrose, should attempt to seduce Olivia, the charming daughter of the family, only to discover that he was legitimately married to her after all; that Mr. Burchell, the *deus ex machina* of the whole affair, should turn out in the end to be the Squire's wealthy uncle in disguise; that Mr. Jenkinson, the bearded rascal who cheated both father and son at the fair, should become a totally reformed character in prison, eager to make amends to the family, prompted readers then and now to conclude of the novel, with Dr. Johnson, "It is very faulty; there is nothing of real life in it, and very little of nature." [7]

Those who relish the "wild regions of romance" will always enjoy the rapid acceleration of the plot, but the "rational enjoyment" of the book resided, no doubt, in the character of Dr. Primrose himself who seems to have taught the world that a patient and cheerful faith in the benevolence of God was enough to combat the misfortunes of nature, social change, and the malignancy of man. The particular combination of "wild romance" and "rational enjoyment" which marked *The Vicar of Wakefield* was a departure from any form of novel and romance known up to that time. The publishers, perhaps aware of the risk involved in bringing out a so-called "novel" which fit into no category, therefore held the manuscript for two years before publishing it. Only about two thousand copies of the book sold in Goldsmith's lifetime, nor did Newbery and Collins clear their expenses until after the fourth edition.

Goldsmith had no model of any sort to follow when he began his experiment in novel writing, but he undoubtedly gathered suggestions from several novelists then popular. Samuel Richardson, in whose printing shop he labored for several unhappy months in 1759, had now been dead for five years. If Goldsmith had learned anything from Richardson's long-drawn-out romance, *Clarissa Harlowe*, it was to laugh at the heroine and her Lovelace as well. Fielding, whom he quoted in *The Citizen of the World*, Goldsmith enjoyed for his vigorous humor and his biting satire. Indeed, Parson Adams, in Fielding's *Joseph Andrews* might be considered an ancestor of Goldsmith's Dr. Primrose; and we know that Olivia Primrose said that the arguing tutors, Thwackam and Square, in *Tom Jones* taught her to reason. However, Goldsmith introduced into his scenes of country life a poetic and sentimental feeling unknown to the more realistic Fielding. Smollett, for whom Goldsmith wrote in the *British Magazine,* had not yet published *Humphrey Clinker;* and Sterne's *Tristram Shandy* Goldsmith criticized as a clear indication of the "depravity of the times" since this "sentimental novel" seemed to Goldsmith more prurient than witty. [8]

Goldsmith was well aware of the peculiar effectiveness of *Can-*

dide and *Rasselas,* the brief novels of Voltaire and Johnson, respectively. Still more important, he saw in *Candide* and *Rasselas* —both published in 1759—finished examples of the philosophic romance, with which he, too, had in a sense been experimenting in his "Chinese Letters." Like Candide, the Chinese Philosopher was, in his study of the West, exploring the familiar eighteenth-century concept that "all is for the best in the best of all possible worlds"; like Rasselas, Lien Chi Altangi was searching for "happiness" far from home, only to discover that it resides in one's own breast, if anywhere. Both Voltaire and Johnson, in *Candide* and *Rasselas,* were as relentlessly clear in their presentations as were Leibniz and Spinoza in stating these philosophic propositions originally.

Addison and Steele, whom Goldsmith admired and frequently quoted, not only suggested in *The Spectator Papers* the city beaux and country squires, the London coquettes and the busy politicians of the coffee-houses, but also hinted at possible plot complications and supplied Goldsmith with an ethical-religious-philosophic premise with which to judge his characters. Indeed, Goldsmith's description of his hero in the "Advertisement" to *The Vicar of Wakefield*—"a priest, an husbandman, and the father of a family"—would have seemed entirely appropriate and familiar to the authors of *The Spectator Papers.* Had Goldsmith, in fact, carried out his announced intentions in his presentation of the good doctor and his family, it is doubtful that he would be read today; for he would have been nothing more than an imitator of others and not the "original" he proved to be. The real aims of *The Vicar of Wakefield* are hardly those described by their author —though they were, no doubt, stated with the same good faith he showed in announcing his intentions in writing *The Traveller* and *The Deserted Village.* In all three instances, Goldsmith—once caught up in his literary visions—was carried to realms of humor, irony, and melancholy, which he himself had no conscious intention of entering when he defined his aims.

Slow to find its public, *The Vicar,* by the end of the eighteenth century, had been translated into French and German. Since that time it has been translated into the language of almost every civilized country of the world and is today one of the most popular novels; perhaps its appeal lies, at least in part, in the fact that no one knows exactly how to interpret the peculiar combination of "beauties" and "faults" that mark this "singular tale," though all are charmed by its apparent simplicity and kindliness. To Goethe, who heard the novel read aloud by Herder four years after its publication, when he himself was twenty years of age, *The Vicar of Wakefield* was a "prose-idyll" that taught him the goodness of the human heart and threw over his own youth the poetic haze which helped him for the remainder of his life.[9] Sir Walter Scott wrote that we return to the *Vicar of Wakefield* again and again, "and we bless the memory of an author who contrives so well to reconcile us to human nature." [10] This romantic interpretation of *The Vicar* was repeated by Thackeray, Irving, and by countless critics and editors up to the present day. It is well summed up by Goldsmith's nineteenty-century biographer, John Forster, who wrote of *The Vicar of Wakefield* that "it is our first pure example of the simple domestic novel. . . . Good predominant over evil, is briefly the purpose and moral of the little story. It is designed to show us that patience in suffering, that perservering reliance on the providence of God, that quiet labour, cheerful endeavour, and an indulgent forgiveness of the faults and infirmities of others, are the easy and certain means of pleasure in this world, and of turning pain to noble uses." [11]

Since Goldsmith probably wrote the first third of his novel as early as 1761, and then put it aside in the confusion of other obligations, it is not surprising that Forster and many others have mistaken the idyllic scenes that mark the quietly ironic opening of what promises to be a "domestic novel" for the whole of the work. Some critics, however, perceived that the novel lacked unity. "The earlier chapters," wrote Macaulay, "have all the sweetness of pastoral poetry, together with the vivacity of comedy." But, as the story progresses, Macaulay pointed out, "It wants not merely the probability which ought to be found in a tale of common English life, but that consistency which ought to be found even in the wildest fiction about witches, giants, and fairies." [12]

II *A Philosophic Romance*

In the opening chapters of the novel Goldsmith again called up the vision of Lissoy and presented the picture of the country parson, made familiar to the reader in *The Citizen of the World,* in *The Traveller,* in *The Deserted Village,* and elsewhere in his writing. Goldsmith was always enchanted with the memory of his father presiding happily over a large family and his entertaining at his generous table friends, neighbors, and passers-by. "The place of our retreat was in a little neighborhood," wrote the Vicar, taking the reader right back to the scenes of *The Deserted Village.* The countryside was owned by farmers, who tilled their own grounds, "and were equal strangers to opulence and poverty."

As they had almost all the conveniences of life within themselves, they seldom visited towns or cities in search of superfluity. Remote from the polite, they still retained the primeval simplicity of manners; and frugal by habit, they scarce knew that temperance was a virtue. They wrought with cheerfulness on days of labour; but observed festivals, as intervals of idleness and pleasure. They kept up the Christmas carol; sent true-love knots on Valentine morning; ate pancakes on Shrovetide; showed their wit on the first of April; and religiously cracked nuts on Michaelmas eve. (I, 84)

Though Goldsmith so often described ironically the simplicity of Dr. Primrose—or allowed the good Doctor to display his own guileless and gullible nature—here, certainly, Goldsmith, too, succumbed to the charms of innocent and cheerful mirth. The mood, however, did not last long. Just as Goldsmith had written to his brother Henry that he envied him his quiet fireside, but that he was impelled by his own restless, romantic nature, to pursue his lonely wanderings, so now the Pastor, his son George, and finally his two daughters, Olivia and Sophia, are loosened from their moorings and sent out into the world to learn by experience what the simple village life could not teach. The "prose-idyll" so loved by Goethe soon becomes a far more interesting philosophical novel, after the manner of Voltaire and Johnson; it also, as Macaulay pointed out, lost any claim to "consistency" and "probability."

In the third chapter of *The Vicar of Wakefield* the Reverend Dr. Primrose, after he has learned of the financial ruin of his family, is saying farewell to his elder son, George. Having assured his wife, Deborah, and the five remaining children, that "we have still enough for happiness if we are wise," he turned to his departing son, and addressed him in words which clearly state with ironic

OLIVER GOLDSMITH

overtones the thesis of the book. George first mingled his tears with those of the weaker members of the family and then asked his father for his blessing. "This I gave him from my heart," wrote the Doctor, for a Bible, "added to five guineas, was all the patrimony I had now to bestow." Though the father had few guineas to spare, he was rich in rhetoric:

"You are going, my boy," cried I, "to London, on foot, in the manner Hooker, your great ancestor, travelled there before you. Take from me the same horse that was given him by the good Bishop Jewel, this staff; and take this book too, it will be your comfort on the way: these two lines in it are worth a million: '*I have been young, and now am old: yet never saw I the righteous man forsaken, or his seed begging their bread.*' . . . As he was possessed of integrity and honour, I was under no apprehension from throwing him naked into the amphitheater of life; for I knew he would act a good part, whether vanquished or victorious." (I, 79)

Goldsmith, in proposing to examine the Psalmist's proposition "that the righteous man is never forsaken," [13] was following the example of Voltaire and Johnson, who, two years before Goldsmith began his novel, had examined with similar irony equally familiar axioms. That "glorious pillar of unshaken orthodoxy," Dr. Primrose, was as perfect a character as either Candide or Rasselas on whom to test a philosophic proposition; moreover, the Doctor was the father of six young Primroses whose adventures could be offered as further proof of the truth or untruth of the text. Since *Candide, Rasselas,* and *The Vicar of Wakefield* are all three philosophic novels, the adventures which crowd the scenes are the very means by which their authors test, with ironic exaggeration, the worth of the texts so blandly accepted by the uncritical.

In the presentation of the Chinese Philosopher, Goldsmith had already experimented with the idea of expressing his own views on various philosophical concepts through the words of a cheerful, educated but simple individual who looked at the world from a certain fixed standpoint. Lien Chi Altangi, a follower of the wisdom of Confucius and trained in the sixteen books of etiquette, and Dr. Primrose, a poor parish priest of the Established Church, perfectly conversant with the rules of Christian-gentlemanly behaviour, both prove to be excellent disguises for Goldsmith. Through them he could be, by turns, eloquent, ironic, pathetic, absurd, or noble. It is significant that both of these spokesmen had sons who, like Goldsmith himself, become poor, philosophic wanderers in the world. They find—again as did Goldsmith—that the simple and perhaps "true" wisdom of their fathers bore small relation to the experiences of life.

Dr. Primrose was as well read and as inquiring a philosopher as Lien Chi Altangi himself. In presenting his son with a staff instead of a horse, the Doctor had in mind an anecdote taken from Izaak Walton's *Life of Hooker,* which would certainly have pleased the Chinese Philosopher. As Bishop Jewel parted with Hooker, he "gave him good Counsel, and his Benediction, but forgot to give him money; which when the Bishop had considered, he sent a Servant in all haste to call Richard back to him, and at Richard's return, the Bishop said to him 'Richard, I sent for you back to lend you a horse, which hath carried me many a Mile, and I thank God with much ease,' and presently delivered into his hands a Walking-staff, with which he professed he had travelled through many parts of Germany." Calmly following the great tradition which places piety above riches, the parson thus cast his son "naked into the amphitheater of life."

George was not seen or heard of by the Primrose family for the next three years. In Chapter XX, appropriately entitled "The History of a Philosophic Vagabond, Pursuing Novelty, but Losing Content," the reader learns of George's wanderings on the Continent, from the time he said good-bye to his family until he settled in London as a bookseller's hack. George's adventures are, indeed, Goldsmith's own until he reached Dover in 1756 and, after attempting to earn a living as an apothecary and as an usher in a boys' school, settled down in London to make a place for himself with his pen. Unlike Goldsmith, however, George Primrose returned home to tell the tale.

In Book I of *The Vicar of Wakefield,* the reader is invited to examine again the proposition of the Psalmist, that the good are always victorious over surrounding evil—this time, by means of the "romance" of the elder daughter and the wicked Squire Thornhill. When the Primroses were forced by circumstances to move from their comfortable parsonage to a humbler one, the

Squire unfortunately became the landlord of the unprotected family. Olivia and her younger sister Sophia are thus described by their father: "Olivia, now about eighteen, had that luxuriancy of beauty with which painters generally draw Hebe; open, sprightly, and commanding. Sophia's features were not so striking at first, but often did more certain execution; for they were soft, modest, and alluring. The one vanquished by a single blow, the other by efforts successfully repeated. . . . The one entertained me with her vivacity when I was gay, the other with her sense when I was serious" (I, 73–74).

Though Olivia was considered by her father as something of a "coquet" and Sophia as a "prude," the father conceded that he had "often seen them exchange characters for a whole day together." Olivia and Sophia are presented as two charming, harmless creatures who mixed "washes" at the fireplace for their complexions (which their father surreptitiously kicked over); made waistcoats for their younger brothers out of the long trains of their gowns (which their father declared inappropriate to their fallen social state); helped their brothers in the hayfield; and (at the request of their father) sang songs to the family over their modest noon repast.

The designing Squire Thornhill, though more experienced in the ways of the world than any of the Primroses, is quite as simple; for he too is hardly more than a factor in a philosophic equation—as well as a rich opportunity for Goldsmith to laugh at the Lovelaces of the world! Immediately after the departure of George, as the family journeyed to its new abode, the landlord of the "obscure inn" in which they spent the first night of the pilgrimage gave the Primroses all the information they needed concerning the "villain," had they been on their guard. This gentleman the landlord described "as one who desired to know little more of the world than its pleasures, being particularly remarkable for his attachment to the fair sex. He observed that no virtue was able to resist his arts and assiduity, and that scarce a farmer's daughter within ten miles round but what had found him successful and faithless" (I, 80). The landlord's account gave Dr. Primrose "some pain," but the effect on his daughters and his wife was far otherwise. The faces of the girls immediately "seemed to brighten with the expectation of an approaching triumph; nor was my wife less pleased and confident of their allurements and virtue."

Not only the landlord, but also a fellow guest at the inn—to whom the Doctor had casually offered his purse to help him pay his reckoning—told the Primroses more of the reputation of Squire Thornhill. The stranger, who bears a striking resemblance to Dr. Goldsmith, soon introduced himself as "Mr. Burchell." He was about thirty years old, and "was drest in cloaths that once were laced. His person was well formed, and his face marked with the lines of thinking. He had something short and dry in his address, and seemed not to understand ceremony, or to despise it."

Jogging along the country road with the family the following morning, Mr. Burchell "lightened the fatigues of the road with philosophical disputes," but he failed to repay the Doctor the money he had borrowed. On a hill beside the road he pointed out "a very magnificent house" belonging to young Squire Thornhill, the nephew of Sir William. The Doctor was astounded to learn that his new landlord was related to "a man whose virtues, generosity, and singularities are so universally known." He had often heard Sir William described "as one of the most generous, yet whimsical men in the kingdom; a man of consumate benevolence." "Something, perhaps, too much so," replied Mr. Burchell, "at least he carried benevolence to an excess when young; for his passions were then strong, and as they all were upon the side of virtue, they led it up to a romantic extreme." Sir William was surrounded by those who sought his aid, and, "no longer able to satisfy every request that was made him, instead of *money* he gave *promises*. They were all he had to bestow, and he had not resolution enough to give any man pain by a denial." The dependents who gathered around him overwhelmed him with "reproaches and contempt" in their disappointment and, "in proportion as he became contemptible to others, he became despicable to himself."

Forgetting his assumed role of "Mr. Burchell," Sir William almost slipped into the first person—a lapse unnoticed by any of the Primrose family. "I found that—that—I forget what I was going to observe: in short, Sir, he resolved to respect himself, and laid down a plan for restoring his falling fortunes." The description of the "plan" makes the reader realize that Mr. Burchell is, in fact, not only Sir William Thornhill in disguise, but also closely related to Goldsmith himself. "For this purpose," said Burchell, Sir William, "in his own whimsical manner," to carry out his plan, "travelled through Europe on foot, and though he has scarce attained the age of thirty, his circumstances are more affluent than ever. At present, his bounties are more rational and moderate than before; but still he preserves the character of an humourist, and finds most pleasure in eccentric virtues" (I, 81–83).

Though Goldsmith was never able to bring about a reform in his character, he at least at the same period in his life proposed to do so. In a letter to a cousin in Ireland, written on August 15, 1758, Goldsmith wrote, in terms not unlike those used by Burchell, that "I have often affected bluntness to avoid the imputation of flattery." Now, at the age of thirty, he found himself in danger of turning into "a perfect Hunks, and as dark and intricate as a mouse-hole," and has given orders to his landlady for "an entire reform in the state of my finances." The fact that in Letter XXVII of *The Citizen of the World* the Man in Black called himself a "saving hunks" and a whimsical, dismal fellow afflicted by a tender heart makes Burchell's description of Sir William—in reality, himself—a perfect portrait of the Man in Black, who, as has been noted, was one of Goldsmith's several projections of one side of his own somewhat perverse personality. Mr. Burchell described Sir William to Dr. Primrose as follows:

He loved all mankind; for fortune prevented him from knowing that there were rascals. Physicians tell us of a disorder in which the whole body is so exquisitely sensible, that the slightest touch gives pain: what some have thus suffered in their persons, this gentleman felt in his mind. The slightest distress, whether real or fictitious, touched him to the quick, and his soul laboured under a sickly sensibility of the miseries of others. Thus disposed to relieve, it will be easily conjectured, he found numbers disposed to solicit: his profusions began to impair his fortune, but not his good nature; that, indeed, was seen to increase, as the other seemed to decay: he grew improvident as he grew poor; and though he talked like a man of sense, his actions were those of a fool (I, 82).

With almost the same words, Goldsmith had described the poet as a man of sense, who, in his actions, was frequently a fool (III,

313). In a phrase as applicable to Goldsmith as to Sir William, Burchell summed up his description of Sir William (himself) as a man who "preserves the character of an humourist, and finds most pleasure in eccentric virtues." [14]

That Dr. Primrose was as mistaken in his reading of the character of Mr. Burchell, as he was wrong in his judgment of his son George, is an indication of the gentle irony of Goldsmith's study of Dr. Primrose, the "righteous man" whom Providence never deserts. The Doctor's patronizing description of Mr. Burchell—whom he later believes to be a villain—is at once a charming character sketch of "A Poor Gentleman" in the seventeenth-century tradition and a somewhat romanticized portrait of Goldsmith himself. "I was pleased with the poor man's friendship for two reasons," Dr. Primrose confided with a certain lordly condescension to his reader, "because I knew he wanted mine; and I knew him to be friendly as far as he was able." Mr. Burchell—or, rather, Sir William Thornhill—was the means by which the whole family was rescued, as, no doubt, Goldsmith would have liked to have rescued his rather feckless Irish family. The Parson's description of Mr. Burchell is a compound of Goldsmith's memories of his evenings in the tavern of Lissoy, and his playful encounters with the children who danced to the tune of his flute in Green Arbour Court and who expected gingerbread, ballads, and stories from the odd gentleman who lived by the gateway. According to Dr. Primrose, Burchell

was known in our neighbourhood by the character of the poor gentleman that would do no good when he was young, though he was not yet thirty. He would at intervals talk with great good sense; but, in general, he was fondest of the company of children, whom he used to call harmless little men. He was famous, I found, for singing them ballads and telling them stories; and seldom went out without something in his pockets for them, a piece of gingerbread, or a halfpenny whistle. He generally came for a few days into our neighbourhood once a-year, and lived upon the neighbours' hospitality. He sate down to supper among us, and my wife was not sparing of her gooseberry-wine. The tale went round; he sung us old songs, and gave the children the story of the Buck of Beverland, with the history of Patient Grissel, the Adventures of Catskin, and then Fair Rosamond's Bower (I, 91).

George Primrose, when he said goodbye to his tearful family and received the staff and the wisdom of the Psalmist from his father, became, as the reader knows, a "philosophic vagabond"; Sir William Thornhill, disguised as Mr. Burchell, had also become a wandering philosopher. Together these two characters supply us with an understanding of Goldsmith's reflections on his life as a meditative traveler. Dr. Primrose himself, in whom Goldsmith portrayed not only his memories of his father and his brother but many of his own experiences, became a third philosophic vagabond. After he learned of the elopement of Olivia, he, too, took up his staff and wandered through the countryside. Dr. Primrose went in search not only of his daughter but also of the meaning of good and evil in a world in which, the Psalmist assured him, the righteous man is never forsaken nor his children left to beg their bread.

III   The Psalmist Tested

Chapter XVII, which is entitled "Scarce Any Virtue Found to Resist the Power of Long and Pleasing Temptation," brings to a tumultuous close the portion of the novel which might be called a "prose-idyll." In this chapter the good Doctor learned that Olivia had, indeed, eloped. Since it is the quill of Dr. Primrose that described the rush of events and feelings which break into the calm opening of the tale, the true answer as to how well God protects his shorn lambs does not lie before the reader on the printed page but hovers elusively between the lines. From the beginning of the chapter, when the Doctor had obtained a promise from Olivia that she would accept the hand of farmer Williams if the Squire failed to make a definite "offer" within a given time, to the end, when Dr. Primrose resolved to pursue the eloping pair in the spirit of Christian temperance, the poor father's faith and moral courage were severely tested. Does Goldsmith intend the reader to admire the Doctor's patience and nobility, or to smile at his simplicity, to weep at his suffering, or to laugh at his wisdom? If one considers on how many levels one can read the following scenes, one need not wonder at the wide variety of interpretations the novel has survived.

After the arrangements for Olivia's marriage have been completed, the family is portrayed in its cozy kitchen, "round a charming fire, telling stories of the past, and laying schemes for the future," for the wedding was but four days off. "Well, Moses," cried the cheerful father, addressing his second son, "we shall soon, my boy, have a wedding in the family; what is your opinion of matters and things in general?"—"My opinion, father, is, that all things go on very well; and I was just now thinking that when sister Livy is married to farmer Williams, we shall then have the loan of his cyder press and brewing tubs for nothing."—"That we shall, Moses," cried the father, "and he will sing us Death and the Lady, to raise our spirits, into the bargain" (I, 139).

When the Doctor learned that Mr. Williams had already taught the song to Dick, he looked around for his little son but failed to discover him in the family circle. "My brother Dick," piped up Bill, age four, "is just gone out with sister Livy; but Mr. Williams has taught me two songs, and I'll sing them for you, Papa. Which song do you choose, *The Dying Swan,* or the *Elegy on the Death of a Mad Dog?*"—"The Elegy, child, by all means," replied the father, "I never heard that yet; and Deborah, my life, grief you know is dry, let us have a bottle of the best gooseberry wine to keep up our spirits. I have wept so much at all sorts of elegies of late, that without an enlivening glass, I am sure this will overcome me; and Sophy, love, take your guitar, and thrum in with the boy a little." Bill arose and thus began,

> Good people all, of every sort,
> Give ear unto my song;
>
> And if you find it wondrous short,
> It cannot hold you long.

Like so many of Goldsmith's humorous "trifles," this one, too, in its proper setting, yields, its own ironic turn. A mad dog, one learns, bites the good man of the town:

> Around from all the neighb'ring streets,
> The wond'ring neighbours ran,
> And swore the dog had lost his wits,
> To bite so good a man.
>
> The wound it seem'd both sore and sad,
> To every Christian eye;

And while they swore the dog was mad,
They swore the man would die.

But soon a wonder came to light,
That show'd the rogues they lied;
The man recover'd of the bite,
The dog it was that died.

Though the reader may ponder the relevance of this odd little poem of the mad dog who bit the good man, Dr. Primrose himself gave it but a passing thought. "A very good boy, Bill, upon my word," he cried, "and an elegy that may truly be called tragical. Come, my children, here's to Bill's health, and may he one day be a bishop." The Doctor then launched forth on a learned conversation on the nature of true poetry, requested a song from Moses, called to his wife for another bottle of wine, and delivered his last happy speech in the book:

What thanks do we not owe to heaven for thus bestowing tranquillity, health, and competence. I think myself happier now than the greatest monarch upon earth. He has no such fire-side, nor such pleasant faces about it. Yes, Deborah, we are now growing old; but the evening of our life is likely to be happy. We are descended from ancestors that knew no stain, and we shall leave a good and virtuous race of children behind us. While we live they will be our support and our pleasure here, and, when we die, they will transmit our honour untainted to posterity. —Come, my son, we wait for your song; let us have a chorus. But where is my darling Olivia? That little cherub's voice is always sweetest in the concert (I, 141).

Where, indeed, was Olivia? The happy father soon learned the bitter news; as he spoke, Dick came running in with the words, "O Papa, papa, she is gone from us, she is gone from us, my sister Livy is gone from us for ever."—"Gone, child!"—"Yes, she is gone off with two gentlemen in a post-chaise, and one of them kissed her, and said he would die for her; and she cried very much, and was for coming back; but he persuaded her again, and she went into the chaise, and said, O what will my poor Papa do when he knows I am undone!"

What "poor Papa" did do gave Goldsmith the end of the thread by which he unravelled his tangled philosophic problem as to whether or not the righteous man can ever be forsaken. The meaning of Bill's song now becomes clear; before the reader is the good man bitten by that mad dog, the Squire.

> The wound it seem'd both sore and sad,
>   To every Christian eye;
> And while they swore the dog was mad,
>   They swore the man would die.

By what stages "the man [Dr. Primrose] recovered from the bite" is, indeed, the "wonder" of the tale.

Dr. Primrose's immediate response to the news of his daughter's flight was to cast aside all of his Christian faith in the benevolence of Providence. Job-like, he now cried to his children: "Now, then, my children, go and be miserable; for we shall never enjoy one hour more. And O may heaven's everlasting fury light upon him and his! Thus to rob me of my child! And sure it will, for taking back my sweet innocent that I was leading up to heaven. Such sincerity as my child was possessed of. But all our earthly happiness is now over! Go, my children, go, and be miserable and infamous; for my heart is broken within me!"

Moses then admonished his father with the same Christian-Stoic platitudes on which he had been nurtured. "Father," cried the son, "is this your fortitude?"—"Fortitude, child!" replied the father, "Yes, he shall see I have fortitude! Bring me my pistols. I'll pursue the traitor. While he is on earth, I'll pursue him. Old as I am, he shall find I can sting him yet. The villain! the perfidious villain!" Before the Vicar had time to take his pistols from the shelf, Deborah caught her husband in her arms. "My dearest, dearest husband," cried she, "The bible is the only weapon that is fit for your old hands now. Open that, my love, and read our anguish into patience, for she has vilely deceived us." Deborah, like Job's wife, broke down at the realization of the family disaster. "She is an ungrateful creature to use us thus," she cried between her sobs. "She never had the least constraint put upon her affections. The vile strumpet has basely deserted her parents without any provocation, thus to bring your grey hairs to the grave, and I must shortly follow."

The "wretched child" was sorely missed at breakfast the next day—she who used to add "life and cheerfulness" to the morning cup of tea. As Mrs. Primrose declared that "that vilest stain of our family" should never again "darken these harmless doors," Dr. Primrose turned to Moses and said, "My son, bring hither my bible and my staff; I will pursue her wherever she is, and, though I cannot save her from shame, I may prevent the continuance of iniquity." Before departing, however, he admonished his wife against hardness of heart; and, while the song of the birds was heard through the kitchen window, he delivered his customary sermon:

Wife, do not talk thus hardly: my detestation of her guilt is as great as yours; but ever shall this house and this heart be open to a poor return- ing repentant sinner. The sooner she returns from her transgression, the more welcome shall she be to me. For the first time, the very best may err: art may persuade, and novelty spread out its charm. The first fault is the child of simplicity; but every other the offspring of guilt. Yes, the wretched creature shall be welcome to this heart and this house, though stained with ten thousand vices. I will again hearken to the music of her voice, again will I hang fondly on her bosom, if I find but repentance there (I, 143).

One is reminded of the Chinese Philosopher's words to his son—it is not the fact that one falls which is so important as that one attempts again to rise (III, 31). The wisdom of Confucius, as well as the wisdom of Christianity, admonishes forgiveness and charity to the repentant sinner. Armed with his staff and his Bible, Dr. Primrose began his pursuit of "a lost child" whom he hoped to reclaim to virtue. In putting to the test the Psalmist's assurance that "the righteous are never forsaken," the Doctor became the third "philosophic vagabond." [15]

IV *Philosophic Travelers*

For the Parson himself, respectable as he was, did become something of a vagabond. He was delighted to travel in the wagon of a group of strolling players, glad to sit before the fire of an inn and to lift a glass with the landlord, pleased to argue the merits of monarchy with the butler whom he mistook for the mas- ter, and willing to accept the financial aid of a stranger when he lay ill for several weeks in a tavern. The fate of the wretched girl is almost forgotten by the reader, as well as by her father, as one wanders with Goldsmith's Vicar once more from town to town, from the fair to the races, from taproom to country home. The Parson, having been persuaded by the Squire that he was not Olivia's seducer, could think of no better plan than to roam the countryside in search of his daughter.

Miraculously enough, though the Vicar did not at that time find Olivia, he did encounter George. While seated near the stage of a country theater with a pleasant group of newly made friends, Dr. Primrose recognized among the actors before him none other than his son George, whom he had not seen for three years. George was so overcome by the sight of his father that he left the stage in the midst of the performance, and joined the Doctor and his friends, who urged him to repair at once to their drawing room and begin the story of his travels. "I fancy, Sir," cried Mrs. Arnold, his hostess, "that the account of your adventures would be amusing." George, who liked to "shine" quite as much as did Goldsmith, replied, "Madame, I promise you, the pleasure you have in hearing will not be half so great as my vanity in repeating them." Again like Goldsmith, he added, "and yet, in the whole narrative, I can scarce promise you one adventure, as my account is rather of what I saw, than what I did." Goldsmith, when he wandered through Europe, gathering material for *An Enquiry Into Polite Learning,* was just such a "philosophic vagabond."

Beginning his story at the point the reader left him in Chapter III, George remarked: "No person ever had a better knack at hoping than I. The less kind I found Fortune, at one time, the more I expected of her at another, and being now at the bottom of her wheel, every new revolution might lift, but could not depress me. . . . [I] comforted myself with reflecting, that London was the mart where abilities of every kind were sure of meeting distinction and reward" (I, 155–56).

Describing George's entrance into life with the very metaphor of the wheel of fortune which he had used in a letter to his friend, Robert Bryanton,[16] concerning his own early struggles in London, Goldsmith leaves one in no doubt that in writing the story of George he was glancing back with a wry smile at his own youth. As surely as Mr. Burchell was describing Goldsmith's efforts to deal with the hangers-on who kept him poor, so now George was speaking in Goldsmith's own bitter tones when he told the assembly about his first experience in Grub Street. "A little man" in a coffee-house attempted to instruct him in the art of collecting fees from noblemen for subscriptions to books which were never published; this experience made him determined to trust no one's advice:

Having a mind too proud to stoop to such indignities, and yet a fortune too humble to hazard a second attempt for fame, I was now obliged to take a middle course, and write for bread. But I was unqualified for a profession where mere industry alone was to ensure success. I could not suppress my lurking passion for applause; but usually consumed that time in efforts after excellence, which takes up but little room, when it should have been more advantageously employed in the diffusive productions of productive mediocrity. My little piece would therefore come forth in the midst of periodical publication, unnoticed and unknown. The public were more importantly employed than to observe the easy simplicity of my style, or the harmony of my periods. Sheet after sheet was thrown off to oblivion. My essays were buried among the essays upon liberty, eastern tales, and cures for the bite of a mad dog; while Philautos, Philalethes, Philelutheros, and Philanthropos, all wrote better, because they wrote faster than I.[17]

George, as well as Goldsmith, "began to associate with none but disappointed authors, like myself, who praised, deplored, and despised each other"; and he found that he was never pleased at the discovery of genius in another: "I could neither read nor write with satisfaction; for excellence in another was my aversion, and writing was my trade" (I, 158–59).

George's account of his London adventures soon took a melodramatic turn which enabled Goldsmith to link together the three characters who had played an important part in the struggles of Dr. Primrose. George's encounter in London with that "very good natured fellow," Ned Thornhill (known to the reader as Squire Thornhill), involved him in the intrigues of the life of a wealthy young gentleman of London and terminated in George's supposed obligation to fight a foolish duel for his patron. Young Thornhill, finding that his affairs had now grown too dangerously complicated, hastily left London for Ireland where, as the reader knows, he was soon once more bringing trouble to the Primrose family. Though Ned Thornhill refused to pay George for his part in the duel, he did leave with him a letter of recommendation to Thornhill's wealthy uncle, Sir William, who was then in London. This honorable gentleman heard George's story to the end, pointed out that his nephew was guilty in the matter of the duel, but so also was George, who willingly entered into his schemes. George meekly accepted Sir William's refusal of a reward, as well as the older man's hope that he would repent. "The serverity of this rebuke I bore patiently, because I knew it was just" (I, 161).

Dr. Primrose, who calmly listened to George's account of his London adventures, was somewhat roused when he heard the name of Ned Thornhill. "What did you say, George?" he interrupted; "Thornhill, was not that his name? It can certainly be no other than my landlord."—"Bless me," cried Mrs. Arnold, "is Mr. Thornhill so near a neighbour of yours? He has long been a friend in our family, and we expect a visit from him shortly." Before the Squire's equipage was heard in the driveway, however, George finished the story of his subsequent adventures as a sailor; as a prisoner; and, finally, like Goldsmith, as a wanderer "among the harmless peasants of Flanders," playing his flute for his supper, or disputing in convents and universities for the promised reward of a dinner.

When the Squire at last arrived, he did seem to "start back" a moment at seeing so unexpectedly the son and father he had harmed; "but I readily imputed that to surprise, and not displeasure," wrote the Parson, now convinced that Sir William and not his nephew was the villain he sought. "Upon our advancing to salute him, he returned our greeting with the most apparent candour; and, after a short time, his presence served only to increase the general good humour" (I, 168). If Goldsmith's "righteous man" was to be saved from his accumulating troubles it was evidently not because of his ability to read the character of those about him! The Squire, indeed, had no difficulty in persuading the poor Parson that he had paid frequent visits to the humble home of his tenant in order to comfort the rest of the family, whom he had left "perfectly well." The next morning Squire Thornhill showed his zeal for the welfare of the family by obtaining for George a commission on a ship that was bound immediately for the West Indies. The Parson again said goodbye to his son who is thus safely disposed of until the final "revelations." As for the Doctor, he "took leave of the good family that had been kind enough to entertain me so long, not without several expressions of gratitude to Mr. Thornhill for his late bounty. I left them in the enjoyment of all that happiness which affluence and good-breeding procure, and returned towards home, despairing of ever finding my daughter more, but sending a sigh to Heaven to spare and to forgive her" (I, 170).

Still weak from his illness, the Doctor hired a horse; and, with the intention of returning to his home and all that he held "dearest upon earth," he moved slowly down the darkening road. When night came on, the traveler turned his horse's head towards a small public house by the roadside and "asked for the landlord's company over a pint of wine." As was his pleasant custom, the Doctor soon found himself chatting before the fire "on politics and the news of the country," which included scandalous stories about Squire Thornhill. But this conversation was interrupted by certain sounds from above which even the guileless Parson could not pretend he did not hear. "Out I say, pack out this moment, tramp, thou infamous strumpet, or I'll give thee a mark thou won't be the better for these three months. What! you trumpery, to come and take up an honest house, without cross or coin to bless yourself with; come along I say."—"O, dear Madam," cried the stranger, "pity me; pity a poor abandoned creature for one night, and death will soon do the rest." Dr. Primrose recognized the voice of his poor ruined Olivia. "I flew to her rescue," wrote the Doctor, "while the woman was dragging her along by the hair, and I caught the dear forlorn wretch in my arms.—'Welcome, any way welcome, my dearest lost one, my treasure, to your poor old father's bosom. Though the vicious forsake thee, there is yet one in the world that will never forsake thee; though thou hadst ten thousand crimes to answer for, he will forget them all'" (I, 171–172).

But the trials of Dr. Primrose were by no means ended. Leaving his daughter reposing in another wayside inn, he slowly made his way to his home in order to prepare his wife for the news of Olivia's return. The parsonage, however, burst into flames just as he turned the corner of the road and distracted the poor Doctor from any thought of Olivia. Soon the family was settled once more in a still humbler shelter, where they welcomed Olivia to what comfort the shed afforded.

In order to restore as well as he could the former serenity of the dejected family gathered together in the cold, damp shed, the Doctor called upon his "strong memory"—for most of his books had been burned—for a tale which should prove once again that man's happiness is in higher hands and cannot be taken from him if his heart is pure. "Our happiness, my dear," said the still unvanquished Rector, turning to Olivia, "is in the power of one who can bring it about in a thousand unforeseen ways that mock our foresight. If example be necessary to prove this, I'll give you a story, my child, told us by a grave, though sometimes a romancing, historian" (I, 179). Thereupon, the intricacies of the romance of Matilda and her Neopolitan lover—not a story from the Bible—held the Primrose family enthralled and made them forget, for the moment at least, that they were cold, hungry, and homeless. Surely Goldsmith was smiling at the absurdity of the well-meaning man of God who found in a "romancing historian" another means of escaping the sad realities of life. Goldsmith was not, as many have thought, creating a "character eminently calculated to inculcate benevolence, humanity, patience in suffering, and reliance on Providence." [18] Once again Goldsmith was affectionately satirizing the father and the brother who were "passing rich on forty pounds a year" and who brought up their children to think that money was but dross.

V *Theory of Romance*

At the same time that Goldsmith was step by step leading the reader to the unavoidable conclusion that the Psalmist erred in stating that the righteous man is never deserted, he was also satirizing the vogue for "romance" by burying the reader's "rational enjoyment" in the accumulating disasters of the Primrose family. Whether Goldsmith found a satire on "wild romance" the simplest method by which to finish the manuscript for which he knew he could collect the remaining forty pounds promised him by the publisher, or whether at the outset he intended to make his philosophic novel a satire both on the Psalmist's text and also on the absurd taste for melodramatic tales, it is impossible to determine. Carried away as usual by his imaginative poetic vision of his happy boyhood in Ireland, his intention—whatever it was— shifted in the lapse of time between his writing of the first third of the novel and the hasty completion of his manuscript. The result was that *The Vicar of Wakefield* became, by the time it was published, not a sentimental, faintly ironic "domestic novel" but a double satire on the religious clichés with which the good Doctor faced life's tragedies and on the form of romance then in vogue, one in which elaborate plot interest took the place of "rational enjoyment."

Goldsmith's ideas on romance had already been set forth both in letters and in essays. Only a year or more before he began writing his only novel, he had half-humorously expressed his views on romance to his brother Henry who had asked his advice concerning the education of his son. Never let the boy read a novel or a romance, Goldsmith had advised, for "those paint beauty in colours more charming than nature, and describe happiness that man never tastes. How delusive, how destructive therefore are those pictures of consummate bliss, they teach the youthful mind to sigh after beauty and happiness which never existed, to despise the little good which fortune has mixed in our cup, by expecting more than she ever gave." [19] Dr. Primrose, it is clear, was administering exactly this anodyne to his desolate family when he attempted to distract them by telling them the romance of Matilda.

That other father, Lien Chi Altangi, had also a word of advice on the reading of romances for his son about to set forth on his struggles in the world. In letter LXXXIII of *The Citizen of the World* (III, 310–13), which began to appear in 1760 at the time Goldsmith was contemplating *The Vicar of Wakefield,* the Chinese Philosopher wrote: "It was a saying of the ancients, that a man never opens a book without reaping some advantage by it. I say with them, that every book can serve to make us more expert, except romances, and these are no better than instruments of debauchery. They are dangerous fictions, where love is the ruling passion."

As has been seen, Goldsmith frequently used Altangi as a means of expressing his own views—as, for example, "To be able to inculcate virtue by so leaky a vehicle [as a romance] the author must be a philosopher of the first rank." Goldsmith perhaps conceived of himself as such an author; for, soon after noting the thought of the Chinese Philosopher, he undertook to illustrate the absurdity of romances by writing one even more absurd—which, however, was saved from inanity by its philosophic intention. Goldsmith knew that romance deals in "intrigue and criminal liberties," "assignations, and even villany" harmful to youth "whose reason is so weak, and whose hearts so susceptible to passion."

To slip in by a back-door, or leap a wall, are accomplishments that, when handsomely set off, enchant a young heart. It is true, the plot is commonly wound up by a marriage, concluding with the consent of parents, and adjusted by every ceremony prescribed by law. . . . But, say some, the authors of these romances have nothing in view, but to represent vice punished, and virtue rewarded. Granted. But will the greater number of readers take notice of these punishments and rewards? Are not their minds carried to something else?

Goldsmith in rushing the Primroses through all sorts of wild adventures, and then in winding up the whole by the marriages of the three older children, hardly expected to "represent vice punished and virtue rewarded" in the manner of the romances against which he inveighed. Instead, he relied on his customary weapons of humor, irony, farce, and tears, judiciously mixed with common sense, to cure the taste for the false and the sentimental. Though Goldsmith was by no means "a philosopher of the first rank," he managed to make use of that "leaky vehicle," the romance, to examine with ironic amusement the Psalmist's axiom. More interesting than the grand finale of *The Vicar of Wakefield*, when rewards and punishments are duly bestowed after the manner of romance, are the scenes scattered throughout the book in which Goldsmith, through his three "philosophic vagabonds"—George Primrose, Mr. Burchell, and the Doctor himself—shows the temper of his own philosophic ideas. These scenes bring the reader close to the mind of Goldsmith, in all its amusing variety.

When George Primrose, for example, returned from his wanderings on the Continent and attempted to explain to his father and to his friends at home how he became a writer in London, he humorously divulged many of Goldsmith's own mental processes. Poverty, as he had observed, being "the nurse of genius," he decided to try his luck at writing; since he was undoubtedly poor, he might also prove to be a genius. "Finding that the best things remained to be said on the wrong side," George "resolved to write a book that should be wholly new." Like Goldsmith, George had discovered the knack of turning accepted truths upside down and examining them on the "wrong" side. "I therefore dressed up three paradoxes with some ingenuity," said George with pride:

They were false, indeed, but they were new. The jewels of truth have been so often imported by others, that nothing was left for me to import but some splendid things, that, at a distance, looked every bit as well. Witness, ye powers, what fancied importance sat perched upon my quill while I was writing! The whole learned world, I made no doubt, would rise to oppose my systems; but then I was prepared to oppose the whole learned world. Like the porcupine, I sate self-collected, with a quill pointed against every opposer.' "—Well said, my son," cried [the Parson] "and what subject did you treat upon? I hope you did not pass over the importance of monogamy.—But I interrupt; go on; You published your paradoxes; well, and what did the learned world say to your paradoxes?"—"Sir," replied [his] son, "the learned world said nothing to my paradoxes; nothing at all, Sir.—Every man of them was employed in praising his friends and himself, or condemning his enemies; and unfortunately, as I had neither, I suffered the cruellest mortification, neglect." (I, 157)

Paradox remained the method used by Goldsmith in order to catch the attention of the reading world—if not that of the learned. Beginning with the somewhat heavy paradoxes in *An Enquiry Into Polite Learning*—perhaps the book which earned only neglect for poor George—Goldsmith learned in *The Bee* to lighten his touch and never to linger too long on any single flower in the garden of mistaken ideas. In *The Citizen of the World* Goldsmith learned how to allow two characters, the Chinese Philosopher and the Man in Black, to explore his paradoxes while they examined the ways of the London world. In *The Vicar of Wakefield*, Goldsmith took the single accepted truth that the good man is never forsaken by Providence and held it up for inspection in the ironically humorous light of his own experience.

Mr. Burchell, the second "philosophic vagabond," was a more morose and at the same time more benevolent character than George Primrose. Though constantly watching over the affairs of the simple Parson, he attacked his ideas with all the bluntness of the Man in Black; for, like Goldsmith, Mr. Burchell had a keen sense of the "false." In the course of one of their dialogues, the Doctor asserted, "Both wit and understanding are trifles, without integrity; it is that which gives value to every character. The ignorant peasant, without fault, is greater than the philosopher with many; for what is genius and courage, without an heart? *An honest man is the noblest work of God!*" Mr. Burchell routed the Parson by calmly replying, "I always held that hackneyed maxim of Pope as very unworthy a man of genius, and a base description of his own superiority." The poor Parson found himself contending with a true scholar who was perfectly familiar with the sources of his battery of maxims and aphorisms.

VI *Dr. Primrose as Dr. Goldsmith*

Satiric as Goldsmith was in his presentation of Dr. Primrose, he also used him to voice many of his ideas and experiences. Though Dr. Primrose was in the early scenes of the novel a portrait of his father and brother, he became Goldsmith himself when the Vicar traveled the country roads in search of his daughter. The first indication of this transference occurred when Goldsmith introduced into his story a portrait of his own publisher and good friend, John Newbery, as the passing stranger who paid for the Doctor's three-week sojourn in the country inn where he fell ill. "This person," wrote the Parson, seizing Goldsmith's quill, "was no other than the philanthropic bookseller in Paul's Churchyard, who has written so many little books for children" (I, 145). Since Francis Newbery, the nephew of John Newbery, was the publisher of *The Vicar of Wakefield,* the delightful little sketch of his uncle was no doubt appreciated.

Of more significance as an indication of how Goldsmith made use of Dr. Primrose himself as his mouthpiece are the conversations which engaged the traveler as he journeyed from inn to inn. Like Goldsmith, the Doctor was an ideal traveler, always cheerful, always curious—in spite of the fact that the object of his journey was the recovery of a lost girl. Meeting a group of strolling players,[20] he remarked, as he exchanged civilities with one of them, " 'Good company upon the road,' says the proverb, 'is the shortest cut:' " he therefore entered into conversation with "the poor players," and discussed with them, as they jogged along in their cart, the writers of the day. The Doctor was soon discanting on Ben Jonson, Shakespeare, antique dialect, humor, wit, taste—in fact, on all the literary topics with which readers of *The Bee* and *The Citizen of the World* had become familiar. The Doctor soon bethought him of "the impropriety of his being in such company" (I, 147) in clerical clothes; however, Goldsmith never considered the impropriety of inserting an essay in the middle of a novel.

Accompanied by one of the players, Dr. Primrose entered the "first alehouse that offered" and took shelter in the commonroom. Here the two men were accosted by a well-dressed gentleman who "was condescending enough to desire me and the player to partake in a bowl of punch, over which he discussed modern politics with great earnestness and interest." Since politics proved to be as absorbing a subject of conversation to the Parson as the theater, he accepted the invitation of his new acquaintance and proceeded with him to a "magnificent mansion" [21] in order to continue the discussion over a good dinner and a warm fire. The fact that the "well-dressed gentleman" conducted his visitors on foot to his mansion, explaining that "the coach was not ready," and that upon entering the "perfectly elegant and modern" drawing room of his home the visitors were introduced to "two or three ladies, in an easy dishabille," warned the reader, if not the Doctor, that the host was an impostor.

What an opportunity for Goldsmith to rehearse his views on liberty, monarchy, wealth, and social classes! The Doctor soon observed that politics proved to be "the subject on which our entertainer chiefly expatiated; for he asserted, that liberty was at once his boast and his terror." After the removal of the dinner-cloth, he quizzed the poor Parson as to his knowledge of the views of the seventeen magazines and two reviews he claimed to read regularly. "Though they hate each other, I love them all," the host remarked, and thus continued: " 'Liberty, Sir, liberty is the Briton's boast; and, by all my coal-mines in Cornwall, I reverence its guardians.'—'Then it is to be hoped,' cried I, 'you reverence the king.'—'Yes,' returned my entertainer, 'when he does what we would have him; but if he goes on as he has done of late, I'll never trouble myself more with his matters. I say nothing; I think only. I could have directed some things better.' " The furious reply of the brave defender of monarchy brought forth the political views of one of the ladies, who exclaimed, "How, do I live to see one so base, so sordid, as to be an enemy to liberty, and a defender of tyrants? Liberty, that sacred gift of heaven, that glorious privilege of Britons!" (I, 148–49). Goldsmith's—or, rather, the Vicar's—reply, which fills several pages of fine print, makes the reader almost forget that he is following what purports to be a novel, for Goldsmith presented his own political views through the Parson whom he had now almost forgotten to satirize for his simplicity.

Goldsmith's well-known views that only under a king, who holds the balance between all classes, can freedom exist, is repeated by the Vicar. "I am for liberty, that attribute of God! Glorious liberty!" cried the Vicar, "I would have all men kings. I would be a king myself. We have all naturally an equal right to the throne: we are all originally equal. This is my opinion, and was once the opinion of a set of honest men who were called Levellers." These men brought confusion in their wake, the Vicar pointed out; for only a king, it was soon discovered, "diminishes the number of tyrants, and puts tyranny at the greatest distance from the greatest number of people." Wealth constantly flowing into the land from foreign trade is bound to accumulate and become "aristocratical." The power of a monarchy is needed to restrain the wealthy lords and to protect the humble poor, who, without the protection of a king, grow steadily poorer as the aristocrats grow increasingly wealthy, powerful, and arrogant. In the "middle order of mankind," the Vicar declared, "are generally to be found all the arts, wisdom, and virtues of society. This order alone is known to be the true preserver of freedom, and may be called the People" (I, 149–51). Without the balance maintained by a monarchy, the voice of the middle group is in danger of being shouted down by the "rabble." Behind this lengthy and not in the least ironic speech of the Parson one hears very clearly the voice of the poet of *The Traveller*.

At last it became apparent to the Vicar that his warmth in defense of monarchy had lengthened his harangue beyond the "limits of good breeding." His "entertainer," who often strove to interrupt the Parson's soliloquy, could be restrained no longer. "What!" cried he, "then I have been all this while entertaining a Jesuit in parson's clothes; but, by all the coal mines of Cornwall, out he shall pack, if my name be Wilkinson." The return of the family in whose home Wilkinson was the butler, relieved the

Vicar of his embarrassment and also set the plot of this hopelessly involved tale on its way to a resolution as false as the romances Goldsmith despised. The "rational enjoyment" supplied by the three "philosophic vagabonds" of this "singular tale" helps the reader journey through the "wild regions of romance"—and discourages any attempt to sort out its "beauties" and its "faults."

Whether, in the end, rational enjoyment or wild melodrama takes precedence is a question for the critic to ponder, for both are supplied in full measure. At the Squire's suggestion that he marry Olivia to one of his tenants and still remain her lover, the Parson dropped his philosophizing for a moment and shouted at the Squire, "Avoid my sight, thou reptile, nor continue to insult me with thy presence." Ned Thornhill's reply was to summon the sheriff and cast the Vicar into prison without more ado. When the weeping wife and all the children implored the Vicar to comply with any terms demanded by the Squire, he remained, as one might expect, inflexible. "Why, my treasures!" cried this righteous man, "why will you thus attempt to persuade me to the thing that is not right. My duty has taught me to forgive him; but my conscience will not permit me to approve" (I, 185).

Though this speech invites an ironic smile, as so many of the poor Vicar's sermons surely do, one is aware that Goldsmith himself was hardly smiling. Rather, he was responding to a kind of poetic rage against the injustices of the proud and the powerful— who also had caused him to suffer. Having, one suspects, spent some time in prison himself, Goldsmith had strong feelings on the subject of prisons, which were expressed by the Vicar, as well as by the Chinese Philosopher.

Goldsmith, unlike Voltaire and Johnson, did not sustain—and perhaps did not wish to—the ironic tone of the opening chapters of his "philosophic novel." Instead, he viewed in many different lights the Psalmist's text, "I have been young, and now am old; yet never saw I the righteous man forsaken, or his seeds begging their bread." Just as he could consider the character of his father, his brother, and other members of his family, including his own, as amusing, ridiculous, charming, satiric, and even tragic, so does he regard the story of the Primrose family. Goldsmith, in the character of the Vicar, illustrated "the folly of being over wise." Never understanding the true nature of the people around him, Dr.

Primrose survived family dishonor, financial ruin, fire, and, finally, imprisonment.

Providence, aided by Mr. Burchell and George Primrose, who were all the while lurking in the wings, rescued the Vicar in his extremity and vindicated the Psalmist's text. "And now, Sir," cried Mr. Burchell, stepping to the center of the prison floor and addressing George in terms intended for the assembled group: "I see you are surprised at finding me here; but I have often visited prisons upon occasions less interesting. I am now come to see justice done a worthy man, for whom I have the most sincere esteem. I have long been a disguised spectator of thy father's benevolence. I have at his little dwelling enjoyed respect uncontaminated by flattery, and have received that happiness that courts could not give, from the amusing simplicity round his fire-side" (I, 217).

Mr. Burchell, that "harmless, amusing companion" of the Primroses, was thus unveiled as the "benevolent"—and wealthy—Sir William Thornhill. He was also one of the three "philosophic vagabonds" who voiced Goldsmith's own views. With what satisfaction Goldsmith must have written, "The poor Mr. Burchell was in reality a man of large fortune and great interest, to whom senates listened with applause, and whom party heard with conviction; who was the friend of his country, but loyal to his king." The second "philosophic vagabond," George Primrose, who had deserted from the army in order to punish "the betrayer of our honour," was also, as has been noted, the mouthpiece of Goldsmith. Before appearing bloody and manacled in the final scene, George had dispatched a reassuring letter to his father which might have been written by Goldsmith to his father for the same purpose—to conceal from the family at home his own distress. "Honoured Sir," began the letter, which was read aloud to the family in prison, "I have called off my imagination a few moments from the pleasures that surround me, to fix it upon objects that are still more pleasing, the dear little fire-side at home. My fancy draws that harmless group as listening to every line of this with great composure. I view those faces with delight which never felt the deforming hand of ambition or distress!" (I, 205).

Mr. Burchell and George Primrose both played upon and deceived the "simplicity" of the Vicar, but both venerated this attribute in the high-minded priest, and, finally, were able to rescue him because of this very quality. With the timely help of these two "philosophic vagabonds," the machinations of the Squire were foiled, the strings of the plot were neatly tied by three marriages, and the Psalmist's text was finally vindicated; for, indeed, the "righteous man" was not deserted.

VII   *The Psalmist Answered*

Did Goldsmith intend the reader to smile at the wisdom of the third "philosophic vagabond," the Vicar himself? Or did he, when he summed up the parson's views, actually express his own Deistic religious beliefs? The Vicar's sermon, delivered in prison to good and bad alike, was reported in full and, indeed, completely filled Chapter XXIX (I, 208–212).

To answer this question, it is helpful to turn again to *The Citizen of the World*, which appeared in 1762, at the time when Goldsmith was writing *The Vicar of Wakefield*. Though "armed with resolution" against calamities, the Chinese Philosopher forgot the teachings of Confucius in the moment of crisis, just as the Vicar, in his final words, discarded the simple teaching of the Psalmist. "Good heavens," cried Altangi at the news that his son had been made a slave, "Why was this? Why was I introduced into this mortal apartment to be a spectator of my own misfortunes, and the misfortunes of my fellow creatures?" In the same mood the Vicar began his sermon: "My friends, my children, and fellow-sufferers: When I reflect on the distribution of good and evil here below, I find that much has been given men to enjoy, yet still more to suffer."

The Doctor delivered his sermon in an actual prison; the Chinese Philosopher found himself in a mental prison: "Wherever I turn, what a labyrinth of doubt, error, and disappointment appears! Why was I brought into being? for what purpose made? from whence come I? whither strayed? or to what regions am I hastening? Reason cannot resolve. It lends a ray to show the horrors of my prison, but not a light to guide me to escape them. Ye boasted revelations of the earth, how little do you aid the inquiry!" "Surely all men are blind and ignorant of truth," the Chinese Philosopher had cried in his distress, "Oh, for a revelation of Himself, for a plan of his universal system! Oh, for the reason of our creation; or why we were created to be thus unhappy!" (III, 84) One may be sure that, in the words of the Chinese Philosopher, as well as in those of the Vicar of Wakefield, one is overhearing Goldsmith's own despair in his quest for "the great architect's design" and is no longer enjoying the "amusing simplicity" which prevailed around the "fire-side at home."

Goldsmith himself turned readily from the book of Confucius to the book of the Bible, finding consolation in both but not a resolution of the problems which beset him.[22] The Vicar's sermon was a statement of Goldsmith's unanswered questions. "Why man should thus feel pain," the Vicar admitted to the assembled prisoners, nobody has yet discovered: "Why our wretchedness should be requisite in the formation of universal felicity; why, when all other systems are made perfect by the perfection of their subordinate parts, the great system should require for its perfection, parts that are not only subordinate to others, but imperfect in themselves? These are questions that never can be explained, and might be useless if known" (I, 208–9).

The Vicar, like Goldsmith and many of his characters, was a philosophic traveler "in a world where almost all men have been taught to call life a passage and themselves travellers." He concluded his sermon on a melancholy note far different from that with which the novel began. "Let us take comfort now," said the Vicar to his audience in the prison court-yard, "for we shall soon be at our journey's end; we shall soon lay down the heavy burthen laid by heaven upon us; and though death, the only friend of the wretched, for a little while mocks the weary traveller with the view, and like his horizon, still flies before him, yet the time will certainly and shortly come, when we shall cease from our toil" (I, 212). Perhaps the most appropriate text for this "singular book," *The Vicar of Wakefield,* is that which Goldsmith placed on the title page, "*Sperate miseri, cavete felices.*"[23]

CHAPTER 4

Two Laughing Comedies

AFTER Goldsmith had written and had produced his two comedies, *The Good-Natured Man* (1768) and *She Stoops to Conquer*, (1773) he brought together his conclusions concerning comedy in an *Essay on the Theatre; or, a Comparison Between Sentimental and Laughing Comedy* (I, 398–402). This essay appeared in the *Westminster Magazine* for January, 1773, several months before *She Stoops to Conquer* was actually produced at Covent Garden. The theater, Goldsmith pointed out in this most important of his many pronouncements on drama, "like all other amusements, has its fashions and its prejudices." No sooner does it reach a certain excellence than audiences grow restive and demand change, whether or not accompanied by improvement. "For some years," wrote Goldsmith, "tragedy was the reigning entertainment; but of late it has entirely given way to comedy." A lighter kind of composition, Goldsmith noted, now seems to attract the London theatergoer. "The pompous train, the swelling phrase, and the unnatural rant, are displaced for that natural portrait of human folly and frailty, of which all are judges, because all have sat for the picture."

However, wrote Goldsmith, when people are observed in their unguarded moments, they are both amusing and sad. Which is more appropriate for the writer of comedy, the laughing or the sentimental mood? Nature presents herself "with a double face, either of mirth or sadness," and "our modern writers find themselves at a loss which chiefly to copy from." Goldsmith's answer to the question was perfectly clear—the more so, no doubt, because of the lively discussion generated by his own two plays. The dramatist, he said, if he intends to write a comedy, should confine himself to mirth and not by any means confuse his audience by the false appeals of the sentimental now in fashion. "Low life and middle life" are, therefore, the province of comedy.

Aristotle had defined comedy once for all, as "a picture of the frailties of the lower part of mankind, to distinguish it from tragedy, which is an exhibition of the misfortunes of the great." One might perhaps wonder, Goldsmith admitted, whether he should laugh or weep over the misfortunes of the lower orders of society. But the answer, Goldsmith reminded the reader, had been clearly stated by all the great masters of dramatic art, from Aristotle to Boileau; it was that "the distresses of the mean by no means affect us so strongly as the calamities of the great, . . . our pity is increased in proportion to the height from which he fell." In comedy, the characters are "originally so mean, that they sink but little from their fall," and hence one may laugh at their follies.

Goldsmith, in writing his comedies, as in composing his poems, was content with "the rules" as handed down from generations of writers. His quarrel with the vogue of the Sentimental Comedy was that, "notwithstanding this weight of authority, and the universal practice of former ages, a new species of dramatic composition has been introduced, under the name of *sentimental* comedy, in which the virtues of private life are exhibited, rather than the vices exposed; and the distresses rather than the faults of mankind make our interest in the piece." The so-called Sentimental Comedy, Goldsmith pointed out, was not comedy at all but "bastard tragedy"—"a kind of *mulish* production, with all the defects of its opposite parents, and marked with sterility." Furthermore, Sentimental Comedy was essentially immoral because the spectator was taught to pardon and even to applaud the very faults and foibles of the characters on the stage, "in consideration of their goodness of hearts."

According to the ancient tradition of comedy, then—with which Goldsmith heartily agreed—the characters are "mean" and the aim is laughter; there is no tiresome moralizing and no false gentility, nor are extraneous songs and dances necessary to the evening's fun. Goldsmith perceived, however, that genuine humor seemed "to be departing from the stage, and it will soon happen that our comic players will have nothing left for it but a fine coat and a song. It depends upon the audience whether they will drive those poor merry creatures from the stage, or sit at a play as

[119]

gloomy as at the tabernacle." In the final sentence of his essay, Goldsmith reminded the reader that "it is not easy to recover an art when once lost"; one cannot hope to enjoy true laughter if one insists on being too genteel in one's tastes. Moreover, "it will be but a just punishment, that when, by our being too fastidious, we have banished humour from the stage, we should ourselves be deprived of the art of laughing."

The story of the production of *The Good-Natured Man* (1768) and *She Stoops to Conquer* (1773) reminds one that behind Goldsmith's *Essay on the Theatre; or a Comparison Between Sentimental and Laughing Comedy,* abstract and conventional as that essay may seem to be, lie five years of struggle and triumph for the playwright, marked by fist fights and tears, as well as by exhilerating first nights, crimson coats, and dinner parties. Goldsmith himself was frequently "deprived of the art of laughing" in his efforts to persuade a London stage manager to produce his comedies, then to cajole the actors and actresses to act the parts, and finally to suffer through the opening nights of his comedies. These experiences made Goldsmith more than once resolve never to write another Laughing Comedy.

I *Goldsmith as Dramatist*

One is tempted to accept Thomas Davies' [1] simple explanation of why Goldsmith turned to the writing of plays, when he had already proved himself successful as an essayist, poet, and novelist. Davies wrote: "Dr. Goldsmith, having tried his genius in several modes of writing, in essays, in descriptive poetry and history [fiction]; was advised to apply himself to that species of writing which is said to have been long the most fruitful in the courts of Parnassus. The writer of plays has been ever supposed to pursue the quickest road to the temple of Plutus."

Though no one would deny that Goldsmith was always in search of the most direct route to the god of wealth, it is happily true that he was frequently waylaid by the god of pleasure. Goldsmith's delight in all forms of the dramatic may be traced to the evenings he spent singing and dancing in the taverns of Lissoy; to his adventures with the strolling players on the road to London; to his pleasure in puppet shows; to his delight in masquerades at Vauxhall; to his enjoyment of a game of charades, or a rollicking evening of songs at the Wednesday Club. Goldsmith's impulse to "shine" on every occasion, recorded by the gentle Sir Joshua Reynolds, as well as by Boswell and many others,[2] suggests that he was himself a frustrated actor, one of the "poor, merry creatures" considered too vulgar for the London stage. Davies reported that Goldsmith went with some friends to see the Fantaccini puppets in Patton Street, and remarked afterwards that "he was surprised at the applause bestowed on the little insignificant creatures, for he could have performed their exercises much better himself." [3]

Goldsmith, in fact, so delighted in masquerades and disguises that he kept a fancy-dress costume hanging in his closet which he donned from time to time in order to frisk without fear of recognition at public festivities. Reynolds is said to have called on Goldsmith one day in his lodging and to have found him kicking a bundle about on the floor, which proved to be an "expensive masquerade dress" that he had foolishly bought for some projected jaunt that never took place. Now, he explained to Reynolds, he was "endeavouring to extract the value in exercise."

Goldsmith, who loved to lose himself in a throng of merrymakers, felt childishly aggrieved when his plans went awry. Like the Chinese Philosopher and the Man in Black, Goldsmith enjoyed the stir and bustle, the music and the glitter of the make-believe world of drama. All serious discussion was forgotten both by Goldsmith and his two philosophers when the London theatrical season opened. In Letter LXXIX of *The Citizen of the World*, Altangi wrote, in words that reflected Goldsmith's feeling:

The two theatres which serve to amuse the citizens here, are again open for the winter. The mimetic troops, different from those of the state, begin their campaign when all the others quit the field. . . . The dancing master once more shakes his quivering feet; the carpenter prepares his paradise of pasteboard; the hero resolves to cover his forehead with brass, and the heroine begins to scour up her copper tail, preparative to future operations; in short, all are in motion, from the theatrical letter carrier in yellow clothes, to Alexander the Great that stands on a stool. (III, 294–95)

"Both houses have already commenced hostilities," commented Altangi, showing that he was perfectly acquainted with the rivalry between Covent Garden, under John Rich, and Drury Lane, under David Garrick, in their presentation of Gay's *Beggars' Opera*. As for the Chinese Philosopher, he smiled ironically at "the generals of either army," Rich and Garrick.

When Goldsmith, as an essayist, wrote a chapter "On the Stage" in *An Enquiry Into Polite Learning*, and referred disdainfully to London theater managers, he had no thought of submitting a play of his own to the actor-manager of Drury Lane. Garrick's name was not mentioned by Goldsmith in this essay as the manager who put the playwright's script through "a process truly chemical" (III, 517) before accepting it. Garrick, however, took the remark as a personal affront and never quite forgave him, though the two later became fellow members of the Literary Club.

Several years before submitting *The Good-Natured Man* to Garrick, Goldsmith had, as editor of *The Bee*, further offended Garrick by observing, in "Remarks on Our Theatres" (II, 309–12), that "all Grub Street is preparing its advice to the managers," most of it dull, learned, or didactic. "We shall, it is feared," wrote the editor, "be told that Garrick is a fine actor; but then as a manager, so avaricious!" It was hardly surprising that when Goldsmith applied to Garrick in person in 1760, asking to be recommended to the Secretaryship of the Society of Arts and Sciences, he was refused (III, 539–540 n.). When Garrick explained that Goldsmith's unprovoked attacks upon him as a manager made it impossible to comply with his request, Goldsmith merely replied that, "in truth, he had spoken his mind, and believed what he said was right." [4]

Goldsmith submitted *The Good-Natured Man* to Garrick after the way was prepared for him by a kindly letter from Sir Joshua Reynolds to the manager of Drury Lane. Garrick kept the manuscript for several weeks without committing himself, but he confided privately to Johnson and Reynolds that he did not think the play would succeed on the boards. Davies remarked in *The Life of Garrick* that the manager was "fully conscious" of the merits of the play, and was willing to accept it; "but he wished to be courted to it; and the doctor was not disposed to purchase his friendship by the resignation of his sincerity." [5] Goldsmith not only grew restive and discouraged by Garrick's delay, but he was, as usual, in need of money. He would have reclaimed the manuscript from Garrick and taken it to his rival but for the inconvenient fact that John Rich was now dead and the affairs of Covent Garden in a state of confusion.

With characteristic lack of discretion, Goldsmith wrote to Garrick to ask him for an advance on one of Newbery's notes. Garrick agreed to lend him the money, with the proviso that Goldsmith alter certain parts in the play, omit others, and submit the final version to William Whitehead, then poet-laureate of England and a friend of Garrick's. These suggestions so incensed Goldsmith that the two men would have come to blows at their next meeting in the summer of 1767 had not Reynolds and Edmund Burke stepped in and separated them. Goldsmith wrote Garrick a note of apology to which Garrick sent a courteous reply; however, no real amends could be made. Goldsmith withdrew his manuscript and, before the month was over, submitted it to George Colman, the new manager of Covent Garden. Colman, who somewhat begrudgingly accepted it, remarked that it could not be produced before Christmas.[6]

The events which followed vindicated Goldsmith's worst thoughts on theater managers and their abuse of mere playwrights. When Garrick learned that the production of *The Good-Natured Man* was to be postponed a few months, he without difficulty induced the new manager to delay the play still further. Garrick then set about to "kill" Goldsmith's comedy by engaging Hugh Kelly, Goldsmith's Irish friend of the Wednesday Club, to write a Sentimental Comedy, *False Delicacy*. Kelly's play was presented at the Drury Lane Theater on January 23, 1768, with much fanfare, just in time to ruin Goldsmith's chances of a triumphant success with *The Good-Natured Man*. Kelly's *False Delicacy*, a flimsy affair, composed of genteel emotions and many tears, in the popular taste of the day, did succeed in partially spoiling the effect of Goldsmith's Laughing Comedy; but Johnson himself attempted to save the situation by writing a Prologue to *The Good-Natured Man*. A more lugubrious introduction to an evening of fun can hardly be imagined than that provided by the good Doctor's Prologue, which begins thus:

> Press'd by the load of life, the weary mind
> Surveys the general toil of human kind,

With cool submission joins the lab'ring train,
And social sorrow loses half its pain.   (II, 147)

II   The Good-Natured Man

Not only did Johnson write the Prologue to Goldsmith's first dramatic production, but he also led the entire Literary Club to the theater on the evening of January 27, 1768, for the opening night of *The Good-Natured Man.* One may picture Goldsmith dressed in a suit of "Tyrian bloom, satin grain, and garter blue silk breeches," standing at the door of the pit, reluctant to enter. Goldsmith described himself only too well in the Epilogue, when he referred to the author

As some unhappy wight, at some new play,
At the pit door stands elbowing a way,
While oft, with many a smile, and many a shrug,
He eyes the centre, where his friends sit snug;
His simpering friends, with pleasure in their eyes,
Sink as he sinks, and as he rises rise:
He nods, they nod; he cringes, they grimace;
But not a soul will budge to give him place.
Since, then, unhelp'd, our bard must now conform
"To 'bide the pelting of this pitt'less storm,"
Blame where you must, be candid where you can,
And be each critic the *Good-Natured Man.*   (II, 214)

The "prejudiced" and the "illiterate" who filled the pit were, however, not in the least "good-natured"; Sentimental Comedy so dominated the stage that "nothing but morality and sententious writing lifted upon stilts" could please a public accustomed to sermons and tears. The audience had sat through the first two acts in silence, but, at the appearance of the bailiff and his "follower" in the third act, these partisans of the genteel suddenly broke forth in loud cries of "low—low—d—mn'd vulgar." Had it not been for the hearty laughter of Dr. Johnson and the loud clapping of Burke, Reynolds, and other members of the Club, "this barbarous judgment" might well have caused Goldsmith's comedy to be jeered off the stage the very first night. By the end of the evening, Cooke reported, Edward Shuter's admirable skill in bringing out the humor of Croaker's lines broke down "even the rigid moral-mongers of the pit [who] forgot their usual severity on this occasion." Finally, "their *nature,* truer than their *judgment,* joined in the full-toned roar of approbation." When the curtain went down at the end of the performance, Goldsmith rushed into the Green Room, wrung Shuter's hand, and said before all the actors that his interpretation of Croaker "had exceeded his own idea of the character, and that the fine comic richness of his colouring made it almost appear as new to him as to any other person in the house." [7] So mixed were Goldsmith's feelings after this trying evening that, when he joined his friends for the dinner given by the Club in honor of the occasion, Goldsmith could swallow hardly a bite. To pretend a gaiety he did not feel, he valiantly sang for the company its favorite Goldsmith song, "An Old Woman Tossed in a Basket Seventeen Times as High as the Moon."

Several years later Goldsmith told the story of that evening at a dinner party given by the chaplain at St. James Palace, which was attended also by Dr. Johnson. After the opening night of *The Good-Natured Man,* said Goldsmith, when the Club gathered at the Turk's Head, "I was suffering horrid tortures, and verily believe that if I had put a bite into my mouth it would have strangled me on the spot, I was so excessively ill; but I made more noise than usual to cover all that, and so they never perceived my not eating, nor I believe at all imagined to themselves the anguish of my heart; but, when all were gone except Johnson here, I burst out a-crying and even swore by——that I would never write again." Johnson, who listened with amazement to Goldsmith's frank description of his suffering, observed quietly to his friend afterwards, "All which, Doctor, ... I thought had been a secret between you and me; and I am sure I would not have said any thing about it for the world." [8]

Goldsmith's Laughing Comedy, which caused him such "horrid tortures," was a moderate success and has remained to the present time one of the most delightful eighteenth-century plays. Though *False Delicacy* was advertised and praised extravagantly by the critics at the time, Goldsmith's play, in spite of adverse criticism, lasted at Covent Garden for ten nights, not including a command performance for the King and Queen, and netted the author between four hundred and five hundred pounds. The *London Chronicler* announced the morning after the opening of *The Good-*

Natured Man that "the language was exceedingly low," and this criticism caused Colman to omit the bailiff scene on subsequent evenings. W. Griffin, however, who published the play as a book eight weeks after its first performance, restored the bailiff scene; and it has remained in the play ever since. The book went rapidly through five editions, earning the author another one hundred pounds. When Boswell spoke slightingly of the play to Johnson, the Doctor with his usual firmness said that it was the best comedy that had appeared since the *Provoked Husband,* and that there had not been of late any such character exhibited on the stage as that of Croaker.[9]

The Preface that Goldsmith wrote for the play when it appeared as a book shows that Johnson, in associating character with humor in Goldsmith's Laughing Comedy, understood the intent of the author. Goldsmith wrote that, when he first undertook to write a comedy, he was strongly under the influence of poets of the last age, notably Congreve and Farquhar, and that he strove to imitate them. He continued:

The term *genteel comedy* was then unknown amongst us, and little more was desired by an audience than nature and humour, in whatever walks of life they were most conspicuous. The author of the following scenes never imagined that more would be expected of him, and, therefore, to delineate character has been his principal aim. Those who know anything of composition, are sensible that, in pursuing humour, it will sometimes lead us into the recesses of the mean: I was even tempted to look for it in the master of a spunging-house*; but, in deference to the public taste—grown of late, perhaps, too delicate— the scene of the bailiffs was retrenched in the representation. In deference also to the judgment of a few frinds, who think in a particular way, the scene is here restored. The author submits it to the reader in his closet; and hopes that too much refinement will not banish humour and character from ours, as it has already done from the French theatre. Indeed, the French comedy is now become so very elevated and sentimental, that it has not only banished humour and Moliere from the stage, but it has banished all spectators too. (II, 145–46)

When Goldsmith set himself the task of delineating character, he actually meant that he intended to explore a characteristic,

* Note: A spunging-house was a house maintained by a bailiff for debtors before their commitment to debtors' prison. *N.E.D.*

such as "good-nature," very much as the seventeenth-century character writers analyzed the characteristics of a certain type. The aim was essentially a moral one; Young Honeywood, or "The Good-Natured Man," represented, therefore, only the moral problem involved in being "a good-natured man" and was not a study of the whole character. In the traditional sense of the term, it might be said that Honeywood's "humour" was to be good-natured. When Goldsmith, however, wrote that he pursued "humour" even "into the recesses of the mean," he was using the word in still another sense. The bailiff, like the gravedigger in *Hamlet,* was comic relief; for only by laughter could an audience, even in the eighteenth century, be persuaded to sit through an evening of moralizing. The characters of Croaker and Lofty combined the two meanings of humor: it was the "humour" of Croaker to be melancholy, as it was the "humour" of Lofty to be a social climber —and, in being so, they managed to be genuinely funny.

Thus Goldsmith, in his first venture in Laughing Comedy, actually fulfilled the traditional purpose of comedy "to castigate the follies of the town" and, at the same time, to sweeten the pill by laughter. The Epilogue of a comedy, said Goldsmith, should be written by one "Who knows each art of coaxing up the town,/ And makes full many a bitter pill go down" (II, 214). In these two lines Goldsmith neatly summarized his concept of comedy. *The Good-Natured Man* shows how he connected his theme, the analysis of good-nature, with his plot, and how he relieved the tedium of moralizing by hilariously funny scenes from low life. One cannot rehearse the plot of the *Good-Natured Man* without, at the same time, stating the theme.

Sir William, recently returned from Italy unbeknownst to his nephew, had become so disgusted with the reports he had heard of "his hopeful nephew," that "strange, good-natured, foolish, open-hearted" young man, that he had determined to disinherit him, unless he succeeded in bringing about his nephew's reform. Young Honeywood's easy generosity and extravagance had caused his uncle, Sir William Honeywood, to devise a scheme whereby his thoughtless nephew would become involved in "fictitious distress," sufficiently serious to make him fear the debtors' prison—he merely planned "to clap an officer upon him," and then let him see which of his friends would come to his relief.

Sir William explained his mistrust of good-nature, and also his plan for the reformation of his heir to Jarvis, the valet, whom he encountered in his nephew's apartment before the arrival of the young man himself. "All the world loves him," urged Jarvis in defense of his master. "Say, rather, that he loves all the world; that is his fault," replied Sir William. How can one "be proud of a place in his heart where every sharper and coxcomb find an easy entrance?"—"I grant you," said Jarvis, "he is rather too good-natured; that he's too much every man's man; that he laughs this minute with one, and cries the next with another. . . . He calls his extravagance, generosity; and his trusting every body, universal benevolence."

To some members of the audience of *The Good-Natured Man* these ideas must have had a strangely familiar ring, for they had been expressed in similar terms just three years earlier in *The Vicar of Wakefield*. In both instances, an elderly, wealthy uncle, named "Sir William"—that "the world allows to be the best of men"—became a "concealed spectator" of the follies of his nephew. Though Ned Thornhill in the novel turned out to be a villain, Mrs. Primrose, at least, thought of him as "very good-natured"; though Honeywood was accepted by all as good-natured, this very quality led him to "dissipation" from which he had to be rescued. Goldsmith was, in fact, working on both the play and the novel in 1766; in the play, since it was a Laughing Comedy, he exonerated the nephew whom he allowed to remain a villain in the novel.

"What a pity it is, Jarvis," remarked Sir William of Honeywood, "that any man's good-will to others should produce so much neglect of himself, as to require correction! Yet we must touch his weaknesses with a delicate hand. There are some faults so nearly allied to excellence, that we can scarce weed out the vice without eradicating the virtue" (II, 150). However, according to Sir William, Honeywood's affability "arises rather from his fear of offending the importunate, than his desire of making the deserving happy." How strange that his nephew was so poorly prepared to guide his life since, during his absence in Italy, the uncle had written him many letters aiming to teach him "only that philosophy which might prevent, not defend his errors." Jarvis very sensibly remarked, "This same philosophy is a good horse in the stable, but an arrant jade on a journey." The play, then, might be taken as another philosophic journey, to determine how far the horse that Young Honeywood rode, that of good-nature, would carry him through the journey of life.

Sir William Honeywood—by frightening his nephew into a realization that he might be thrown into prison for his debts, and by guiding the beautiful Miss Richland into helping in the reform of her lover—brings all to the happy conclusion seldom achieved in actual life. Sir William Thornhill, in his turn, had also brought order and happiness out of the confused fortunes of the Primrose family as, in the cold reality of actual circumstances, Goldsmith had never been able to accomplish for his family in Ireland. Sir William's speech to his nephew in *The Good-Natured Man* is closely related to Goldsmith's descriptions of other "good-natured" characters throughout his writings; one cannot but read it as an analysis of Goldsmith's own errors and follies which he knew he could never correct. Uncle William, at the end of the play, told his nephew—as Uncle Contarine might have told Goldsmith had he lived—how earnestly he desired to correct the follies of his nephew in whom he saw many redeeming traits. "I saw, with indignation," Sir William began,

the errors of a mind that only sought applause from others; that easiness of disposition which, though inclined to the right, had not the courage to condemn the wrong. I saw, with regret, those splendid errors, that still took name from some neighbouring duty; your charity, that was but injustice; your benevolence, that was but weakness; and your friendship, but credulity. I saw, with regret, great talents and extensive learning only employed to add sprightliness to error, and increase your perplexities. I saw your mind with a thousand natural charms; but the greatness of its beauty served only to heighten my pity for its prostitution. (II, 212)

These high-minded sentiments, characteristic as they are of one side of Goldsmith's temperament, seem more related to the moralizing Sentimental Comedy than to the Laughing Comedy which Goldsmith was attempting to introduce in *The Good-Natured Man*. The drunken butler; the conniving, thieving valet; and, above all, the irrepressible bailiff and his "follower," who brought reproving cries from the pit—all reflect another side of the playwright's taste for "convivializing" at the Wednesday Club, as well as his enjoyment of the plain-speaking, the knavery and the merry joking of the throngs on London streets. Goldsmith's humorous characters lent a pungency all their own to the play, which shocked the audience into laughter in spite of disapproval of the "low."

The juxtaposition of the "low" and the "genteel" in the first scene of Act III can hardly affect a twentieth-century audience as it seems to have moved its ancestors two hundred years ago. No doubt cries and hisses began to be heard from the pit when, at the urging of Honeywood, the bailiff and his attendant hastily dressed themselves in Honeywood's gayly colored silk suits at the approach of Miss Richland. Seated decorously in a circle, Honeywood, Miss Richland, and the two "gentlemen" floundered through a conversation on French criticism, the price of bread, and English justice, which finally elicited from Honeywood the desperate aside, "Ah! the vulgar rogues; all will be out." After one of Miss Richland's elegant speeches "about severity, and justice, and pardon, and the like of they," the bailiff ended the discussion by calmly remarking, "That's all my eye." The curtain soon went down on the scene which, next evening, was removed from the performance. Since the bailiff scene was merely tossed into this Laughing Comedy for the fun to be extracted from the intermingling of social classes by displaying the absurdity of their views, prejudices, and language, the removal had no effect whatever on the plot of the play.

The humor of the characters of Croaker and Lofty, on the other hand, is not only pervasive throughout the five acts of the play but essential to the unfolding of the plot. Both of these minor personages are strictly in the tradition of English comedy from Ben Jonson to Oscar Wilde. As their names suggest, they are types designed to teach a lesson, as well as to provoke laughter. Davies remarked that the conception of these two characters showed the "happy originality which distinguishes the writings of Dr. Goldsmith." He did not mean that the idea of types was in the least new to comedy but that Goldsmith had presented two hitherto unexploited though familiar characters—one who "is almost always lamenting misfortunes he never knew"; the other, "a man who boasts an intimacy with persons of high rank whom he never saw." [10]

To the reader familiar with *The Citizen of the World*, it is evident that Goldsmith was merely putting on the stage, with an added humorous twist, the well-known characters of the Man in Black and of Beau Tibbs. Croaker, a "fretful poor soul" who is "always complaining, but never sorrowful," has "a new distress for every hour" on which he discants with a voice like a "passing bell." The Man in Black was known as "Mr. Drybone"; Jarvis called Croaker "a raven that bodes nothing but mischief—a coffin and cross bones—a bundle of rue—a sprig of deadly nightshade —a—" Honeywood, who agreed immediately with his valet, admitted that "there is something in my friend Croaker's conversation that quite depresses me." Just as the man himself stepped into the room, Honeywood remarked, "His very mirth is an antidote to all gaiety, and his appearance has a stronger effect on my spirits than an undertaker's shop."

True to form, Croaker, after wishing Honeywood a pleasant morning and commenting on how "shockingly" he was looking, complained of the weather and then added, "Indeed, what signifies what weather we have in a country going to ruin like ours? taxes rising and trade falling; money flying out of the kingdom, and Jesuits swarming in." Like the Chinese Philosopher conversing with the Man in Black, Honeywood agreed on "the vanity of our existence," which is only exceeded by "the folly of our pursuits." Croaker quoted Sir William Temple's famous observation that "Life, at the greatest and best, is but a froward child, that must be humoured and coaxed a little till it falls asleep, and then all the care is over," and added, "Ah! my dear friend, it is a perfect satisfaction to be miserable with you" (II, 153–55). Garrick wished himself to act the part of Croaker—if only Goldsmith could be prevailed upon to curtail the merriment which his rival, William Powell, might derive from the part of Lofty!

Croaker attempted to arrange a marriage with the heiress, Miss Richland, for his son Leontine, who was secretly engaged to another girl; Jack Lofty, however, eager to improve his connections among the powerful, himself aspired to marry the beautiful heroine. Just as one sees in the character of Croaker the shadow of the Man in Black, so in Lofty one finds echoes of Beau Tibbs and his false aspirations. When Mrs. Croaker, on whom Lofty was calling, observed that "The world is no stranger to Mr. Lofty's eminence in every capacity," the great little man replied, "I vow to gad, Madam, you make me blush. I'm nothing, nothing, nothing in the world; a mere obscure gentleman. To be sure, indeed, one or two of the present ministers are pleased to represent me as a formidable man. I know they are pleased to bespatter me at all their little dirty levees. Yet, upon my soul, I wonder what they see in me to treat me so!" (II, 168)—and more in the same vein. In the character of Jack Lofty, as in the character of Croaker, Goldsmith was following the tradition of comedy.

III Goldsmith as "The Good-Natured Man"

Several years before the success of Goldsmith's comedy, *The Good-Natured Man,* he had written an essay, entitled "The Anecdotes of Several Poets, Who Lived and Died in Circumstances of Wretchedness" (Letter XXXIV), in which he expressed the opinion that only a writer of "no merit" should be content to remain in obscurity. "A writer of real merit now may easily be rich," be observed: "He may now refuse an invitation to dinner, without fearing to incur his patron's displeasure, or to starve by remaining at home. He may now venture to appear in company with just such clothes as other men generally wear, and talk even to princes with all the conscious superiority of wisdom. Though he cannot boast of fortune here, yet he can bravely assert the dignity of independence" (III, 316). With the wish to assert "the dignity of independence," Goldsmith spent most of the money he earned from *The Good-Natured Man* on enlarged quarters in the Temple, which he filled with elegant furniture. A man servant, some new suits from Filby's, elaborate dinner parties soon put him hopelessly in debt to the booksellers. Though Dr. Johnson had cautioned him to stay within his means and never to apologize for humble quarters, Goldsmith was more sensitive to "the ridicule of living in a garret" than to the peril of remaining in debt.

Goldsmith's taste for expensive and inappropriate coats was a reflection of his desire to assume the "disguise" of a man of the world, which he could by no means sustain. The love of masquerade that often made him appear at a disadvantage in real life was closely related to his sense of the comic in the imaginary life of the stage. The Epilogue that Goldsmith wrote at this time for *The Sisters* (1762), a play by Mrs. Charlotte Lennox, makes clear in what sense Goldsmith looked upon comedy as a kind of "speaking masquerade." The Epilogue began:

> What? five long acts—and all to make us wiser!
> Our auth'ress sure has wanted an adviser.
> Had she consulted *me*, she should have made
> Her moral play a speaking masquerade.

This device, said Goldsmith, would have "warm'd up each bustling scene," and kept the play from "sinking"—as, in fact, it did after only one performance. "Well," continued Goldsmith,

> Well, since she thus has shown her want of skill,
> What if I give a masquerade?—I will.
> But how? ay, there's the rub [pausing] I've got my cue:
> The world's a masquerade! the masquers, you, you, you.
>   [To Boxes, Pit, and Gallery]
> Lud! what a group the motley scene discloses!
> False wits, false wives, false virgins, and false spouses!
> . . . .
> Thus 'tis with all: their chief and constant care
> Is to seem every thing—but what they are.   (II, 92–93)

Goldsmith himself assumed so many disguises in his life that he never discovered who he really was; only occasionally, in the best of his writing, did his simple, poetic, humorous self come through for a time, only to disappear again in rhetorical heroic couplets, in didactic moralizing, in farcical horseplay, or in self-pitying melancholy and bitterness. Davies wrote of Goldsmith that he was "such a compound of absurdity, envy and malice, contrasted with the opposite virtues of kindness, generosity, and benevolence, that he might be said to consist of two distinct souls, and influenced by the agency of a good and bad spirit." [11]

Experience itself—even a holiday trip to France with Mrs. Horneck and her daughters—was always a mixed affair. A long letter addressed to Sir Joshua Reynolds on July 29, 1770,[12] listed "the various mortifications" of the trip, such as "our lying in barns, and of my being half poisoned with a dish of green peas, of our quarelling with postillions and being cheated by Landladies"—experiences which even the pleasure of traveling with the Hornecks could hardly offset. "I find that travelling at twenty and at forty are very different things, I set out with all my confirmed habits about me and can find nothing on the continent so good as when I formerly left it." Having been poor in Paris when young, Goldsmith could now afford—on money advanced by the booksellers— to indulge his taste a little. However, he wrote, the whole of his purchases in Paris was "one silk coat which I have put on and which makes me look like a fool." The most cheering thought that Goldsmith entertained was that of putting his Paris experiences into a play, thus recapturing his lost power to laugh. "I wish I could send you some amusement in this letter," he wrote; "But I protest I am so stupified by the air of this country (for I am sure it can never be natural) that I have not a word to say. I have been thinking of the plot of a comedy which shall be entitled a journey to Paris, in which a family shall be introduced with a full intention of going to France to save money. You know there is not a place in the world more promising for that purpose."

"A Journey to Paris," whimsically suggested in his letter to Reynolds, was never written because Goldsmith's obligations to the booksellers were accumulating. "As soon as I arrive at Dover," he wrote Reynolds, "I intend to let the ladies go on, and I will take a country lodging for a couple of months somewhere near that place in order to do some business. I have so out run the constable that I must mortify a little to bring it up again." The "business" Goldsmith had in mind was *Animated Nature* in eight volumes (for which William Griffin had already given him an advance on the first five volumes) and the *History of England* in four volumes which he had promised Davies he would complete by June, 1771. In spite of the burden of work, Goldsmith was able to steal time from his labors to find relief in the writing he really enjoyed, that of comedies.

IV She Stoops to Conquer

On September 4, 1771, Goldsmith wrote to Bennet Langton, a member of the Literary Club, that he had "been almost wholly in the country at a farmer's house quite alone trying to write a Comedy. It is now finished but when or how it will be acted, or whether it will be acted at all are questions I cannot resolve." The house where Goldsmith stayed for long periods at this time of his life was that of Farmer Selby at the six-mile stone, Edgeware Road; and the play which he had completed was *She Stoops to Conquer*. All of his friends had either gone off to Paris or were enjoying visits in country houses, he lamented: "Every soul is visiting about and merry but myself. And that is hard too as I have been trying these three months to do something to make people laugh. There have I been strolling about the hedges studying jests with a most tragical countenance." As usual, Goldsmith was torn, not only by a sort of melancholy that settled down on him even while engaged in writing a comedy, but also by the pressure of the compiling he now thoroughly hated. "The natural History is about half finished and I will shortly finish the rest," he wrote. "God knows Im tired of this kind of finishing, which is but bungling work, and that not so much my fault as the fault of scurvy circumstances." [13]

Goldsmith finished the comedy in September, 1771, but it was not produced until a year and a half later. When Goldsmith submitted the play to George Colman, he justified once more Goldsmith's worst opinion of managers by keeping the play so long that at last Dr. Johnson took it upon himself to call upon Colman and, "by much solicitation, nay, a kind of force," [14] prevailed upon him to accept the play and to begin rehearsals.

The play went through many revisions and alterations during the weeks of rehearsal before it was produced on March 15, 1773. On March 4, Dr. Johnson wrote a friend, the Reverend Mr. White: "Goldsmith has a new comedy in rehearsal at Covent Garden, to which the manager predicts ill success. I hope he will be mistaken. I think it deserves a very kind reception" (II, 216 n.). A letter from Goldsmith to his friend Joseph Cradock, written the day after the triumphant opening, indicates that Johnson's hopes were fulfilled. Cradock, a wealthy literary and musical dilettante whom Goldsmith had come to know at this time, had written an Epilogue for the play which had arrived too late to be used. Goldsmith lost no time in thanking his friend for his efforts and in reporting on the opening night. "My dear Sir," he wrote, "The Play has met with a success much beyond your expectations or mine. I thank you sincerely for your Epilogue, which, however could not be used." The remainder of the letter was filled with the worries and harassments of a playwright—dissension between the actors and actresses, a persistent hesitation on the part of Colman as to the merits of the play, innumerable changes and revisions made up to the last rehearsal. "Such," wrote Goldsmith, "is the history of my Stage adventures, and which I have at last done with. I cannot help saying, that I am very sick of the stage; and though I believe I shall get three tolerable benefits, yet I shall upon the whole be a loser, even in a pecuniary light; my ease and comfort I certainly lost while it was in agitation." [15]

Though Goldsmith actually seems to have cleared over five hundred pounds from his three benefits, the strain and worry so affected him that the sum was hardly a sufficient compensation for his suffering. When the play was brought out as a book on March 26, 1773, Goldsmith inscribed it to Johnson, as well he might, with the remark that "I have, particularly, reason to thank you for your partiality to this performance. The undertaking a comedy, not merely sentimental, was very dangerous; and Mr. Colman, who saw this piece in its various stages, always thought it so. However, I ventured to trust it to the public; and, though it was necessarily delayed till late in the season, I have every reason to be grateful" (II, 216).

When the opening evening of *She Stoops to Conquer* arrived, Johnson arranged a dinner party at the Shakespeare Coffee-house before the performance, and led the entire Literary Club to Covent Garden.[16] He himself sat in the front row of a side-box, so that when he laughed the whole house would obey the signal and join in. Goldsmith, for his part, ate nothing at dinner, slipped away afterwards, and was nowhere to be found until, just before the close of the fourth act, he was discovered pacing the Mall of St. James Park by a friend. He was led back to the theater and entered by the stage door in time to hear a single hiss from a critic who refused to believe that Mrs. Hardcastle, in her own garden on a dark night, could be convinced by Tony that she was on Crackskull Common. "What's that?" demanded Goldsmith in terror. Colman, who happened to be nearby, replied, "Psha, Doctor! Don't be fearful of squibs, when we have been sitting almost these two hours upon a barrel of gunpowder!" William Cooke, who told the story, said that Goldsmith "never forgave it to Colman to the last day of his life." [17]

Goldsmith's second Laughing Comedy was a complete success,

and it has remained one of the few eighteenth-century plays that has been persistently and successfully revived. Performed for twelve nights at Covent Garden before the theater closed for the season, it was resumed again at the Haymarket during the summer. The critics praised it and were soon lampooning Colman for his hesitation in putting on a play which had met with such popular approval. Command performances were given before the king and queen on May 5, and again on November 10. Horace Walpole, after seeing the comedy, admitted that "it makes you laugh very much"; on sober afterthought, however, Walpole decided that he did not approve of his own laughter, for he considered the play "wretched" and "low." " 'Stoops', indeed!" he wrote to his friend, John Monck Mason, "So she does—that is, the Muse. She is draggled up to her knees, and has trudged, I believe, from Southwark Fair." In a letter to the same friend on May 27, 1773, his remarks on *She Stoops to Conquer* were still more critical:

Dr. Goldsmith has written a comedy—no, it is the lowest of all farces. It is not the subject I condemn, though vulgar, but the execution. The drift tends to no moral, no edification, of any kind. . . . What disgusts me most is, that though the characters are very low, and aim at low humour, not one of them says a sentence that is natural or marks any character at all. . . . Garrick would not act it but bought himself off by a poor prologue.[18]

A convincing reply to Walpole's comment is to be found in a brief exchange between Goldsmith and Reynolds' pupil and friend, James Northcote, after the opening night. "Did it make you laugh?" Goldsmith asked. "Exceedingly," was the reply. "Then," said Goldsmith, "that is all I require," giving him a handful of tickets for the benefit night.[19] Johnson's praise, which he pronounced in Goldsmith's presence a few days after the opening of the play, was to the same effect: "I know of no comedy for many years that has so much exhilarated an audience, that has answered so much the great end of comedy—making an audience merry." [20] Johnson's words were corroborated by *The Evening Post* which reported on March 16, 1773, that "the audience is kept in a continual roar." Since the aim of Laughing Comedy, as Goldsmith had pointed out in his *Essay on the Theatre,* was laughter rather than tears or morals, *She Stoops to Conquer* was a perfect fulfillment of the playwright's intention "to hunt after *nature* and *humour* in whatever walks of life they were most conspicuous." [21]

The Prologue that Garrick wrote for *She Stoops to Conquer* was a half-hearted salute to Goldsmith; the playwright was represented as coming to the rescue of the Comic Muse, now ill and stretched upon her couch:

> One hope remains:—hearing the maid was ill,
> A Doctor comes this night to show his skill:
> To cheer her heart, and give your muscles motion,
> He, in Five Draughts prepar'd, presents a potion—
> A kind of magic charm—for, be assur'd,
> If you will swallow it, the maid is cur'd.   (II, 219)

The maid was not really cured by Goldsmith's play; as Garrick also wrote in his Prologue, "Who deals in Sentimentals, will succeed." Sentimental Comedy held its own even after Goldsmith's effort to clear the air with laughter. However, Garrick had been asked to join the Literary Club in 1773, and he and Goldsmith were on as friendly terms as was possible for these two sparring personalities to be. The least Garrick could do was to agree to write the Prologue. Why Garrick had no part in *She Stoops to Conquer* is not known; perhaps he still feared the rivalry of Edward Shuter who had saved *The Good-Natured Man* by his admirable rendering of the part of Croaker and who now performed with equal power the part of Hardcastle.

The prevailing "gentility" of the theater made it difficult for Colman to persuade the actors to "stoop" to act in such a farce. Lee Lewis, famous as a harlequin, was commandeered to do the part of Young Marlow after it had been refused by an actor known as "Gentleman Smith"; the character of Tony Lumpkin first brought fame to John Quick, who accepted the part on a venture when Woodward, who pronounced the Prologue, disdained to take the role. Mrs. Bulkley became Miss Hardcastle after the refusal of an actress with a voice, for whom Goldsmith had written a song. Goldsmith himself, affecting the soft voice of his heroine, later sang the song for the pleasure of his friends:

> Ah me! when shall I marry me?
> Lovers are plenty; but fail to relieve me.

[138]

> He, fond youth, that could carry me,
> Offers to love, but means to deceive me.
>
> But I will rally, and combat the ruiner:
> Not a look, not a smile shall my passion discover.
> She that gives all to the false one pursuing her,
> Makes but a penitent—loses a lover.   (II, 110)

Many of Goldsmith's friends, who attended the rehearsals and freely offered their advice and suggestions, were so alarmed by the defection of actors that they advised him to postpone the production. "No," said Goldsmith to this suggestion, thinking perhaps that the season was drawing to a close, "I'd rather my play were damned by bad players, than merely succeed by good acting." [22]

Once launched into their parts, the actors were so caught up by the fun of the scenes that they apparently surpassed themselves and even made the audience forget the current argument over Sentimental and Laughing Comedy long enough to roar their approval. What actors would not enjoy bustling into "A Chamber in an Old-fashioned House," and beginning the ancient husband-wife argument thus:

MRS. HARDCASTLE: I vow, Mr. Hardcastle, you're very particular. Is there a creature in the whole country, but ourselves, that does not take a trip to town now and then to rub off the rust a little? There's the two Miss Hoggs, and our neighbour Mrs. Grigsby, go to take a month's polishing every winter.

HARDCASTLE: Ay, and bring back vanity and affectation to last them the whole year. I wonder why London cannot keep its own fools at home. In my time, the follies of the town crept slowly among us, but now they travel faster than a stage-coach. Its fopperies come down not only as inside passengers, but in the very basket.

MRS. HARDCASTLE: Ay, *your* times were fine times, indeed; you have been telling us of them for many a long year. Here we live in an old rumbling mansion, that looks for all the world like an inn, but that we never see company. Our best visitors are old Mrs. Oddfish, the curate's wife, and little Cripplegate, the lame dancing-master; and all our entertainment your old stories of Prince Eugene and the Duke of Marlborough. I hate such old-fashioned trumpery.

HARDCASTLE: And I love it. I love everything that's old: old friends, old times, old manners, old books, old wine; and, I believe,

Dorothy, (*taking her hand*), you'll own I have been pretty fond of an old wife. (II, 220)

With this half-remembered quotation from an old author, Sir William Temple, Goldsmith set the tone of *She Stoops to Conquer; or, The Mistakes of a Night* in the same old mansion, which he, as a boy, had been persuaded to enter, supposing it to be an inn. The characters of Mr. and Mrs. Hardcastle remind the reader at once of Mr. and Mrs. Primrose; in his comedy, however, Goldsmith achieved a unity and direction lacking in his novel.

She Stoops to Conquer struck the farcical note with the entrance of Tony Lumpkin with his "tricks and mischief." At the mention of his wife's son by a former marriage, Mr. Hardcastle exclaimed, "ay, you have taught *him* finely!"

MRS. HARDCASTLE: No matter; Tony Lumpkin has a good fortune. My son is not to live by his learning. I don't think a boy wants much learning to spend fifteen hundred a-year.

HARDCASTLE: Learning, quotha! a mere composition of tricks and mischief.

MRS. HARDCASTLE: Humour, my dear; nothing but humour. Come, Mr. Hardcastle, you must allow the boy a little humour.

HARDCASTLE: I'd sooner allow him a horse-pond. If burning the footman's shoes, frightening the maids, and worrying the kittens be humour, he has it. It was but yesterday he fastened my wig to the back of my chair, and when I went to make a bow, I popt my bald head in Mrs. Frizzle's face.

Mrs. Hardcastle suggested that, when the boisterous and riotous boy had grown a little sturdier, perhaps a year or two of Latin might then "do for him."—"Latin for him!" shouted Mr. Hardcastle, "A cat and a fiddle. No, no; the alehouse and the stable are the only schools he'll ever go to" (II, 221).

Tony Lumpkin, whom Davies called "a diverting picture of ignorance, rusticity and obstinancy," [23] must have been suggested to Goldsmith by his "low" companions of the old Lissoy days. The second scene is in the alehouse of The Three Pigeons (the name of the tavern frequented by Goldsmith in his youth was The Pigeon), where several merry but shabby fellows are sitting around a table, enjoying their punch and tobacco. When the "First Fellow", quells the general hullabaloo with the shout, "Now, gentlemen, silence for a song. The Squire is going to knock himself down for a song," Tony at once steps forward and sings one of Goldsmith's favorite songs. Boswell recorded in the *Life of Johnson*[24] a description of an evening with General Oglethorpe, in the course of which "we drank tea with the ladies; and Goldsmith sung Tony Lumpkin's song in his comedy, *She Stoops to Conquer*." One can easily supply the Irish tune and the Irish brogue to Tony's drinking song, which must have added to the good cheer of many an evening. It begins,

> Let schoolmasters puzzle their brain,
> With grammar, and nonsense, and learning;
> Good liquor, I stoutly maintain,
> Gives *genus* a better discerning.
> Let them brag of their heathenish gods,
> Their Lethes, their Styxes, and Stygians,
> Their *quis*, and their *quaes*, and their *quods*,
> They're all but a parcel of pigeons,
> Toroddle, toroddle, toroll.

"Bravo, bravo," cry all the merry companions at the end of the three stanzas, and lift their mugs to the "health of the Three Jolly Pigeons." Then follows a discussion of the "low" that now brought laughter rather than hisses from the audience:

FIRST FELLOW: The Squire has got spunk in him.

SECOND FELLOW: I loves to hear him sing, bekeays he never gives us nothing that's *low*.

THIRD FELLOW: Oh, damn anything that's *low*, I cannot bear it.

FOURTH FELLOW: The genteel thing is the genteel thing at any time; if so be that a gentleman bees in a concatenation accordingly.

FIFTH FELLOW: I like the maxum of it, Master Muggins. What though I am obligated to dance a bear, a man may be a gentleman for all that. May this be my poison, if my bear ever dances but to the very genteelest of tuncs; 'Watcr Partcd,' or the minuet in 'Ariadne.' [25]

What a pity, remarks Master Slang, that Tony has not yet come into his own money. Tony, who agrees heartily with this opinion, promises that, when he does, he will show the world what it is "to keep good company." He assures his friends, "Ecod, and when I'm of age, I'll be no bastard, I promise you. I have been thinking of Bet Bouncer and the miller's gray mare to begin with. But come, my boys, drink about and be merry, for you pay no reckoning. Well, Stingo, what's the matter?" (II, 226–27).

Stingo, the landlord, enters to announce the arrival from London of "two gentlemen in a post-chaise" who are looking for the home of one Mr. Hardcastle. This news gives Tony just the opportunity he needs for a practical joke. He addresses himself at once to the two new arrivals, Marlow and Hastings, and assures them that "it's a damned long, dark, boggy, dirty, dangerous way" to the home of Mr. Hardcastle of Quagmire Marsh, and that they had better plan to spend the night at "the old Buck's Head on the hill, one of the best inns in the whole country"—which, as the company knew, was the home of the Hardcastles.

Thus begin the "Mistakes of a Night" in this Laughing Comedy. The incidents, said Dr. Johnson, "are so prepared as not to seem improbable,"; but, he admitted, the play "borders upon farce." [26] Indeed, laughter alone could make the incidents seem in the least probable! During four acts, Marlow never suspected that he was in the home of his father's old friend, Mr. Hardcastle, whose daughter Kate he was supposed to woo. Nor did Mr. Hardcastle guess that the two imperious young men who order him and his servants about so freely were Charles Marlow and his friend, George Hastings, both of whom were expected by the Hardcastles. *She Stoops to Conquer* is really a frolic on the stage, akin to those capers Goldsmith enjoyed in the realms of his own imagination between his sober bouts with his *History of Greece* and his *Animated Nature.*

Just as Tony Lumpkin was a projection of one of Goldsmith's early tavern companions—if not of Goldsmith himself—so the hero, Charles Marlow, was a reflection of Goldsmith in another mood. Marlow's insufficient acquaintance with the respectable women of London society was shared by Goldsmith. According to Joseph Cradock, "Goldsmith's turn was for very low humour, always dangerous; but when some authors hinted to him, that for a man to write genteel comedy, it was necessary that he should be well acquainted with high life himself;—'True,' says Goldsmith; 'and if any of you have a character of a truly elegant lady in high life, who is neither a coquette or a prude, I hope you will favour me with it.'"[27]

The only reason that Marlow did not perceive that the Miss Hardcastle—he was too shy to glance at her—was the same person as the supposed barmaid in the supposed inn, was that Marlow, like Goldsmith (until he had met the Horneck sisters), had never known women in society. "My life," he explained to his friend George, "has been chiefly spent in a college, or an inn, in seclusion from that lovely part of the creation that chiefly teach men confidence. I don't know that I was ever familiarly acquainted with a single modest woman, except my mother—But among females of another class, you know." Hastings reluctantly agreed that Marlow, "in the company of women of reputation," was "a trembler" and "an idiot." A glance from a lady with a pair of fine eyes was enough to render Marlow completely tongue-tied; "an impudent fellow may counterfeit modesty," said he, "but I'll be hanged if a modest man can ever counterfeit impudence." Hastings tried in vain to encourage his awkward friend:

HASTINGS: If you could but say half the fine things to them, that I have heard you lavish upon the bar-maid of an inn, or even a college bed-maker—

MARLOW: Why, George, I can't say fine things to them—they freeze, they petrify me. They may talk of a comet, or a burning mountain, or some such bagatelle; but to me a modest woman, drest out in all her finery, is the most tremendous object of the whole creation.

Hastings had himself made the journey to the country for the purpose of courting Constance Neville, the girl whom Mrs. Hardcastle had designated as Tony's bride; not unnaturally his thoughts were fixed on matrimony. As to himself, Marlow said, "I'm doomed to adore the sex, and yet to converse with the only part of it I despise. This stammer in my address, and this awkward unprepossessing visage of mine, can never permit me to soar above the reach of a milliner's 'prentice, or one of the duchesses of Drury-lane" (II, 233–35). Fortunately, Miss Hardcastle perceived her suitor's difficulty and "stooped to conquer" by assuming the role of a barmaid until Marlow had declared his love.

Marlow, when an opportunity offered, addressed the lady with his customary freedom toward servants, and bragged to Hastings later, "Didn't you see the tempting, brisk, lovely little thing, that runs about the house with a bunch of keys to its girdle?"—"Well," replied Hastings, hiding a smile, "and what then?" "She's mine, you rogue, you," answered Marlow. "Such fire, such motion, such eyes, such lips—but, egad! she would not let me kiss them though" (II, 264).

When Marlow finally learned, through Miss Hardcastle, that the mansion was not an inn, and that "the lovely little thing" was not a barmaid, he assumed that she must then be a "poor relation" employed as housekeeper by the family. He resolved at once to leave the house where he had been "damnably imposed upon" and had played the part of a "swaggering puppy." Observing tears in the eyes of the "poor relation" at the thought of never seeing him again, he murmured in an aside worthy of Sentimental Comedy, "By Heaven! she weeps. This is the first mark of tenderness I ever had from a modest woman, and it touches me." Then with the true dignity and decorum of an eighteenth-century hero, Marlow turned to the lady and said, "Excuse me, my lovely girl; you are the only part of the family I leave with reluctance. But, to be plain with you, the difference of our birth, fortune, and education, make an honourable connection impossible; and I can never harbour a thought of seducing simplicity that trusted in my honour, of bringing ruin upon one, whose only fault was being too lovely."

"Generous man!" murmured Miss Hardcastle in an equally sentimental aside, "I now begin to admire him." When Marlow bade her goodbye, lest he be undone by her bewitching charm, Miss Hardcastle remarked thoughtfully to the audience: "I never knew half his merit till now. He shall not go, if I have power or art to detain him. I'll still preserve the character in which I stoop't to conquer, but will undeceive my papa, who, perhaps, may laugh him out of his resolution" (II, 269).

Nothing "low" is to be discerned in these familiar attitudes and gestures which are quite in the tradition of the most "genteel" of comedies. Nor is there anything approaching the "low" in the love affair of Hastings and Constance Neville. Their plan to elope in a post-chaise stationed at the end of the garden was frustrated by the discovery of the scheme by Mrs. Hardcastle who immediately decided to transport her niece to the home of an aunt forty miles away.

For the truly "low" one has to depend on Tony Lumpkin. In order to rid himself of his mother's protégé, and be free to ally himself with Bett Bouncer, Tony hit upon the idea of pretending to escort his mother and Miss Neville to the home of her aunt, while driving them in circles around their own rough neighborhood roads in the dark of a murky night.

Soon all disguises were thrown off, confusions were cleared away, and the proper pairs brought together. "So now to supper," said Mr. Hardcastle to mark the end of the frolic. "To-morrow we shall gather all the poor of the parish about us, and the Mistakes of the Night shall be crowned with a merry morning" (II, 289).

She Stoops to Conquer is certainly a farce; but surely not, as Horace Walpole said, "the lowest of all farces." The humor was genuine because it grew out of the life that Goldsmith knew in Ireland. Walpole was too harsh in his judgment when he observed that, "though the characters are very low, and aim at low humour, not one of them says a sentence that is natural or marks any character at all." Had Walpole been more sympathetic with the awkward, fun-loving, erratic Goldsmith, he would perhaps have recognized that the speech in the play was very "natural" to those who knew the taverns and the country houses of Lissoy, as did Goldsmith, and that the medley of characters Goldsmith presented were, as usual in the writing of this author, various sides of his own complex, unresolved nature.

Goldsmith again reached into the repository of his subconscious for the characters who became hopelessly involved in the "Mistakes of a Night" in *She Stoops to Conquer*. The "incidents" that mark the main plot and the sub-plot bear little relation to "real life"; by the clever interweaving of the love affairs of Marlow and Hastings, Goldsmith finally achieved a unified and balanced comedy that depended on laughter rather than probability. By choosing his characters from "low and middle life," as he explained in his "Essay on the Theatre," Goldsmith was adhering to the tradition of comedy, as set forth by Aristotle and all followers of the Classical tradition; and he was also making use of the life he knew to produce his own Laughing Comedy.

The advance in plot control from the writing of *The Good-Natured Man* to *She Stoops to Conquer* may be measured by the fact that the "low" scene of the bailiffs in the earlier play could readily be removed when it seemed to offend public taste, but Tony Lumpkin's part in the later play was essential. Similarly, an advance in the character studies of the two heroes, Honeywood and Marlow, may be seen; Honeywood's reformation, brought about by a wealthy heiress, is less convincing than Marlow's gain in confidence by the encouragement of Miss Hardcastle. "In which of your characters, Sir, will you give us leave to address you?" Kate asked Marlow when he finally recognized his many mistakes. "As the faltering gentleman, with looks on the ground, that speaks just to be heard, and hates hypocrisy; or the loud confident creature, that keeps it up with Mrs. Mantrap, and old Miss Biddy Buckskin till three in the morning?"—"O, curses on my noisy head! I never attempted to be impudent yet that I was not taken down!" (II, 286). Goldsmith, who shared the failings of his hero, never had the good fortune to meet a heroine willing to undertake the task of reforming him; whatever harmony he achieved was in writing Laughing Comedies.

V *Dramas of Everyday Life*

Goldsmith's painful encounter with an acrimonious Grub Street journalist, William Kenrick, shows all too clearly his inability to deal with the dramas of everyday life. Within a week of the opening of *She Stoops to Conquer,* Kenrick, whom Goldsmith had known in Ralph Griffiths' workroom, attacked him in a "Letter" to the *London Packet* (March 24, 1733) signed "Tom Tickle." Goldsmith might have disregarded his unfriendly criticism had Kenrick not gone one step too far in dragging in a reference to a lady, probably Mary Horneck. "Your poetic vanity," wrote Kenrick, "is as unpardonable as your personal; would man believe it, to be told, that for hours, the *great* Goldsmith will stand surveying his grotesque ourang-outang figure in a pier-glass? Was but the lovely H———k as much enamoured, you would not sigh, my gentle swain, in vain."

Cold rage seems to have taken possession of Goldsmith when he read this "lampoon"; accompanied by a "friend," he lost no time in making his way to the office of the publisher of the paper,

Two Laughing Comedies

Thomas Evans. What happened when the two men reached the shop of Evans was later described by Harris, Evans' assistant, to James Prior, Goldsmith's early biographer. Goldsmith is reported to have said: "I have called in consequence of a scurrilous attack in your paper upon me (my name is Goldsmith) and an unwarranted liberty taken with the name of a young lady. As for myself, I care little, but her name must not be sported with." Evans professed to know nothing about the letter by Tom Tickle; but, as he was reaching down to a lower shelf to get a copy of the *Packet*, Goldsmith "struck him sharply with his cane across the back." Evans, a large Welshman, was amply able to defend himself; in the ensuing scuffle, an oil lamp hanging from the ceiling was knocked from its chain to add to the confusion. Suddenly no other than Kenrick himself stepped from an anteroom where he had been lurking throughout the interview, separated the struggling pair, and sent poor Goldsmith, bruised and bleeding, back to his lodgings in a coach.[28]

Garrick and Topham Beauclerk stopped by Goldsmith's chambers in the Temple that evening to accompany him to a meeting of the Literary Club and discovered their friend in his bloody bandages. They persuaded him to go with them, despite his discomfort, in order "to show the world how little he was affected by his late encounter." Boswell, who musingly considered the whole painful affair, said to Dr. Johnson afterwards: "I fancy, Sir, this is the first time that he has been engaged in such an adventure." Johnson replied, "Why, Sir, I believe it is the first time he has *beat;* he may have *been beaten* before. This, Sir, is a new plume to him." [29]

While Goldsmith's Laughing Comedy was still filling Covent Garden every night, his personal "comedy" grew daily more threatening. The *Packet* of March 29, 1773, accompanied by a taunting letter signed "Pasquin," contained a full account of Goldsmith's fight in Evans' shop. Evans, meanwhile, threatened to sue; since Goldsmith had no defense to offer for his behaviour, he was content to settle for a fine of fifty pounds to be used for Welsh charities. Like Marlow in *She Stoops to Conquer,* Goldsmith might here have uttered, "Oh, confound my stupid head, I shall be laughed at all over the town! I shall be stuck up in caricature in the print shops."

Goldsmith had the poor judgment of writing a letter to the *Daily Advertiser* (March 31, 1773) in which he raised the whole question of personal libel in journalism. The press, he said, "has turned from defending public interest to making inroads upon private life." Goldsmith's admirable statement of the problem so struck Boswell that he decided Dr. Johnson must have written it for his friend. When Boswell suggested the possibility to Johnson, he replied:

Sir, Dr. Goldsmith would no more have asked me to write such a thing as that for him, than he would have asked me to feed him with a spoon, or to do anything else that denoted his imbecility. I as much believe that he wrote it, as if I had seen him do it. Sir, had he shewn it to any one friend, he would not have been allowed to publish it. He has, indeed, done it very well; but it is a foolish thing well done. I suppose he has been so much elated with the success of his new comedy, that he has thought every thing that concerned him must be of importance to the publick.[30]

Easily elated by success, hurt to the quick by ridicule and malice, Goldsmith exclaimed to a friend at this time, "Sir, I am as a lion baited with curs." [31] Perhaps had he not, at the wrong moment, roared like a lion, the curs would have left him alone. Perhaps, too, had he not been equally adept at acting the part of a monkey, his more elegant friends might not have dubbed him a fool.

Such an unsympathetic observer of Goldsmith's antics was Horace Walpole. In a letter to Lady Ossory, Walpole described a dinner party which took place at the home of Topman Beauclerk on December 11, 1773. As an after-dinner stunt, Goldsmith and Garrick had planned an entertainment that, as far as Walpole was concerned, fell very flat. "I was most thoroughly tired, as I knew I should be, I who hate the playing of a butt," he wrote, and continued:

Goldsmith is a fool, the more wearing for having some sense. It was the night of a new comedy, called The School for Wives, which was exceedingly applauded, and which Charles Fox says is exccrable. Garrick has at least the chief hand in it. I never saw anybody in a greater fidget, nor more vain when he returned, for he went to the play-house at half an hour after five, and we sat waiting for him till ten, when he was to act a speech in Cato with Goldsmith! that is, the latter sat on t'other's lap, covered with a cloak, and while Goldsmith spoke, Garrick's arms that embraced him made foolish actions. How could one laugh when one had expected this for four hours? [32]

Goldsmith, while playing the buffoon for the dinner guests, was fighting his mounting envy of the new Sentimental Comedy, *The School for Wives*, by his old rival, Hugh Kelly. It is possible that, out of pity for Goldsmith, Garrick at that time offered to revive *The Good-Natured Man* at Drury Lane. Thus encouraged, Goldsmith wrote to Garrick, on December 24, 1773, asking for an advance on the production, that he might have enough money to spend Christmas in the country with the Horneck family.

Garrick, apparently, sent him the sixty pounds and received the next day, which was Christmas, the following note from Goldsmith, containing still more promises never to be fulfilled. "My Dear Friend," Goldsmith began, "I thank you!" and continued:

I wish I could do something to serve you. I shall have a comedy for you in a season or two at the farthest that I believe will be worth your acceptance, for I fancy I will make it a fine thing. You shall have the refusal. . . . Im sorry you are ill. I will draw upon you one month after date for sixty pound, and your acceptance will be ready money part of which I want to go down to Barton with. May God preserve my honest little man for he has my heart.[33]

Garrick wrote "Goldsmith's Parlaver" across the letter and put it away in his files. Goldsmith, for his part, was now able to accept the invitation from the Hornecks to join them over the New Year's holiday at their country place in Barton. The invitation had been written by Catherine Horneck, whom Goldsmith named "Little Comedy," and it began:

> I hope, my good Doctor, you soon will be here,
> And your spring-velvet coat very smart will appear,
> To open our ball the first day of the year.

The jingle that continued down the page described all the joys of shooting in the country, sitting by the fire, dancing, and playing at "Loo." It ended with the thought that Goldsmith would "greatly oblige his very good friends" if he would consent to forgo the pleasures of the town and lend them his "cheerful company."

To Goldsmith, who had lately fought a battle for the honor of the Hornecks, the invitation was irresistible. On the day he heard from Garrick that his sixty pounds was secure, he sent off a letter of acceptance partly in verse and partly in prose. Of all the "simple sports" named over by "Little Comedy," the card game "Loo" was the most attractive to Goldsmith. In anticipation of the coming pleasures, he wrote:

> First let me suppose, what may shortly be true,
> The company set, and the word to be—Loo:
> All smirking, and pleasant, and big with adventure,
> And ogling the stake which is fix'd in the centre.
> Round and round go the cards, while I inwardly damn,
> At never once finding a visit from Pam°
> I lay down my stakes, apparently cool,
> While the harpies about me all pocket the pool.   (II, 107–9)

"Cautious and sly" as Goldsmith attempted to be, he usually lost: "Ah! the Doctor is loo'd. Come, Doctor, put down": "Thus playing and playing, I still grow more eager,/And so bold, and so bold, I'm at last a bold beggar." No doubt Goldsmith lingered at the card table with the gentlemen before the fire and continued to play after the ladies had withdrawn—and perhaps for higher stakes. As Joseph Cradock observed of Goldsmith, his "greatest real fault . . . was, that if he had thirty pounds in his pocket, he would go into certain companies in the country, and in hopes of doubling the sum, would generally return to town without any part of it." [34]

Cradock also reported in his *Memoirs* that "Goldsmith at that time greatly wished to bring out a comedy, but he had powerful rivals to contend with, who were in full possession of the town." The Laughing Comedy for which Goldsmith had stood was soon out of favor among the London theatergoers. "It was the fashion to say," wrote Cradock, "that Goldsmith's turn was merely for low humour; and that his Vicar, his Moses, and his Tony Lumpkin, were characters now obsolete." [35] No one at Beauclerk's dinner

° *Pam*, the knave of clubs in the game of Loo.

party that so bored Walpole could know that Kelly's *School for Wives* would soon be forgotten, but audiences are still delighted with Goldsmith's two Laughing Comedies, *The Good-Natured Man* and *She Stoops to Conquer.*

"Everything of Goldsmith seems to bear the magical touch of an enchanter," wrote Tom Davies in his *Life of David Garrick.* Why, then, did Goldsmith attempt no more comedies? Davies, as one of Goldsmith's publishers, knew him well; he gave an answer, which is no doubt near the truth. "Though the money gained by this play," he wrote, referring to *She Stoops to Conquer*, "amounted to a considerable sum; more especially so, to a man who had been educated in straits and trained in adversity; yet his necessities soon became as craving as ever." Goldsmith had decided early in his writing career to depend on the booksellers rather than on noble patrons for his living, and "they rewarded his labours generously," wrote Davies. Nevertheless,

his squabbles with booksellers and publishers were innumerable; his appetites and passions were craving and violent; he loved variety of pleasures, but could not devote himself to industry long enough to purchase them by his writings: upon every emergency half a dozen projects would present themselves to his mind; these he communicated to the men who were to advance money on the reputation of the author; but the money was generally spent long before the new work was half finished, or perhaps before it was commenced.

Sometimes Goldsmith met the reproaches of the booksellers with "fair promises," and often with "anger and vehemence." [36]

With no lucrative project in sight after the success of his comedies, Goldsmith had to return to the overwhelming burden of hackwork. The seventh and eighth volumes of his *History of the Earth and Animated Nature* were advertized in 1773 for immediate publication; his *Grecian History* and the second edition of *The History of England* were overdue at the publishers; a revision of *An Enquiry Into Polite Learning* had been partly paid for; and Goldsmith had also agreed to undertake a translation of Paul Scarron's *Roman Comique.* As Davies observed, "Goldsmith never wanted literary employment; the booksellers understood the value of his name, and did all they could to excite his industry." Unable to cope with these obligations, Goldsmith not only indulged in a round of pleasures, bought new waistcoats at Filby's, and gave extravagant dinner-parties in his Temple apartment, but also gambled more deeply than his friends of the Literary Club knew. Davies, who had a practical reason for observing his habits, wrote that "his love of gaming involved him in many perplexing difficulties, and a thousand anxieties; and yet he had not the resolution to abandon a practice for which his impatience of temper and great unskilfulness rendered him totally unqualified." Goldsmith's power to write another Laughing Comedy was dissipated in the growing confusion of his affairs.

Unwilling to borrow from his friends and unable to persuade the booksellers to give him advances on his unfinished work, Goldsmith, in the last year of his life, devised a plan for a *Dictionary of Arts and Sciences,* which would be made up of articles on various subjects by Sir Joshua Reynolds, Dr. Charles Burney, Edmund Burke, Dr. Johnson, and Garrick, all of whom were eager to help Goldsmith by contributing to the undertaking. The booksellers, however, Davies wrote, "were startled at the bulk, importance, and expence of so great a project," dependent on a man whose "indolence of temper and method of procrastination" they had long known. The proposal was rejected, and Goldsmith suffered thereafter from "continual vexation of mind, arising from his involved circumstances." He neglected his health and lost interest in his writing; "Death, I really believe, was welcome to a man of his great sensibility," Davies concluded.[37]

Garrick, whose feeling for Goldsmith remained mixed, expressed his sense of the complexity of the man he knew both professionally and personally, in "Jupiter and Mercury, A Fable," a work written "to provoke Goldsmith to a retaliation" a few weeks before Goldsmith's death. Too eager to be the center of the stage himself to look upon Goldsmith with sympathy, Garrick here referred to Goldsmith as "this scholar, rake, Christian, dupe, gamester, and poet." He conceded, however, that Jupiter looked on him with favor, and ordained that, "Tho' a mixture so odd, he shall merit great fame,/And among brother mortals be Goldsmith his name." Jove, moved by a whimsical impulse to make an "odd fellow," had, with the help of Hermes, fashioned him out of a strange assortment of ingredients:

Two Laughing Comedies

> Here, Hermes, says Jove, who with nectar was mellow,
> Go fetch me some clay—I will make an odd fellow.
> Right and wrong shall be jumbled, much gold and some dross;
> Without cause be he pleas'd; without cause be he cross:
> Be sure as I work to throw in contradictions;
> A great lover of truth, yet a mind turn'd to fictions.
> Now mix these ingredients, which warm'd in the baking,
> Turn to learning and gaming, religion and raking.

Apparently pleased with the result, Jove ended his instruction to Hermes by telling him that, "When on earth this strange meteor no more shall appear,/You, Hermes, shall fetch him to make us sport here." [38] On Parnassus, then, one may suppose that Goldsmith, freed from "some dross," is still writing Laughing Comedies for the sport of the gods.

CHAPTER 5

"Masters of Our Revels"

I *The Writing of Biography*

"REASON and appetite are . . . masters of our revels in turn," wrote Goldsmith, in *An Enquiry Into Polite Learning,* "and as we incline to the one, or pursue the other, we rival angels, or imitate the brutes. In the pursuit of intellectual pleasure lies every virtue; of sensual, every vice. It is this difference of pursuit which marks the morals and characters of mankind; which lays the line between the enlightened philosopher and the half-taught citizen" (III, 527).

The two biographies that Goldsmith published anonymously a few years later, the *Memoirs of M. de Voltaire* (1761) and *The Life of Richard Nash, Esq.* (1762),[1] may be regarded as Goldsmith's full-length studies of an "enlightened philosopher" and a "half-taught citizen" in whom "reason and appetite" were, in turn, "masters of our revels." But, when Goldsmith studied more closely the actual lives of these two men living in his own time, he could no longer draw so clear a line between "reason and appetite"; for he soon saw that his philosopher was not always an angel and that the citizen was anything but a brute. The concept of "reason and appetite" as "masters of our revels in turn" was particularly fascinating to Goldsmith, for he knew that he himself often inclined to the one while he "pursued" the other. In the study of the lives of the great, the famous, or the amusing men and women of the past or present, Goldsmith came not only nearer to an understanding of "man," in his vanity, pride, and glory, but also to an awareness of himself.

Goldsmith's first book, *The Memoirs of a Protestant* (1758), in two volumes, was, in fact, a biography; but it was hardly more than a translation of the French original. Because of eighteenth-century taste for biography, and because of the amazing facility of Goldsmith's pen, the booksellers of London kept him constantly engaged on historical-biographical studies, varying in importance from *The Mystery Revealed: Containing a Series of Translations and Authentic Testimonials Respecting the Supposed Cock Lane Ghost* (1762), to *A Survey of Experimental Philosophy, Considered in Its Present State of Improvement,* which did not appear until 1776, two years after his death. *Plutarch's Lives,* in five volumes (1762); *An History of England, in a Series of Letters From a Nobleman to his Son* (1764); *The Geography and History of England,* in two parts (1765); *The Roman History From the Foundation of the City of Rome to the Destruction of the Western Empire,* in two volumes (1769); *The History of England, From the Earliest Times to the Death of George II,* four volumes (1771); *The Grecian History, From the Earliest State to the Death of Alexander the Great,* two volumes (1774); *The History of the Earth, and Animated Nature,* in eight volumes (1774)—not to mention various abridgments of his histories of England, Rome, and Greece, which Goldsmith did for the use of schools—all of these tomes, and a good many more not mentioned, give one an appalling sense of the midnight labors of this London hack who happened to be a genius in his own right.

Determined to live by his pen and not by the favor of the rich or noble, Goldsmith compiled, translated, pillaged, the writings of others, and engaged still humbler writers to complete the work he had begun. Overworked though he was, his skill in rapidly analyzing his material and in then expressing it with intelligence, lucidity, and wit never seems to have deserted him. Goldsmith was quick to seize upon a theme, to simplify his presentation of it, and to connect his material to his central concept. Thus his biographies of Voltaire and of Nash are still good reading, not only because the facts of the lives of these men are interesting but also because they are a part of the debate in Goldsmith's own mind as to the relationship of "reason and appetite." Goldsmith considered this favorite eighteenth-century question not only in his essays, poems, plays, and novel, but also in biographies.

At the busiest time of Goldsmith's brief writing career, he agreed to compile for John Newbery an edition of *Plutarch's Lives, Abridged From the Original Greek, and Illustrated with Notes and Reflections for the Use of Young Gentlemen and Ladies,* in five volumes (1762). He actually wrote, single-handed, the first four volumes of the series and then, because of illness and the accumulation of other work, asked for assistance on the last volume. The brief "Introduction" that Goldsmith composed for the boys and girls of several generations is worth quoting, for in it he stated in simple terms his notion of the purpose of biography:

Biography has ever since the days of Plutarch been considered as the most useful manner of writing, not only from the pleasure it affords the imagination, but from the instruction it artfully and unexpectedly conveys to the understanding. It furnishes us with an opportunity of giving advice freely, and without offence. It not only removes the dryness and dogmatical air of precept, but sets persons, actions, and their consequences before us in their most striking manner, and by that means turns even precept into example. (V, 65)

Because of "perverseness, folly, and pride," wrote Goldsmith, men seldom take the advice of their appointed counselors; advice, therefore, must be tendered in "an indirect and oblique manner." Biography, as well as fable, since the beginning of time, has proved "a most convenient vehicle for instruction." An "ingenious gentleman" was once asked what was the best lesson that could be taught to young people. "The life of a good man," he replied. When he was then asked what was the next best lesson for youth, his immediate response was "The life of a bad man," (V, 65–66). Thus Goldsmith distinguished between the "angels" and the "brutes," whose biographies might be studied with equal profit by readers of all ages.

The *Memoirs of M. de Voltaire* and *The Life of Richard Nash, Esq.* were, in a sense, "vehicles for instruction," the first being "the life of a good man"; the second, "the life of a bad man." But, since the anonymous author of these two studies was addressing himself to adults rather than to children, one is prepared to find that folly, vanity, and malice mar the picture of the "good" Frenchman, whereas benevolence, generosity, and decorum redeem the portrait of the "bad" gambler and beau of the city of Bath. Although both biographies purport to be didactic in intent, they are actually for the "entertainment" of the reader, whose imagination is stirred by the persons and actions set before him so "artfully and unexpectedly" by the author that the precept is turned to example. The "entertainment" lies in the fact that the "enlightened philosopher" and the "half-taught citizen" are both "good" and "bad," neither quite an angel nor altogether a brute.

Goldsmith insisted, in both of these biographies, that "truth" was his only aim and that he attempted never to deviate from an impartial view of history. It is clear, however, that in these studies, as in all of his writing, Goldsmith was the philosopher who was concerned with the nature of man in general and his own in particular. That Voltaire was both the scholar and the man of the world, and that he was as remarkable for "the fine productions of his retirement" as he was for "the busy incidents of his life," interested his biographer particularly; for Goldsmith, too, divided his time between his retreat in the country and his chambers in London. That Richard Nash was not only a professional gambler, but also the uncrowned "King of Bath," under whose reign the architecture, the streets, and the laws of the town were improved; that he was not only a vain and dissipated man of the world but also the regulator of manners and morals, as well as protector of the young, the old, and the helpless, caused Goldsmith to reflect, one suspects, upon his own unresolved conflicts and contradictions.

Goldsmith himself was aware of the analogy between his experiences and those of the men he studied. "I am not insensible," he remarked in the midst of his tale of Voltaire's youthful adventures, "that by recounting these trifling particulars of a great man's life, I may be accused of being myself a trifler" (IV, 8). He then made use of a figure of speech which he had already introduced into *An Enquiry*, the *Chinese Letters, The Vicar of Wakefield*, and elsewhere. "These useful follies," he wrote, "like the fermentation of liquors, often disturb the mind only in order to [add to] its future refinement: a life spent in phlegmatic apathy resembles those liquors which never ferment, and are consequently always muddy." [2] With the youthful follies of Voltaire and of Nash, then, Goldsmith opened his biographies, not so much to apologize for them as to show how they contributed—as no doubt did Goldsmith's—to the "future refinement" of these remarkable men, and to prove once more that "reason and appetite" are not totally unreconcilable.

II *The Life of Voltaire*

Voltaire, the son of a wealthy provincial, and Goldsmith, the son of a poor clergyman, both found themselves, by the time they reached the universities, "enamoured with poetry and eloquence"; and both felt an "utter aversion to all that wore the appearance of study." Goldsmith must have smiled when he found that Voltaire, too, "neglected severer studies" because he was "wound up in no other pursuit than that of poetry." Voltaire was "ridiculed for his backwardness in the sciences by the whole university," but neither ridicule, exhortation, nor punishment could make him change his ways: "Anything that wore the face of industry he carefully avoided, and wherever pleasure presented, he was foremost in the pursuit." Voltaire could hardly have found a biographer more sympathetic with his "youthful follies" than was Goldsmith!

But unlike Goldsmith, Voltaire had the good fortune to encounter an understanding tutor who helped him change his whole course of study and thus to become a poet. As a result, Voltaire, loaded with prizes, returned to the home of his father at the age of eighteen. There Voltaire was indulged and flattered, for "the old man mistook his son's knowledge for prudence, and imagined that a lad so very wise in conversation would be equally so in action. In this he was deceived." Voltaire, like his biographer, "was a youth of exquisite sensibility"; and, observed Goldsmith from his own experience, "men of such disposition generally feel pleasure with a double relish" (IV, 6).

Whether Voltaire's wealth or Goldsmith's poverty were the greater hindrance in the lives these two young poets led for a while in Paris or London is an open question. Goldsmith's description of Voltaire's experiences in Paris remind one of the hints he has given in letters and essays of the life he had led in London before he had found a place for himself in the literary world. "There are in every great city," wrote Goldsmith of the corresponding period in Voltaire's youth, "a set of battered beaus, who, too old for pleasure themselves, introduce every young fellow of spirit into what they call polite company": "A kept mistress, an actress, or an opera dancer, generally compose the society. These are all perfectly skilled in the arts of coquetting, teach the young beginner how to make love, set his features, adjust his bow, and—pick his

pocket. Into such company as this Voltaire was quickly introduced; and they failed not, according to custom, to flatter him
into a high opinion of his parts, and to praise his wit, though incapable of relishing its delicacy" (IV, 6–7).

Goldsmith was well prepared to understand Voltaire, for he
had only to substitute the music halls and the taverns of London
for the operas and the cafés of Paris to understand the tempta-
tions that surrounded Voltaire. Goldsmith had no difficulty in
summoning up the picture of his subject, for the two poets were
also akin in temperament. "Imagine," he wrote of Voltaire,

a youth pleased with himself and everything about him, taking the lead
in all conversation, giving a loose to every folly that happened to occur,
uttering things which, when spoken, seemed to please, but which, upon
reflection, appeared false or trivial:—such was the gay, thoughtless,
good-natured Voltaire, in a circle of close, designing beings, who ap-
proved his sallies from flattery and not from their feelings; who despised his efforts to please, or enjoyed his folly with tacit malignity.
(IV,7)

Goldsmith described himself in a letter to his brother written at
this time as living in London "among a parcel of cool designing
beings" who had spoiled for him "the pleasure of a revel" and had
deprived him of his former "jollity." Voltaire, the "gay libertine,"
and Goldsmith, the Man in Black, with "a pale melancholy visage," [3] found that their quest of pleasure among the "wretches" of
Paris and London led the former to a term in prison and the latter
to a miserable existence in a cold garret. Both stood in need of
reformation.

Voltaire, at least according to Goldsmith, actually underwent a
reform after his father welcomed him home when he thought his
son sufficiently punished. Voltaire now determined to establish his
life on a firmer basis; "here he united the characters of the man of
pleasure and the philosopher; dedicated the morning to study,
and the evening to society. His companions now were very different from those he had some time before associated with; he began
to have a reputation for genius, and some of the politest of either
sex in Paris were pleased to admit him among the number of his
intimates" (IV, 11). Goldsmith too attempted—but without success—to bring about a harmony between "the man of pleasure"

within himself and the "philosopher," as he imagined Voltaire had done in reconciling the two sides of his nature. In the *Memoirs of M. de Voltaire*, the conflict between "reason" and "appetite", which Goldsmith had recognized in his *Enquiry Into Polite Learning*, disappeared after Voltaire's reformation.

Like Goldsmith, Voltaire had always "a desire of thinking differently from other people," [4] and was "particularly fond of controversy, and often mistook paradox for refinement." [5] Goldsmith never overcame the habit—maddening to his friends—of attempting to "shine" in conversation by means of proposing paradoxical propositions for discussion. Voltaire, however, was guiltier of this fault "in his youth than in riper age; for it was about this time that he thought proper to confine himself to his chamber, to draw up a new system of religion, and abolish the old" (IV, 11). Such a bold position was beyond the reach of Goldsmith, who remained content with old truths; however, having discovered (with George Primrose) that "generally what was new was false," he, too, attempted to give up the use of paradox: "Nothing can be a more certain sign that genius is on the wane, than its being obliged to fly to paradox for support, and attempting to be erroneously agreeable." [6] Goldsmith himself, one is told, had frequently earned his evening meal during his two wander-years in Europe by debating just such paradoxical propositions in convents and monasteries.

Whether Goldsmith met and talked with Voltaire in Paris or in Switzerland during his travels is debatable; that he intended the reader to think that he had "had the honour and the pleasure of being his acquaintance," certainly is clear. Not only did he make the assertion in his *Memoirs of M. de Voltaire*, but he follows up his claim by writing that "he remembers to have seen him in a select company of wits of both sexes at Paris," [7] and he even names the subject of the conversation—"English taste and learning." Since Voltaire was absent from Paris between 1750 until his death in 1778, the conversation might possibly have taken place at "Les Délices," Voltaire's retreat near Geneva. Fontenelle, whom Goldsmith described as a very vigorous member of the group, was ninety-eight years old, however, when Goldsmith was in Switzerland, and could hardly have maintained his superiority to Voltaire in the dispute which, Goldsmith said, lasted past midnight. No doubt, in order to add vividness to his scene, Goldsmith imagined himself seated in a corner of the drawing room, listening to the discussion of English culture by two remarkable French philosophers whom he probably knew only through books. "Fontenelle continued his triumph till about twelve o'clock," he wrote,

when Voltaire appeared at last roused from his reverie. His whole frame seemed animated. He began his defence with the utmost elegance mixed with spirit, and now and then let fall the finest strokes of raillery upon his antagonist; and his harangue lasted till three in the morning. I must confess, that, whether from national partiality, or from the elegant sensibility of his manner, I never was so much charmed, nor did I ever remember so absolute a victory as he gained in this dispute. (IV, 25)

Though the young Goldsmith was probably not present when the conversation between Fontenelle and Voltaire took place, Goldsmith was but following Voltaire himself in thus making his biography more "entertaining." In a review of Voltaire's enormously popular "Essai Sur Les Moeurs," [8] Goldsmith, after praising Voltaire's "beauties," commented on his methods as a biographer in terms which make one suspect that he imitated Voltaire when he himself turned to the writing of biography. "It is certain," he wrote, "Mr. Voltaire often colours too strongly. Fond of character and anecdotes that may serve to strike the reader, he generally raises or depresses both, as best suits the point of representation he has in view; and if he does not find his facts and personages sufficiently remarkable, or to his purpose, he generally makes them so. His maxims are commonly drawn from too small a number of instances, to be always true" (IV, 280).

The greatest proof of Goldsmith's admiration for Voltaire, in spite of these strictures on his methods as a biographer, is that he quoted, pillaged, imitated Voltaire in *An Enquiry*, in many numbers of *The Bee* and *The Citizen of the World*, and especially in his own *History of England in a Series of Letters From a Nobleman to His Son* (1764). Here Goldsmith translated page after page from Voltaire's "Essai Sur Les Moeurs," changing words here and there, connecting sentences in order to make the style more harmonious and easy, and filling in the paragraphs with sections from other historians. Goldsmith never acknowledged publicly this two-volume work written for school boys, but he admitted to his friends that he was the author. Moreover, the ideas expressed by the Nobleman to his son Charles in the first of these letters are exactly those of Goldsmith who habitually conceived of history not as the dull chronology of kings and dynasties, but rather as the contemplation of the lives of outstanding men. "To study history is to weigh the motives, the opinions, the passions of mankind, in order to avoid a similitude of errors in ourselves, or profit by the wisdom of their example." "To understand history is to understand man, who is the subject" (V, 256). With what pleasure Goldsmith must have written the final paragraph of the letter to Charles, in which he suggested, by making use of a famous quotation from Sir William Temple, that he was not only an elderly nobleman but, indeed, a member of the Temple family. The Nobleman assured his son that he would look forward to his reply with "the highest amusement." And

amusement is all that I can now expect in life, for ambition has long forsaken me; and perhaps, my child, after all, what your noble ancestor has observed is most true:—*When all is done, human life is, at the greatest and the best, but like a froward child, that must be played with and humoured a little to keep it quiet till it falls asleep, and then the care is over.*

I am, my dear boy, your most tender friend and affectionate father (V, 259).

Since Goldsmith had already used this sentence in *An Enquiry,* in *The Bee,* and in the *Citizen of the World* (and was soon to use it again in *The Good-Natured Man*) the quotation must have served as an identification to his more knowing readers who were familiar with him as the author of many other anonymous essays.

Goldsmith was fully aware of the fact that Sir John Hawkins and others regarded him as a mere hack, and he therefore smiled no doubt as he wrote in the guise of the nobleman to his son, "I would advise you to consult the original historians in every relation. Abridgers, compilers, commentators, and critics, are in general only fit to fill the mind with unnecessary anecdotes, or lead its researches astray." Remember, said he, shaking a parental finger at Charles, "not the history of kings, but of men, should be your principal concern; and such a history is only to be acquired by consulting those originals who painted the times they lived in" (V, 257).

A description of how Goldsmith, wrote history is supplied by Goldsmith's friend, William Cooke,[9] who reported that Goldsmith "first read in a morning, from Hume, Rapin, and sometimes Kennet, as much as he designed for one letter, marking down the passage referred to on a sheet of paper, with remarks. He then rode or walked out with a friend or two, who he constantly had with him, returned to dinner, spent the day generally convivially, without much drinking (which he was never in the habit of), and when he went up to bed took up his books and paper with him, where he generally wrote the chapter or the best part of it, before he went to rest." Thus this history for boys, in a way, wrote itself, "with as much facility as a common letter," hardly interferring with its author's need for daily "convivializing." Dr. Johnson, who loved Dr. Goldsmith and who, after his death, thought that he well deserved a place in Westminster Abbey, frequently remarked on the fact that Goldsmith was deficient in the kind of knowledge in which he and the rest of the Literary Club rejoiced. Considering the number of volumes on the history of England, Rome, and Greece which continued to appear even after Goldsmith's death, it is interesting to hear the learned Johnson say of his friend, "He had, indeed, been at no pains to fill his mind with knowledge. He transplanted it from one place to another; and it did not settle in his mind; so he could not tell what was in his own books." [10]

Scattered throughout Boswell's *Life* one finds Johnson's comments on Goldsmith's store of knowledge, such as, "Sir, he knows nothing; he has made up his mind about nothing"; "It is amazing how little Goldsmith knows"; "Goldsmith had no notions on any subject; so he talked away at random." Goldsmith's "ideas," such as they were, were not indeed the informative, pungent nuggets of pertinent information which enlivened the talk of Johnson, Burke, and other members of the Literary Club. They were, rather, the more intuitive, diffuse, "philosophic" notions of liberty, learning, monarchy, the clergy, history, civilization, concerning which Goldsmith, at the very beginning of his career, had "made up his mind" though, in conversation, he was easily confused both by the smiles and gibes of others. "No man was more foolish when he had not a pen in his hand, or more wise when he had." [11] Joseph Cradock, in his *Memoirs*, presents a picture of Goldsmith in society. "I dined yesterday," Goldsmith told Cradock on one occasion, "in company with three of your friends, and I talked at everything." "And they would spare you in nothing."—"I cared not for that, I persisted; but I declare solemnly to you, that though I angled the whole evening, I never once obtained a bite."

"You are all of you," continued Goldsmith, "absolutely afraid of Johnson,—now I attack him boldly, and without the least reserve."—"You do, Doctor, and sometimes catch a Tartar."—"If it were not for me, he would be insufferable; if you remember, the last time we ever supped together, he sat sulky and growling, but I resolved to fetch him out."—"You did; and at last he told you that he would have no more of your fooleries." [12] Goldsmith, of course, was once again talking like "poor Poll." That he also "wrote like an angel" was apparent to all of his friends, who alternately lamented and enjoyed Goldsmith's rattling tongue.

Goldsmith's "Apostrophe on the Supposed Death of Voltaire," [13] written in 1760 when he heard the false report of the death of Voltaire, is a rhetorical rhapsody which Goldsmith put into the mouth of his Oriental philosopher, Lien Chi Altangi. Such expression came easily to his pen, but never to his tongue. Comparing Voltaire with Confucius, the Chinese Philosopher exclaimed:

Let others, my friend, bestrew the hearses of the great with panegyric; but such a loss as the world has now suffered, affects me with stronger emotions. When a philosopher dies, I consider myself as losing a patron, an instructor, and a friend. I consider the world as losing one who might serve to console her amidst the desolations of war and ambition. Nature every day produces in abundance men capable of filling all the requisite duties of authority, but she is niggard in the birth of an exalted mind, scarcely producing in a century a single genius to bless and enlighten a degenerate age. (III, 162)

In spite of the efforts of the Man in Black during his visit to Westminster Abbey (Letter XIII) to persuade the traveler from China to take a more realistic view of the awards accorded genius by the world, he still hoped to win appreciation for Voltaire. Neither Altangi nor Goldsmith could forgive the "journalists and illiterate writers of the age" who characterized Voltaire "as a monster, with a head turned to wisdom, and a heart inclining to vice; the powers of his mind and the baseness of his principles forming a detestable contrast." Among his fellow writers, however, Voltaire seemed "possessed of good-nature, humanity, greatness of soul, fortitude, and almost every virtue." One is aware of Goldsmith's unconscious identification of himself with Voltaire when he exclaimed, through Altangi, "Whence, my friend, this malevolence, which has ever pursued the great, even to the tomb? whence this more than fiend-like disposition of embittering the lives of those who would make us more wise and more happy?" (III, 162–63).

Though Goldsmith to many seemed a man with no "fixed principles" who had "made up his mind about nothing," he admired and insisted upon the principles which seemed to him to form the basis of the character of Voltaire and which far outweighed his minor faults. Voltaire showed, according to Goldsmith, "an inflexible perseverance in what he thought was right, and a generous detestation of flattery, formed the groundwork of this great man's character. From these principles many strong virtues and few faults arose; as he was warm in his friendship, and severe in his resentment, all that mention him seem possessed of the same qualities, and speak of him with rapture or detestation" (III, 163). Voltaire "was born free, and had imbibed the privileges of a man and a philosopher" (IV, 35). Though Goldsmith can hardly be said to be "possessed of the same qualities" of the hero he wrote of with "rapture," it is clear that these were the principles he admired and to which he aspired. At least in writing the *Memoirs of M. de Voltaire,* Goldsmith discovered a character temperamentally akin to himself in many ways but superior in strength and power; to his study of this "good man," Goldsmith, at the very time when he was forming his own "principles," gave his best self. "A person of his eminence can have few indifferent as to his character: every reader must be an enemy or an admirer" (III, 163).

Goldsmith, who remained an admirer of Voltaire all of his life, came to his defense when Reynolds painted a picture of the Frenchman as "Sophism." Goldsmith rebuked his good friend, Sir Joshua, for a canvas depicting James Beattie[14] in scarlet robes with his "Essay on Truth" under his arm and Truth herself standing by his side, driving out Sophistry, Scepticism, and Infidelity, who were represented by the countenances of Voltaire, Gibbon, and Hume. Goldsmith wrote to Reynolds: "It very ill becomes a man of your eminence and character, Sir Joshua, to condescend to be a mean flatterer, or to wish to degrade so high a genius as Voltaire before so mean a writer as Dr. Beattie; for Dr. Beattie and his book together will, in the space of ten years, not be known ever to have been in existence, but your allegorical picture, and the fame of Voltaire will live forever to your disgrace as a flatterer." [15] For his amazingly popular "Essay on Truth," which was lauded even by Dr. Johnson, Beattie had in 1762 been awarded a pension of three hundred pounds by George III; but Goldsmith, who knew full well by that time the worth of his own works, never received the slightest recognition from the government. Goldsmith, of course, was unable to conceal his envy of Beattie. As Mrs. Thrale wrote to Johnson, "Everybody rejoices that [Beattie] will get his pension; every one loves him but Goldsmith, who says he cannot bear the sight of so much applause as we all bestow upon him. Did he not tell us so himself, who could believe he was so amazingly ill-natured?" [16]

"The folly of others is ever more ridiculous to those who are themselves most foolish," is the last sentence of the Chinese Philosopher's "Apostrophe on the Supposed Death of Voltaire." The remark might well be the reply to those who take too seriously the follies of Goldsmith. His other, wiser self is reflected in Altangi's concluding paragraph on Voltaire: "let his errors rest in peace, his excellencies deserve admiration; let me with the wise admire his wisdom; let the envious and the ignorant ridicule his foibles" (III, 164). The philosophy of Voltaire and that of Confucius became curiously related in the mind of Altangi. "Between Voltaire and the disciples of Confucius," he wrote, "there are many differences; however, being of a different opinion does not in the least diminish my esteem: I am not displeased with my brother, because he happens to ask our father for favours in a different manner from me." The study of the life of Voltaire became for Goldsmith one of the nature of man in his greatness and weakness; and, through many shifts and disguises, it reflects Goldsmith himself in his loftier, more rational and disciplined moments. Lien Chi Altangi and the lively Frenchman whose "Apostrophe" he wrote eighteen years before he died, are related in as much as they represent the side of their author which we have come to recognize as the "philosopher," as opposed to "the man of pleasure."

III   The Life of Nash

The Life of Richard Nash, Esq., which appeared in 1762, was a more ambitious undertaking than the *Memoirs of M. de Voltaire.* Though published anonymously, it seems to have been recognized at once as the work of Goldsmith. The biography of Beau Nash, "a little King of a little people," came out in a separate volume, two years after the death of the "late master of the ceremonies at Bath." A serious study, it purported to be "extracted principally from his original papers," as the author announced on the title page.[17] Goldsmith's health was somewhat impaired at this time; it was perhaps both to restore his vigor, and also to write *The Life of Nash* for John Newbery, that he visited the watering place of southern England during the summer of 1762. Whether he had gathered some of his material before then, and what use he made at that time of the manuscripts in the possession of two citizens of Bath, is known only through a footnote by Goldsmith himself which reads: "This account of his parentage is confirmed by the following memorandum, written by Mr. Nash himself in a book belonging to Mr. Charles Morgan, at the Coffee House in Bath; whence it was transcribed by George Scott, Esq., to whom we are indebted for this and many other anecdotes respecting the life of Mr. Nash" (IV, 55). The "Advertisement," added in the second edition of the biography in December, 1762, assured "the Public" that all the papers concerning Nash's life were handed over to "the editor of this volume; so that the reader will at least have the satisfaction of perusing an account that is genuine, and not the work of imagination, as biographical writings too frequently are" (IV, 50).

The impression of the accuracy of all the details of Goldsmith's *Life of Nash* was supposed to be further enhanced in the mind of the reader by such phrases as "I have before me a bundle of letters, all addressed from a pack of flattering reptiles, to 'his Honour,' and even some printed dedications in the same servile strain." From some of these Goldsmith quoted as though they were only to be found in manuscript form, when, as a matter of fact, the book, which he himself named in the next paragraph, was available. It was entitled "The Discoveries of John Poulter, *alias* Baxter, who was apprehended for robbing Dr. Handcock of

Salisbury, on Claverton Down, near Bath. Written wholly by Himself." [18]

Though Nash died in February, 1761, before Goldsmith's visit to Bath, he implied that he himself had personally encountered the Beau. "I have known him, in London," he wrote, "wait a whole day at a window in the Smyrna Coffee-house, in order to receive a bow from the Prince, or the Duchess of Marlborough, as they passed by where he was standing; and he would then look round upon the company for admiration and respect" (IV, 112–13). Since Goldsmith was a boy of fifteen, who had never been out of Ireland when the Duchess of Marlborough died in 1744, one may accept this anecdote as another example, similar to those he inserted in his *Memoirs of M. de Voltaire,* of the biographer's attempt to enliven his study. Many little phrases—such as, "among other stories of Nash's telling, I remember one, which I the more cheerfully repeat, as it tends to correct a piece of impertinence" (IV, 123)—lure the reader into believing that Goldsmith was actually present when the events he described took place.

He was "injudicious" enough, however, to insert a spurious letter purporting to be by the old retired actor Quin, still living at the time in Bath, to an unidentified lord, in which Quin supposedly was impugning Nash's reputation in an effort to supplant him. Since Goldsmith was attacked in journals for the implications of his suggestions, he added this note in the second edition of the biography:

Can any one who reads what precedes and what follows this letter, suppose that we thought it was written by Mr. Quin, or that it would give any uneasiness either to him or his friends? The letter was really found among Mr. Nash's papers, as the editor can at any time prove, and it was inserted here to show what artifices were used by those who had more levity than good nature to impose upon a poor old man, and to embitter his last moments. (IV, 127)

There is no evidence, however, that such a letter ever existed. Quin, who lived in Bath until his death in 1766, was buried in the Abbey Church, with an epitaph on his tomb by Garrick (IV, 127). A still more elaborate fabrication was a letter concerning a "Mr. Jenners," addressed to an unknown lord.

A Letter from Mr. *** *in Tunbridge to Lord——in London,*

[168]

found among the Papers of Mr. Nash and prepared by him for the press: inserted among the documents reproduced at the end of Goldsmith's biography, which he declared to be genuine, is of particular interest (IV, 142–50). The letter, which all scholars agree was written by Goldsmith himself, throws light not only on the real author of the letter but also suggests the Man in Black, whose shadow falls across so much of Goldsmith's writing. The letter, which fills six pages of fine print, begins as follows:

My Lord:—What I foresaw has arrived, poor Jenners, after losing all his fortune, has shot himself through the head. His losses to Bland were considerable, and his playing soon after with Spedding contributed to hasten his ruin. No man was ever more enamoured of play, or understood it less. At whatever game he ventured his money, he was most usually the dupe, and still foolishly attributed to his bad luck those misfortunes that entirely proceeded from his want of judgment.

After finding that he had brought on himself irreparable indigence and contempt, his temper, formerly so sprightly, began to grow gloomy and unequal: he grew more fond of solitude, and more liable to take offence at supposed injuries; in short, for a week before he shot himself, his friends were of opinion that he meditated some such horrid design. . . .

You remember, my lord, what a charming fellow this deluded man was once. How benevolent, just, temperate, and every way virtuous; the only faults of his mind arose from motives of humanity: he was too easy, credulous, and good natured, and unable to resist temptation, when recommended by the voice of friendship. These foibles the vicious and the needy soon perceived, and what was at first a weakness they soon perverted into guilt; he became a gamester, and continued the infamous profession till he could support the miseries it brought with it no longer. (IV, 142–43)

How clearly Goldsmith understood that "our youth, our time, those moments that may be laid out in pleasure or improvements, are foolishly squandered away in tossing cards, fretting at ill-luck, or, even with a run of ill-luck in our favour, fretting that our winnings are so small"! The stages by which "the young beginner" is cheated by the sharper are described in detail in this extraordinary document, as well as the faces, the clothes, and the manners of those who inhabit the underworld of the gamester. "I entreat you," wrote Goldsmith, "to examine the faces of all the noted gamblers round one of our public tables; have you ever seen anything more haggard, pinched, and miserable?" In words reminiscent of his description to his brother in 1759 of his own "pale melancholly visage," Goldsmith one year later wrote that "passion" flushes the cheeks of the players while the game is in progress, but "all such flushings are ever succeeded by consequent paleness; so that a gamester contracts the sickly hue of a student, while he is only acquiring the stupidity of a fool."

How pathetically suggestive of Goldsmith and his taste for "fine clothes" are his words on the bearing of a gentelman of breeding. The "great error" of the young beginner, Goldsmith wrote in his letter, "lies in imagining every fellow with a laced coat to be a gentleman. The address and transient behaviour of a man of breeding are easily acquired, and none are better qualified than gamesters in this respect," observed the man who, in fact, was never quite accepted as "a man of breeding" by Mrs. Thrale, Horace Walpole, or, indeed, by Dr. Johnson himself. Though he loved him, he always complained of his friend's want of learning and his lack of principle. To continue with Goldsmith's own astute analysis of the nature of a gamester: "At first, their complaisance, civility, and apparent honour is pleasing, but upon examination, few of them will be found to have their minds sufficiently stored with any of the more refined accomplishments which truly characterize the man of breeding."

Goldsmith's friends and acquaintances have remarked on the fact that he was not himself a successful card-player; he merely understood the wiles of the notable gamesters, whose lure he could not escape; for "a sharper, when he plays, generally handles and deals the cards awkwardly, like a bungler; he advances his bets by degrees, and keeps his antagonist in spirits by small advantages and alternate success at the beginning; to show all his force at once would but frighten the bird he intends to decoy."

That Goldsmith was all too often that "bird" himself must have been evident to his family and friends from the days when he returned home empty handed to his later years when he would disappear from time to time leaving no word behind and forgetful of his obligations to the booksellers who had advanced him money on unwritten books. Though Goldsmith never bent the knee to the "great," he always had a respectful veneration for "the man of the world" and aspired to maintain that status in his personal bearing. He was far more astute in discerning the false claims of gamesters than in coping with their cleverness in cards. Like his milder shadow, Beau Tibbs, the card-sharper "talks of honour and virtue, and of his being a gentleman, and that he knows great men"; and, like Wilkinson, he "mentions his coal-mines, and his estate in the country." However, like the butler, he proves to be merely "the well-dressed gentleman"; for

he is totally divested of that masculine confidence which is the attendant of real fortune; he turns, yields, assents, smiles, as he hopes will be most pleasing to his destined prey; he is afraid of meeting a shabby acquaintance, particularly if in better company; as he grows richer he wears finer clothes; and if ever he is seen in an undress, it is most probable he is without money; so that seeing a gamester growing finer each day, is a certain symptom of his success. (IV, 145)

Goldsmith himself considered fine coats and an elegantly furnished apartment in the Temple to be symbols of his success. Winning independence through his own pen, he was unable to keep the position he achieved because he was the very victim he describes as being hopelessly entangled in the toils of professional gamblers, even though he perfectly understood that he was sure to be the loser. "A life of gaming must necessarily be a life of extravagance; parties of this kind are formed in houses where the whole profits are consumed." "A man with a healthful complexion, how great a philosopher soever he be would not willingly exchange it for a sallow, hectic phyz, pale eyes, and a sharp wrinkled visage." As he wrote his brother, he was no longer "that strong active man" he used to be; now he had "two great wrinkles between the eye brows," a pale complexion, and "an eye disgustingly severe." The beginner never realized his danger, but "the person once listed as a gamester, if not soon reclaimed, pursues it through his life; no loss can retard, no danger awaken him to common sense; nothing can terminate his career but want of money to play, or of honour to be trusted."

Goldsmith, though praised and even petted by "the great," never gave up his association with the scoundrels and wretches of London,[19] and, indeed, who is to say that his final contribution to literature might not have been impaired had he not, throughout his life, maintained this peculiar duality, that of the man who knows the better way, but never foregoes the worse? Goldsmith loved the riff-raff of society, and could not give up the gaming table where he was sure to be the loser and where

the company are superficial, extravagant, unentertaining; the conversation flat, debauched, and absurd; the hours unnatural and fatiguing; the anxiety of losing is greater than the pleasure of winning; friendship must be banished from that society the members of which are intent only on ruining each other; every other improvement, either in knowledge or virtue, can scarce find room in that breast which is possessed by the spirit of play; the spirit becomes vapid, the constitution is enfeebled, the complexion grows pale, till, in the end, the mind, body, friends, fortune, and even the hopes of futurity sink together! Happy, if nature terminates the scene, and neither justice nor suicide are called in to accelerate her tardy approach. (IV, 149–50)

Thus poor Jenners' companions were described by "Mr. ° ° °" after Jenners had shot himself through the head; to "Lord———" with far more moralizing concerning the evils of gambling than my Lord, no doubt, cared to hear.

Goldsmith, in the Preface to *The Life of Richard Nash*, his most ambitious and popular biography, recommended the book as "well calculated to supply a vacant hour with innocent amusement." The reader, he warned, must not expect "a romantic history, filled with warm pictures and fanciful adventures"; instead, he must "rest satisfied with a genuine and candid recital, compiled from the papers he [Nash] left behind and others equally authentic; a recital neither written with a spirit of satire nor panegyric, and with scarce any other art than that of arranging the materials in their natural order." Without doubt, Goldsmith assured the reader, he might have made this "history more pleasing at the expense of truth" had he not taken great pains to study his sources and "to describe the man as he was, not such as imagination could have helped in completing his picture." He had also "given an exact account of the rise, regulation, and nature of the amusements of the city of Bath," and to these he had added many anecdotes "commonly known," though often "extracted" from remote and unnamed sources. Such was "the entertainment that may be expected from the perusal of this performance." So successful, in-

deed, was Goldsmith's presentation of the *Life of Richard Nash,*
the year after the death of the man who had dominated the social
life of Bath for more than fifty years, that it has been accepted
uncritically by all biographers of Nash since Goldsmith and even
today forms the basis of the life of Nash in the *Dictionary of
National Biography.*

IV   Apologia Pro Vita Sua

Part of the interest of Goldsmith's *Life of Richard Nash* lies in
the fact that the author was composing an elaborate *apologia pro
vita sua,* just as he was when he wrote the *Memoirs of M. de
Voltaire.* In this instance he is not showing the reader that even
the "good man" was guilty of little vices, but rather that this "bad
man" had "an honest benevolent mind, with the vices that spring
from too much good nature." Goldsmith's defense of Nash is all
too familiar to the reader of his "life of the Man in Black," his
account of Mr. Burchell's reformation, his story of the wanderings
of George Primrose, not to mention the drama of *The Good-
Natured Man,* and the erring hero of *She Stoops to Conquer.* The
defense of all of these characters was that their "hearts" were better than their "heads." Beau Nash, like the rest, as well as Goldsmith, "had pity for every creature's distress, but wanted prudence in the application of his benefits. He had generosity for the
wretched in the highest degree, at a time when his creditors complained of his justice. He often spoke falsehoods; but never have
any of his harmless tales been tinctured with malice" (IV, 59).

Like Voltaire and Goldsmith, Nash distinguished himself at
college, "not by application to study, but by his assiduity in intrigue." Near the gates of any university were to be found girls
with some beauty and more coquetry who lie in wait for "every
raw amorous youth," nor was our hero an exception. Having tried
the army, Nash became a student in the Temple where he "went to
the very summit of second-rate luxury" by spending the little
money he had on fine clothes and by cultivating every contact he
could make with the nobility. Living the life that poor little Beau
Tibbs only dreamed of, Nash launched himself into a course "of
gaiety and dissipation" and became "steady in nothing but in pursuit of variety." Goldsmith might have been referring to himself
when he wrote of Nash, "He was thirty years old, without fortune

or useful talents to acquire one. He had hitherto only led a life of expedients; he thanked chance alone for his support; and having been long precariously supported, he became, at length, totally a stranger to prudence or precaution. Not to disguise any part of his character, he was now, by profession, a gamester, and went on from day to day, feeling the vicissitudes of rapture and anguish, in proportion to the fluctuations of fortune" (IV, 62).

How could a serious historian, such as Goldsmith claimed to be, justify an interest in a "man of the world"—no matter how greatly he had improved the manners of Bath—who was secretly in connivance with the group of actual criminals in control of the gaming tables of that famous spa? Goldsmith's justification was that "the great and the little" are of equal importance to the historian, who knows that "nothing very great was ever yet formed from the little materials of humanity." "Thus none can properly be said to write history, but he who understands the human heart, and its whole train of affections and follies. Those affections and follies are properly the materials he has to work upon." Court intrigues, the movements of armies, and the relation of great political events "may surprize indeed," but they instruct only "those very few who govern the million beneath." The "generality of mankind find the most real improvement from relations which are levelled to the general surface of life," and profit from a perusal of "the history of a man placed in the middle ranks of life," of one who was "ever assiduous without industry, and pleasing to his superiors without any superiority of genius or understanding."

In fact, wrote Goldsmith, "every man's life would perhaps furnish the most pleasing materials for history, if he only had candour enough to be sincere, and skill enough to select such parts as once making him more prudent, might serve to render his readers more cautious." Since few men—and certainly not Goldsmith—are capable of such a combination of candor and sincerity, how fortunate one is to be able, with the help of all of Nash's papers, to attempt "the delineation of a mind without disguise." In the *Life of Richard Nash,* Goldsmith declared: "I attempt the character of one who was just such a man as probably you or I may be, but with this difference that he never performed an action which the world did not know, or ever formed a wish which he did not take pains to divulge" (IV, 53–54).

Accounts of Bath were readily available to Goldsmith; his defense of the man who "was generous, humane, and honourable, even though by profession a gamester" required something more than the art of the historian; indeed, in his *Life of Richard Nash,* Goldsmith soon became the teller of anecdotes and incidents in the style he had found successful in *The Bee* and in *The Citizen of the World.* "A thousand instances might be given of his integrity, even in this infamous profession, where his generosity often impelled him to act in contradiction to his interest," Goldsmith wrote of Nash (IV, 77). An account of "a giddy youth" who came to Bath in 1725 and was "at last undone" because he did not heed the advice of Nash was one such incident. Stories of "the late Duke of B." and "the late Earl of T——d" introduce the reader to the character of Nash as a victim of more experienced cardplayers. Though he had long practice in all the games then popular, he, like Goldsmith, "was never formed by nature for a successful gamester." Like his biographer, Nash "was constitutionally passionate and generous," and therefore could not remain sufficiently "reserved and cool" to prevail over the hardened gambler. For success in cards, "every passion must learn to obey control: but he frequently was unable to restrain the violence of his, and was often betrayed by this means into unbecoming rudeness, or childish impertinence." Thus Nash remained "a minion of fortune," always in "the power of chance"; and, though favored by "the great," he was never able to establish himself in "a state of independence" (IV, 79).

Nash was soon in the power of professional gamblers who saw their opportunity of gaining control of the gaminghouses of Bath by offering him a partnership in the business. The first year Nash was paid, but each succeeding year he received a smaller sum, nor did he ever concern himself with the books of these "infamous men" because, says Goldsmith, "the low and timid are ever suspicious; but a heart impressed with honourable sentiments expects from others sympathetic treatment." "King of Bath" though Nash was, as far as regulating the decorum of the morning levees and the evening balls, he was caught in the toils of men more knowing than himself who continued to deceive "the public and each other" until, in 1745, the legislature decided "to suppress these seminaries of vice" (IV, 82). From that time until his death,

Goldsmith wrote, "I find this poor, good-natured, but misguided man involved in continual disputes, every day calumniated with some new slander, and continually endeavouring to obviate its effects" (IV, 83).

But now having seen the "unfavourable" side of Nash, that of a gambler, wrote Goldsmith, one turns to those "brighter parts of his character" that gained for him the affection of many friends and the esteem of the corporation. Though he was first introduced into "polite company" by gaming, that alone would not have "carried him forward." Good manners, fine clothes, humor, wit, vivacity, and a general air of gentility are necessary for admittance into "the circle of the *beau monde.*" To·be sure, only "moderate talents" are requisite; and "in a state of tranquil society," such talents are more apt to bring success than greater ones. "Trifling opportunities of shining are almost every hour offered to the little sedulous mind," especially if he has the address to "enter into the service of the fair sex, and set up for a man of gallantry and intrigue," as did Nash early in life.

Since so little is known of Goldsmith's claims to a medical degree, not to mention his successes as a lover, it is interesting to hear him assert that "the business of love somewhat resembles the business of physic; no matter for qualifications, he that makes vigorous pretensions to either is surest of success." Goldsmith followed this remark with a description of Nash's appearance which proved to be not unlike that of Goldsmith. "Nature had by no means formed Mr. Nash for a *beau garçon,*" he wrote; "his person was clumsy, too large and awkward, and his features harsh, strong, and peculiarly irregular" (IV, 87). "He chose rather to be thought an odd fellow than a well-bred man" (IV, 142).

In spite of these disadvantages, Nash "became an universal admirer of the sex, and was universally admired," for he did possess some of the qualities of a lover. "He had assiduity, flattery, fine clothes, and as much wit as the ladies he addressed. Wit, flattery, and fine clothes, he used to say, were enough to debauch a nunnery" (IV, 87). After a delightful paragraph on the ways to court, known to three generations, Goldsmith ended with the casual remark, "the only way to make love now, I have heard Mr. Nash say, was to take no manner of notice of the lady; which method was found the surest way to secure her affections" (IV, 87–88). Since

[176]

Goldsmith never, as far as is known, made the acquiantance of Nash, he was perhaps remembering here the character of Beau Tibbs which he had recently drawn in Letter LIV of *The Citizen of the World*. The bragging little Beau of London had declared to the Chinese Philosopher that perfect indifference was his method with women. "That's my way," he told the Duke of Piccadilly, "I take a fine woman as some animals do their prey—stand still, and swoop, they fall into my mouth" (III, 205).

In expanding upon Nash as a lover, Goldsmith seemed to forget his role as an historian. "Were I upon the present occasion to hold the pen of a novelist," he wrote,

I could recount some amours, in which he was successful. I could fill a volume with little anecdotes, which contain neither pleasure nor instruction; with histories of professing lovers, and poor believing girls deceived by such professions. But such adventures are easily written, and as easily achieved. The plan even of fictitious novels is quite exhausted; but truth, which I have followed here, and ever design to follow, presents in the affair of love hardly any variety. (IV, 88)

Goldsmith, the historian, was plainly at war with Goldsmith, the novelist, in his reluctance to embark on the tales of "professing lovers" and "poor believing girls."

Foregoing the lure of enlarging upon Nash as a "universal gallant," Goldsmith told the reader that, "in the early years of his reign," Nash "entirely gave up his endeavours to deceive the sex, in order to become the honest protector of their innocence, the guardian of their reputation, and a friend of their virtue" (IV, 88). Like Mr. Burchell in his effort to protect Olivia and Sophia Primrose, Nash made it his "constant practice to do every thing in his power to prevent the fatal consequences of rash and inconsiderate love." Many persons "now alive," wrote Goldsmith, "owe their present happiness" to the fact that Nash (like Burchell) "interrupted the progress of an amour that threatened to become unhappy, or even criminal, by privately making their guardians or parents acquainted with what he could discover." Again, Goldsmith could not resist the temptation to make his "history" more vivid by pretending to have been present at the crisis of one of these dramas: "One night when I was in Wiltshire's room, Nash came up to a lady and her daughter, who were people of no inconsiderable fortune, and bluntly told the mother, *she had better be at home.*" The lady was at first "piqued and disconcerted," but Nash persisted and at last the mother returned to her lodging to find "a coach and six at the door, which a sharper had provided to carry off her eldest daughter" (IV, 89)—even as Olivia was carried off by Ned Thornhill.

Goldsmith, the novelist, was by now so carried away with his anecdotes of ill-starred love affairs that he wrote, "I shall beg leave to give some other instances of Mr. Nash's good sense and good-nature on these occasions, as I have had the accounts from himself" (IV, 89). Then followed the stories of "Miss L." and "Colonel M." and finally of "Miss Sylvia S——," whose unhappy love affair with "the celebrated S——" formed, it is thought, the basis for *The Good-Natured Man* (IV, 92, n.). Though there is a basis of fact in these stories, Goldsmith's interest in their historical truth was secondary to his interest in them as the source of romances with a moral meaning.

In his *Memoirs of M. de Voltaire,* Goldsmith described the *good* man who, after the dissipations of his youth, was able to achieve a balance between "the man of pleasure" within him and "the philosopher." In writing *The Life of Richard Nash,* Goldsmith strove to prove that the actual vices which marked this "man of pleasure" were balanced, if not by his wisdom, at least by his charity and generosity. Though Goldsmith did not succeed in thus making a hero of the "King of Bath," he achieved what is more important in terms of biography—the balanced portrait of a man "who had too much merit not to become remarkable, yet too much folly to arrive at greatness." Did his "merit" finally overbalance his "folly"? This is the question with which Goldsmith struggled, for it was directly applicable to himself. The sentence from Horace's *Art of Poetry* (lines 351–52) quoted by Goldsmith—"I will not take offence at a few blemishes against which human nature has failed to be on its guard"—was his appeal for charity in the judgment of weak human nature, always more bent on the pursuit of pleasure than of reason.

Nash lived to the age of ninety when he was "past the power of giving or receiving pleasure," being by then "poor, old, and peevish." He was never, however, able to "turn from his former manner of life" to pursue real happiness; "the old man endeavoured to practice the follies of the boy; he spurred on his jaded passions after every trifle of the day" (IV, 129). The aged Beau was not "permitted to run on thus without severe and repeated reproof." The clergy of Bath sent him frequent admonitions and "calls to reformation." But the "asperity" of their advice made him turn away from religion, wrote Goldsmith, who had himself suffered from the over-zealous clergy. "They threatened him with fire and brimstone, for what he had long been taught to consider as foibles, and not vices; so, like a desperate debtor, he did not care to settle an account, that, upon the first inspection, he found himself utterly unable to pay."

At this point Goldsmith quoted a long letter, supposedly written to Nash by "one of his monitors" and preserved among the "papers of Mr. Nash." This exhorting document, sent to him by "a friend" in the spirit of "benevolence," might, of course, have been genuine, as Goldsmith claimed; it might, on the other hand, have been a dramatized version of one of his father's sermons remembered from his boyhood and echoed by the Vicar of Wakefield. Curiously enough, the writer of the letter made a macabre use of the phrase "dry bones," which suggests the origin of the name of the Man in Black, "Mr. Drybone." Rising to the customary pitch of the eighteenth-century evangelical preacher, Nash's "monitor" wrote: "You are as odious to God as a corrupt carcase that lies putrefying in the churchyard. You are as far from doing your duty, or endeavouring after salvation, . . . as a heap of dry bones nailed up in a coffin is from vigour and activity. . . . Think, Sir, I conjure you, think upon this if you have any inclination to escape the fire that will never be quenched" (IV, 130).[20] One might conclude that the Man in Black was a ghost which dwelt in Goldsmith's conscience, one with whom he vainly struggled all of his life. He was, in fact, a gamester, and not so mysterious as he seemed to the Chinese Philosopher. In the life of Nash, Goldsmith wrote "every gamester is a rake, and his morals worse than his mystery" (IV, 148).

In the first edition of *The Life of Richard Nash*, Goldsmith wrote a defense of his hero against this gloomy onslaught from the clergy, which was omitted from the second edition.[21] "Such

repeated admonitions served to sting, without reforming him,"
wrote Goldsmith, who had heard all too many of the same variety
himself:

They made him morose, but not pious. The dose was too strong for the
patient to bear. He should have been met with smiles, and allured into
reformation; if indeed he was criminal. But, in the name of piety, what
was there criminal in his conduct? He had long been taught to consider
his trifling profession as a very serious and important business. He went
through his office with great gravity, solemnity, and care; why then de-
nounce peculiar torments against a poor harmless creature, who did a
thousand good things, and whose greatest vice was vanity? He deserved
ridicule, indeed, and he found it; but scarce a single action of his life,
except one, deserves the asperity of reproach.

These "admonitions of the grave" only served to aggravate his
follies into vices. Had not the corporation of Bath granted him a
pension, wrote Goldsmith, who had not received one, "the poor
man of pleasure might have terminated his life very tragically"
(IV, 131).

Goldsmith would willingly have overlooked, if he had been able
to manage it, the fact that Nash did secretly ally himself with the
professional gamblers who were fleecing the visitors to Bath for,
according to his biographer, Nash did "a thousand good things"
which more than paid for his one error of judgment. Goldsmith's
defense is the more poignant because, in referring to Nash, he
uses the same phrase which he tells us was so frequently used to
describe him—"a poor harmless creature." Here, as in *The Vicar
of Wakefield*, Goldsmith struggled to believe in the redemptive
power of unconscious charity and simple goodness. Goldsmith, in
fact, was already brooding upon his tale of *The Vicar of Wakefield* while he was writing *The Life of Richard Nash*, and one
finds a hint of the romance in an anecdote told about Nash.[22] One
of the "thousand good things" that he hoped might redeem the
character of the Beau had to do with a poor clergyman and his
family who were rescued by the charity of their benefactor, Nash,
who assumed the role of protector of the worthy. The story begins
as follows:

About six and thirty years ago, a clergyman brought his family to
Bath for the benefit of the waters. His wife laboured under a linger-

ing disorder, which it was thought nothing but the Hot-wells could remove. The expenses of living there soon lessened the poor man's finances; his clothes were sold, piece by piece, to provide a temporary relief for his little family, and his appearance was at last so shabby, that, from the number of holes in his coat and stockings, Nash gave him the name of Doctor Cullender. Our beau, it seems, was rude enough to make a jest of poverty, though he had sensibility enough to relieve it. The poor clergyman combated his distresses with fortitude; and instead of attempting to solicit relief, endeavoured to conceal them. Upon a living of thirty pounds a-year he endeavoured to maintain his wife and six children; but all his resources at last failed him, and nothing but famine was seen in the wretched family. The poor man's circumstances were at last communicated to Nash; who, with his usual cheerfulness, undertook to relieve him. (IV, 102)

As a "cool biographer, unbiased by resentment or regard," Goldsmith came to a balanced judgment of Nash, who was neither "truly great" nor "strongly vicious" (IV, 141). As an apologist who shared many of his good and his bad qualities, Goldsmith wrote:

He could not stifle the natural impulse which he had to do good, but frequently borrowed money to relieve the distressed; and when he knew not conveniently where to borrow, he has been often observed to shed tears, as he passed through the wretched supplicants who attended his gate.

This sensibility, this power of feeling the misfortunes of the miserable, and his address and earnestness in relieving their wants, exalts the character of Mr. Nash, and draws an impenetrable veil over his foibles. His singularities are forgotten when we behold his virtues, and he who laughed at the whimsical character and behaviour of this Monarch of Bath, now laments that he is no more. (IV, 153–54)

The two biographies that Goldsmith published early in his career,[23] the first concerned with a great philosopher, and the second with a notable man of the world, gained in depth and psychological insight because Goldsmith discovered his own inner conflicts in Voltaire and in Nash. That Voltaire learned to balance his "reason and appetite" and became a triumphant exponent of the rational, the witty, and the sceptical influenced Goldsmith in the writing of his own histories of England, Rome, and Greece; that

Nash, a man of the "middle rank," never resolved the conflict of his nature supplied Goldsmith with material for the novel and the plays he immediately turned to after the appearance of his biography of a gamester and a rake. Nash, the "weak" man, inspired Goldsmith the novelist and playright, as well as Goldsmith the historian. For the next few years, as has been noted, Goldsmith stole time from his reviewing and compiling to write *The Vicar of Wakefield* and *The Good-Natured Man*, the suggestions for which are to be found in the biography of the erring but generous Beau Nash.

V *Evaluations*

When Dr. Johnson began to write his introductory essay on Parnell for his *Lives of the English Poets*, he observed in discussing the works of the poet: "of these Goldsmith has given an opinion, and his criticism it is seldom safe to contradict." He would very willingly have declined the assignment given him by the bookseller of writing Parnell's life, since it had already been written by Goldsmith, "a man of such variety of powers, and such felicity of performance, that he always seemed to do best that which he was doing; a man who had the art of being minute without tediousness, and general without confusion; whose language was copious without exuberance, exact without constraint, and easy without weakness. What such an author has told, who could tell again?" (IV, 156). The list of poets about whom Johnson was asked to write his prefatory essays did not include the name of Goldsmith. Though Johnson somewhat altered the list, in the main he followed the suggestions of his publishers; for he, like Goldsmith, wrote all of his life for the booksellers.

Why Johnson had not written a separate life of Goldsmith in the five years that had intervened between the death of Goldsmith and the appearance of the first volume of the *Lives of the English Poets*, no one can say. Bishop Percy wrote to Goldsmith's family in Ireland, immediately after the death of the poet, and collected as much biographical material on Goldsmith as he could, all of which he turned over to Johnson.[24] Edmund Malone, too, recorded that he was sure that Johnson intended to write a life of Goldsmith, "for I collected some material for it by his desire" (I, 64). Malone wrote to Percy on March 2, 1785, concerning their mutual desire to see Doctor Johnson set to work on Goldsmith's life: "Dr. Johnson used to say that he never could get an accurate account of Goldsmith's history while he was abroad." Percy reported in a letter to Malone, that, when he reminded Johnson of his undertaking, he confessed that he had "utterly forgotten them [the materials left with him], and the subject." [25]

Much as one would have valued a *Life of Goldsmith* comparable to Johnson's earlier *Life of Savage*, one is indebted to Johnson, nevertheless, for his staunch defense of Goldsmith—though he not infrequently grew impatient with his "fooleries"—from his earliest acquaintance with him in 1761 until his death and afterwards. Boswell never tired of baiting Johnson on his estimate of Goldsmith. "But, Sir," Boswell remonstrated on one occasion, "He is much indebted to you for his getting so high in the publick estimation."—Johnson: "Why, Sir, he has, perhaps, got *sooner* to it by his intimacy with me." [26] Though Boswell was the rival of Goldsmith for Johnson's favor, he seems to have reported justly Johnson's admiration for the man whose lack of "principles" and insufficiency of knowledge annoyed him. "Goldsmith," Johnson said, "had great merit," and excelled in every literary area he cared to enter. "Whether, indeed, we take him as a poet, as a comic writer, or as an historian, he stands in the first class," declared the Doctor. Boswell replied in astonishment:

'An historian! My dear Sir, you surely will not rank his compilation of the Roman History with the work of other historians of this age?' Johnson, 'Why, who are before him?' Boswell, 'Hume,—Robertson,—Lord Littleton.' Johnson . . . 'I have not read Hume; but doubtless, Goldsmith's *History* is better than the *verbiage* of Robertson, of the foppery of Dalrymple . . . it is the great excellence of a writer to put into his book as much as his book will hold. Goldsmith has done this in his *History* . . . Goldsmith tells you shortly all you want to know . . . Goldsmith's plain narrative will please again and again . . . Sir, he has the art of compiling, and of saying everything he has to say in a pleasing manner. He is now writing a *Natural History* and will make it as entertaining as a Persian Tale'.[27]

At Goldsmith's death, it was, of course, Johnson who was chosen by the Literary Club to write his epitaph, every member of which loved and venerated the man whom they had so often ridiculed. The only line from the long Latin epitaph which one remembers now—"Nullum quod tetigit non ornavit"—sums up Johnson's view of Goldsmith; and this verdict has been accepted by successive generations. Goldsmith improved all that he touched, whether as essayist, poet, novelist, dramatist, or biographer. No one can thumb through the volumes of hackwork that he left behind—much of it unsigned and unidentified—without being impressed by the courageous struggle of this versatile Irishman to achieve a position in the London world or without lamenting the wastefulness of genius.

Goldsmith's gay and sociable nature was crossed by a strain of melancholy that kept him something of an enigma to himself as well as to his friends. The very complexity of his temperament perhaps prevented him from being candid with himself or others, and it impelled him to conceal himself in the characters of his books through which he also sought to discover a kind of harmony. A penniless youth, he stumbled into writing to keep from starving; a successful author, he continued to write at a furious pace in order to pay for his extravagance as a "man of the world." He achieved a permanent place in literature as the author of half a dozen books, written in time stolen from his endless editing, compiling, and "convivializing." Though in his last year he is thought to have earned as much as eighteen hundred pounds, he died in debt to the extent of two thousand pounds. "He died of a fever," said Johnson, "made, I am afraid, more violent by uneasiness of mind. His debts began to be heavy, and all his resources were exhausted. Sir Joshua is of opinion that he owed not less than two thousand pounds. Was ever poet so trusted before?" [28] Was ever genius so foolish before? one might ask in sheer exasperation at the futile expenditure of so much power.

In all of Goldsmith's permanent works—*The Citizen of the World, The Deserted Village, The Vicar of Wakefield, She Stoops to Conquer,* and *The Life of Richard Nash,* varied though their form may be—he was asking an essentially philosophical question as to the moral values of life and the nature of man. The tension between "reason and appetite," the "good man" and "the bad man," was always felt by Goldsmith, whether his language was humorous, rhapsodic, rational, or melancholy. Many of Goldsmith's characters were made to go through a "reformation," which, one may suppose, turned them into "enlightened philosophers." Goldsmith, never able to reform himself, more nearly described his own restless spirit in Letter XLVII of *The Citizen of the World.* Here he wrote that the "good man" is frequently helpless:

When misfortunes therefore oppress, when tyrants threaten, it is our interest, it is our duty to fly even to dissipation for support. . . . The soul may be compared to a field of battle where two armies are ready every moment to encounter: not a single vice but has a more powerful opponent, and not one virtue but may be overborne by a combination of vices. Reason guides the bands of either host; nor can it subdue one passion but by the assistance of another. Thus, as a bark on every side beset with storms, enjoys a state of rest, so does the mind, when influenced by a just equipoise of the passions, enjoy tranquillity. (III, 179)

Goldsmith died, at the age of forty-six,[29] from sheer intemperance, both in work and in pleasure, when he seemed to be at the height of his success. He had, throughout his life, responded to the call of the two "masters of our revels," reason and appetite; finally, he found it impossible to respond to either. Though a remarkably strong man physically, he contracted what doctors now believe to have been Bright's Disease, and died on April 4, 1774, after a brief illness in his apartment in the Temple. Characteristically, he refused to follow the advice of several apothecaries and doctors who attended him, and insisted on swallowing a double dose of "Dr. James's Powders," sold in the bookstore of his old employer, John Newbery. Though it is probable that the pills did not actually cause his death, they undoubtedly hastened it. Dr. Johnson told the story that "when Goldsmith was dying Dr. Turton said to him, 'Your pulse is in greater disorder than it should be, from the degree of fever which you have: is your mind at ease?' Goldsmith answered it was not" (I, 39).

Goldsmith was buried on April 9, 1774, not in Westminster Abbey, but in the Temple Church-yard. The exact spot where he lies is not known, but a marble slab was placed in 1860 near where the grave is supposed to have been. After his funeral Goldsmith's friends of the Literary Club raised a subscription to pay for a marble bust of Goldsmith executed by the sculptor Joseph Nollekens. The monument was placed in the Poets' Corner of

Westminster Abbey in a spot chosen by Sir Joshua Reynolds. The inscription, by Dr. Johnson, is in Latin; for Johnson thought that only the universal language was worthy either of Westminster Abbey or of Goldsmith.[30] Translated into the English which Goldsmith might have preferred, the inscription reads:

To the memory of Oliver Goldsmith, poet, naturalist and historian, who left scarcely any species of writing untouched or unadorned by his pen: a powerful but gentle master of the passions, both in exciting mirth, and in drawing forth tears: of a genius sublime, penetrating, versatile; in expression noble, elegant, and graceful:—this monument has been consecrated by the affection of his companions, the attachment of his friends, and the veneration of his readers. (I, 41)

In death as in life, Goldsmith remained divided; his mortal parts lie in an unidentified grave in the Temple Church-yard, and his immortal spirit is to be sought in the Poets' Corner of Westminster Abbey. But Goldsmith's real self is fixed neither in a marble bust nor a Latin inscription; it is to be found in the plain English of the few books known and loved in almost all parts of the world.

Notes and References

Preface

1. All quoted passages in the text of this book will be taken from *The Works of Oliver Goldsmith*, 5 vols. (London, 1884–86), ed. by J. W. M. Gibbs. References to volume and page will be indicated in the text.

2. Katharine C. Balderston, *The History and Sources of Percy's Memoir of Goldsmith* (Cambridge, 1926).

3. See "On the Proper Enjoyment of Life," *British Magazine*, August, 1761. Gibbs, IV, 469–97. The authorship of this essay has been disputed. See Morris Golden, "Two Essays Erroneously Attributed to Goldsmith," *Modern Language Notes*, LXXIV (1959), 13–16.

4. This supposition is based on his essay, "Adventures of a Strolling Player," *British Magazine*, (October, 1760). Gibbs, I, 290–99.

5. Sir John Hawkins, *The Life of Samuel Johnson, LL.D.* Ed. by Bertram H. Davis, (New York, 1961), p. 179.

Chapter One

1. When the "Chinese Letters" appeared as a book in 1762, the volume was entitled *The Citizen of the World*.

2. *The Collected Letters of Oliver Goldsmith*, ed. by Katharine C. Balderston. (Cambridge, 1928), 56–62.

3. In 1758 Goldsmith published a translation of *The Memoirs of a Protestant*, under the pseudonym of "James Willington."

4. 12 Green Arbour Court.

5. Between 1759 and 1762 Goldsmith contributed to at least ten periodicals. See *The Cambridge Bibliography of English Literature, 1660–1800*, II (New York, 1941), 638–45.

6. *Letters*, p. 64. Goldsmith reprinted this poem in *The Citizen of the World*, Letter XXX, Gibbs, III, 113–14, with six lines added at the opening and two at the close.

7. Percy had been introduced to Goldsmith on February 21, 1759, by Dr. James Grainger of *The Monthly Review* at the Temple Exchange Coffee House.

8. Thomas Percy, Bishop of Dromore, "Memoir of Goldsmith," *Miscellaneous Works of Olive Goldsmith*. 4 vols. (1801), I, p. 61.

9. *Letters*, 32–36; 41–48.

10. *Letters*, 27–28.

11. See Elizabeth E. Kent, *Goldsmith and His Booksellers*. (Ithaca, 1933).

12. On the title page was the following quotation from Lucretius' *De Rerum Naturae:* "Floriferis ut Apes in saltibus omnia libant," See also Gibbs, III, 504–5.

13. Much of the material Goldsmith used in *The Bee* was taken from the *Encyclopédie* and the *Biographia Britannica*.

14. Charles Welsh, *A Bookseller of the Last Century* (London, 1885).

15. *Letters*, 36–41.

16. Gibbs, II, 376–78. This essay appeared in *The Citizen of the World* as Letter CXVII. Note that the last sentence was not included. Gibbs, III, 422–24.

17. This use of the word goes back to the Classical concept, popular in the medieval ages, of the four humors (blood, phlegm, yellow bile, and black bile) to explain the variations of personalities. The Man in Black suffered from black bile and was therefore a "melancholy" man, subject to "the spleen."

18. Goldsmith's sister considered the Man in Black's story her brother's account of his own youth. *Letters*, 169–70.

19. See Martha P. Conant, *The Oriental Tale in England in the Eighteenth Century* (New York, 1908).

20. *Letters*, 36–41.

Chapter Two

1. See R. S. Crane, "Oliver Goldsmith, M. B.," *Modern Language Notes*, XLVIII (1933), p. 462.

2. William Cooke, *Table Talk*, "Anecdotes of Dr. Goldsmith," *The European Magazine*, XXI (February, 1792), p. 86.

3. Hawkins' words were, "As he wrote for the booksellers, we, at the Club, looked on him as a mere literary drudge, equal to the task of compiling and translating, but little capable of original, and still less of poetical composition," *op. cit.*, p. 182.

4. Gibbs, II, 3.

5. This anecdote was told originally by James Prior, in *The Life of Oliver Goldsmith* (1837) who said he had it from Mary Horneck (the "Jessamy Bride"), II, p. 33.

6. See *The Cambridge History of English Literature, 1660–1800*, II, 641.

Notes and References

7. Percy's "Memoir of Goldsmith," *op. cit.*, I, p. 62.
8. See Gibbs, II, 20–21. The original ballad from which both Percy and Goldsmith borrowed is in *The Reliques of Ancient Poetry* (1765); the title is "Gentle Herdsmen, Tell to Me."
9. Joseph Cradock, *Literary and Miscellaneous Memoirs*, 4 vols. (1828), II, p. 20.
10. Birkbeck Hill, II, 231.
11. Cooke (August, 1793), p. 95.
12. *Ibid.*, p. 93.
13. Cooke (September, 1793), p. 173.
14. Temple Scott, *Oliver Goldsmith Bibliographically and Biographically Considered* (New York, 1928), p. 201.
15. Cooke (August, 1793), p. 94.
16. Cooke (September, 1793), p. 172.
17. Scott, 274–76.
18. Scott, 241–42.
19. Goldsmith made this remark to the Earl of Lisburn at a Royal Academy dinner. Gibbs, I, p. 28.
20. Mrs. Horneck, her two daughters, and her son, maintained a home in London, as well as a house in the country.
21. Scott, p. 227.
22. Edward Purdon and Goldsmith both wrote for the *Busy Body*. Gibbs, I, p. 2.
23. William Ballantyne, who edited a collection of songs and poems, entitled *Mackniana*. Scott, p. 206.
24. Various accounts of this occasion are given by different editors, some asserting that Goldsmith was not present at the coffee-house at any time during the evening. Cooke wrote that Goldsmith read "Retaliation" aloud at the Club. (September, 1793), p. 174. See also Richard Cumberland's account of the writing of "Retaliation." *Memoirs Written by Himself* (1807), I, 369–72.

Chapter Three

1. Birkbeck Hill, I, p. 416.
2. *Ibid.*, (Appendix F), 520–22.
3. Welsh, p. 58.
4. Johnson made this remark to Fanny Burney. Birkbeck Hill, I, p. 415 (note 3).
5. The remark was made to Dr. William Farr. Gibbs, I, 237.
6. Quoted by John Forster, *The Life and Times of Oliver Goldsmith,* 2 vols. (London, 1854), I, p. 423.
7. See note 4, above.
8. Gibbs, III, 199–203.

9. *Truth and Poetry From My Own Life,* tr. by John Oxenford, (London, 1867–68), Bk. X, 368–70.

10. Quoted by Forster, I, p. 411.

11. *Ibid.,* p. 412.

12. Thomas Babington Macaulay, *Miscellanies,* 4 vols. (London, 1900), III, p. 44.

13. Psalm 37:25.

14. Note that the initials of Sir William Thornhill are the same as those of Sir William Temple, from whom Goldsmith frequently quoted his most famous sentence, "When all is said and done, human life is, at the greatest and the best, but like a froward child, that must be played with and humoured a little to keep it quiet till it falls asleep, and then the care is over." Gibbs, II, p. 155; III, p. 526. Temple was also known for his words on English "humourists," and was certainly a man of "eccentric virtues."

15. The term "philosophic vagabond" had already been used by Goldsmith in *The Bee,* October 6, 1759. Gibbs, II, p. 320.

16. *Letters,* p. 38.

17. In the Prefaces to *Essays* (1765) Goldsmith made the same complaint against the public. The list of names is identical except that "Philautos" is "Philantos" in the *Essays.*

18. "Preface," *The Vicar of Wakefield, A Tale, by Dr. Goldsmith.* 1817.

19. *Letters,* p. 60.

20. Cf. "The Adventures of a Strolling Player." Gibbs, I, 290–99.

21. Goldsmith as a youth once strayed into a gentleman's mansion, having been told by a mischievous acquaintance that the mansion was an Inn. "Mrs. Hodson's narrative," *Letters,* 166–68. This episode is used again in *She Stoops to Conquer.*

22. "Misery Best Relieved by Dissipation," Letter XLVII, *The Citizen of the World.* Gibbs, III, 178–79.

23. "Hope on, ye wretched; beware, ye happy." Found at the end of Burton's *Anatomy of Melancholy.*

Chapter Four

1. Thomas Davies, *Memoirs of the Life of David Garrick,* 2 vols. (1780), II, p. 141.

2. Sir Joshua Reynolds, *Portraits.* Edited by F. W. Hilles (London, 1952), pp. 43–44. See also Birkbeck Hill, I, 412–15.

3. Davies, II, p. 145.

4. *Ibid.,* p. 143.

5. *Ibid.,* 146–47.

6. *Letters,* 74–77. See note 3, p. 74.

7. Cooke (August, 1793), p. 94.

8. Mrs. Hester Lynch Piozzi (Mrs. Thrale) *Anecdotes of the Late Samuel Johnson, LL.D.* (1786), 245–46.

9. Birkbeck Hill, II, p. 48.

10. Davies, II, p. 147.

11. *Ibid.*, p. 141.

12. *Letters*, 93–97.

13. *Ibid.*, 102–06.

14. Birkbeck Hill, III, 320–21.

15. Cradock, I, 224–26.

16. James Northcote, *Memoirs of Sir Joshua Reynolds*, 2 vols. (1813), I, 286. See also Cumberland, I, 366–69.

17. Cooke (September, 1793), p. 173.

18. *Letters of Horace Walpole*, edited by Mrs. Paget Toynbee, 16 vols. (Oxford, 1903–08), VIII, 381. See also pp. 184, 269, 440.

19. Northcote, I, p. 286, note.

20. Birkbeck Hill, II, p. 233.

21. Cooke (September, 1793), p. 173.

22. Scott, p. 296.

23. Davies, II, p. 153.

24. Birkbeck Hill, II, p. 219.

25. From Arne's opera, "Artaxeres." Minuet from Handel's opera, "Ariadne."

26. Birkbeck Hill, II, p. 207.

27. Cradock, IV, p. 282.

28. Prior, II, p. 411. Gibbs, I, 34–35.

29. Birkbeck Hill, II, p. 210.

30. *Ibid.*

31. Scott, p. 290.

32. *Letters of Horace Walpole, op. cit.*, VIII, p. 381.

33. For the two letters that follow, see *Letters*, 125–28.

34. Cradock, I, p. 232.

35. Cradock, IV, 282–83.

36. See Davies, II, 150–160, for further comments on Goldsmith. To Richard Cumberland, Goldsmith once said, "You and I have very different motives for resorting to the stage; I write for money, and care little about fame" *Memoirs*, I, 366.

37. Cradock, who knew Goldsmith during the last few weeks of his life, observed: "I believe he died miserably, and that his friends were not entirely aware of his distress." *Memoirs*, IV, p. 287.

38. Davies, II, 155–56.

Chapter Five

1. Goldsmith began his *Memoirs of M. de Voltaire* in 1758, presumably to pay off his debt to Ralph Griffiths. *Letters,* p. 63. For an account of the publication of these two biographies, see Gibbs, IV, p. 2 and p. 48.

2. Gibbs, IV, 8–9.

3. *Letters,* 57–58.

4. "Those who know me at all, know that I have always been actuated by different principles from the rest of Mankind." *Letters,* p. 43.

5. Goldsmith also wrote of Voltaire, "he had refined by study all that paradox of which he was once so fond." Gibbs, IV, p. 45.

6. *An Enquiry,* Ch. VII, Gibbs, III, p. 496.

7. Gibbs, IV, 24–25. See Gibbs' footnote on p. 25, for comment on the truth of Goldsmith's claim. See also *ibid.,* p. 470; here Goldsmith again asserted that he conversed personally with Voltaire.

8. *The Monthly Review,* August, 1757.

9. Cooke (August, 1793), p. 94.

10. Birkbeck Hill, III, p. 253.

11. *Ibid.,* II, p. 236, note 1. See also pp. 215, 235; IV, p. 252.

12. Cradock, I, p. 231. See also footnote. Boswell wrote of Goldsmith, "It has been generally circulated and believed that he was a mere fool in conversation; but, in truth, this has been greatly exaggerated." Birkbeck Hill, I, 412. Sir Joshua Reynolds wrote, "Goldsmith's mind was entirely unfurnished. When he was engaged in a work, he had all his knowledge to find, which when he found, he knew how to use, but forgot it immediately after he had used it." *Portraits, op. cit.,* p. 50.

13. Voltaire died in 1778.

14. James Beattie (1735–1803), Professor of Moral Philosophy at Aberdeen. His "Essay on Truth" was written to expose Hume and Voltaire.

15. Northcote, I, 299–303. See also Gibbs, IV, p. 20, note.

16. Hester Lynch Piozzi, *Letters to and from the Late Samuel Johnson, LL.D.,* 2 vols. 1788, I, p. 186.

17. About one-tenth of Goldsmith's biography of Nash came from John Wood's *Essay Toward a Description of Bath.* Arthur Friedman, "Goldsmith and Wood," *Times Literary Supplement* (November 2, 1956), p. 649. See also Oliver W. Ferguson, "The Materials of History: Goldsmith's *Life of Nash,*" *Publications of the Modern Language Association,* LXXX (Sept., 1965), 372–86.

18. This book appeared in many editions, the seventh being dated 1753, and the twelfth, 1761. Gibbs, IV, p. 114, footnote 3.

Notes and References

19. Cooke (September, 1793), p. 172; Hawkins, 182–83.

20. Beau Tibbs, in Letter LIV, *The Citizen of the World*, addressed the Man in Black as "My dear Drybone." Gibbs, III, p. 204, note.

21. Restored by Gibbs. See his footnote, IV, p. 131.

22. Morris Golden, "Another Manufactured Anecdote in the 'Life of Nash'?" *Notes and Queries*, XXII (1957), 120–21.

23. The other two biographies for which Goldsmith is known, *The Life of Thomas Parnell, D.D.* and that of *Henry St. John, Viscount Bolingbroke*, both appeared in 1770, and both were written at the request of Thomas Davies, Goldsmith's publisher at that time.

24. Gibbs, I, p. 64.

25. Arthur Tillotson, "Dr. Johnson and the Life of Goldsmith," *Modern Language Review*, XXVIII (1933), 439–43.

26. Birkbeck Hill, II, p. 216. See also *ibid.*, I, p. 413; II, p. 215, 236; III, p. 252.

27. *Ibid.*, II, 236–37.

28. Birkbeck Hill, II, p. 280. See also note 2.

29. This calculation is based on the assumption that 1728 was the date of Goldsmith's birth.

30. See Birkbeck Hill, III, 81–85.

Selected Bibliography

BIBLIOGRAPHIES

BALDERSTON, KATHARINE C. *A Census of the Manuscripts of Oliver Goldsmith.* New York: The Brick Row Book Shop, 1926.

CRANE, RONALD S. "Oliver Goldsmith (1730?–1774)," in *The Cambridge Bibliography of English Literature*, II, pp. 636–50. New York: The Macmillan Company, 1941.

————. *An Exhibition in the Yale University Library of the Works of Oliver Goldsmith.* New Haven: The Yale University Press, 1928.

SCOTT, TEMPLE. *Oliver Goldsmith Bibliographically and Biographically Considered.* New York: The Bowling Green Press, 1928.

WILLIAMS, IOLO A. *Seven XVIIIth Century Bibliographies.* London: Dulau and Company, 1924.

PRIMARY SOURCES

BALDERSTON, KATHARINE C. *The Collected Letters of Oliver Goldsmith.* Cambridge: The University Press, 1928.

CRANE, RONALD S. *New Essays by Oliver Goldsmith.* Chicago: The University of Chicago Press, 1927.

DOBSON, AUSTIN. *The Poems and Plays of Oliver Goldsmith*, 2 vols. London: J. M. Dent and Company, 1889.

DOUGHTY, OSWALD. *The Vicar of Wakefield.* London: Scholartis Press, 1928.

GIBBS, J. W. M. *The Works of Oliver Goldsmith*, 5 vols. London, 1884–1886.

HILLES, FREDERICK W. *The Vicar of Wakefield and Other Writings.* New York: Random House, 1955.

SECONDARY SOURCES

1. *Biographical Sources*

BOSWELL, JAMES. *The Life of Johnson*, 6 vols. Edited by George Birkbeck Hill. Revised by L. F. Powell. Oxford: The Clarendon Press, 1934–1950. Unsympathetic portrait of Goldsmith contrasted with that of Johnson.

COOKE, WILLIAM. *Table Talk.* "Dr. Goldsmith," *The European Maga-*

zine, XXIV, XXI (February, 1792; August-October, 1793). A rich repository of anecdotes bearing on the life of Goldsmith in London, by one who knew him.

CRADOCK, JOSEPH. *Literary and Miscellaneous Memoirs*, 4 vols. London: J. B. Nichols, 1828. A wealthy dilettante records the visits of Goldsmith to his homes in London and in Leicestershire.

CUMBERLAND, RICHARD. *Memoirs . . . Written by Himself*, 2 vols. London: Lackington, Allen, & Co., 1807. A personal account by a fellow dramatist of his meetings with Goldsmith, with stress on his "foibles."

DAVIES, THOMAS. *Memoirs of the Life of David Garrick*, 2 vols. London: The Author, 1780. Davies for many years the publisher of Goldsmith was also a bookdealer and an actor. His study of Garrick includes important material on Goldsmith.

G(*lover, Richard*). "Authentic Anecdotes of the Late Dr. Goldsmith," *Universal Magazine*, LIV, May, 1774, 252–55. Written a month after the death of Goldsmith, "G." records many details of Goldsmith's continental experiences.

HAWKINS, SIR JOHN. *The Life of Samuel Johnson, LL.D.* London: J. Buckland, 1787. The author presents Goldsmith as a "literary drudge."

NORTHCOTE, JAMES. *Memoirs of Sir Joshua Reynolds*, 2 vols. London: Printed for H. Colburn, 1813. Anecdotes of "many distinguished persons," including Goldsmith.

PERCY, THOMAS. "Memoir of Goldsmith. *The Miscellaneous Works of Oliver Goldsmith*. 4 vols. J. Johnson, C. and J. Robinson, etc., 1801. Bishop Percy was designated by Goldsmith as his biographer.

REYNOLDS, SIR JOSHUA. *Portraits*. Edited by Frederick W. Hilles. London: William Heinemann, 1952. Character sketches by Sir Joshua Reynolds of his friends: Oliver Goldsmith, Samuel Johnson, David Garrick.

THRALE, HESTER LYNCH. *Anecdotes of the Late Samuel Johnson, LL.D.* London: T. Cadell, 1786. Inaccurate, prejudiced account of the publication of *The Vicar of Wakefield*.

WELSH, CHARLES. *A Bookseller of the Last Century. Being Some Account of the Life of John Newbery*. London: Griffith, Farran, Okeden & Welsh, 1885. Careful accounts of Newbery's business relations with Goldsmith.

2. *Biographical and Critical Studies*

DOBSON, AUSTIN. *Life of Oliver Goldsmith*. London: W. Scott, 1888.

Selected Bibliography

The earliest, and best of the shorter biographies of Goldsmith. Bibliography by J. P. Anderson.

FORSTER, JOHN. *The Life and Times of Oliver Goldsmith,* 2 vols. London: Bradbury & Evans, etc. 1854. Forster presented in his study new material on Goldsmith's life in London.

FREEMAN, WILLIAM. *Oliver Goldsmith.* London: Herbert Jenkins, 1951. Brief, factual account of Goldsmith's life, based on many quotations from original sources.

GAUSSEN, ALICE C. C. *Percy: Prelate and Poet.* London: Smith, Elder & Co., 1908. Chapter VIII is an account of the friendship of Percy and Goldsmith.

KENT, ELIZABETH E. *Goldsmith and His Booksellers.* Ithaca: Cornell University Press, 1933. Story of Goldsmith's relation to his publishers.

PITMAN, JAMES HALL. *Goldsmith's 'Animated Nature': A Study of Goldsmith.* New Haven: The Yale University Press, 1924. Scholarly study of the circumstances under which Goldsmith compiled *Animated Nature.*

PRIOR, JAMES. *The Life of Oliver Goldsmith,* 2 vols. London: J. Murray, 1837. The first full life of Goldsmith, "from a variety of original sources."

SELLS, ARTHUR LYTTON. *Les Sources Françaises de Goldsmith.* Paris: E. Champion, 1924. A presentation, in parallel columns, of Goldsmith's writing and his French sources.

SHERBURN, GEORGE, "The Periodicals and Oliver Goldsmith," *A Literary History of England.* Edited by A. C. Baugh. III, 1050–1062. New York: Appleton, 1950.

SMITH, HAMILTON JEWELL. *Oliver Goldsmith's The Citizen of the World: A Study.* Yale Studies in English, LXXI. New Haven: The Yale University Press, 1926. Scholarly account of *The Citizen of the World,* in relation to his Sources.

STEPHEN, LESLIE. "Goldsmith, Oliver." *Dictionary of National Biography.* London: Oxford University Press, 1921–1922. A fourteen-column account of the life and works of Goldsmith.

WARDLE, RALPH MARTIN. *Oliver Goldsmith.* Lawrence, Kansas: The University of Kansas Press, 1957. Though the author does not claim to present any new Goldsmith material, he does make use of the scholarship of the twentieth century on Goldsmith.

Index

Index